## *Praise for*
## Start Making Sense

"A beautiful, deep, thoughtful book. *Start Making Sense* is for anyone who has asked themselves: Yes, yes—but what is the meaning of my existence? That's everyone, I think—including me. Steven J. Heine, a pioneer in the new field of existential psychology, offers no glib prescriptions. Instead, Heine probes the evolutionary origins and contemporary implications of our species' hardwired need for meaning. Will you know what to do with the rest of your life after reading this book? Maybe not. But as Heine so beautifully argues, sometimes understanding the questions is even more important."

—Angela Duckworth, *New York Times*–bestselling author of *Grit*

"In *Start Making Sense*, Heine reveals the hidden centrality of 'meaning' in human life as he harvests the first fruits from the new field of existential psychology. In communities with historically unprecedented levels of wealth, health, and security, what many of the dislocated and depressed need is not more drugs or counseling per se—though those can help, as he notes. They hunger for meaning in their lives. In this new age of anxiety, what we all need is not boundless opportunities but a story that weaves us into both a thick social network of friends and a rich cultural tapestry, one that conveys to us why we want to get up every day. In this important book, Heine has put his finger on what might be the most pernicious plague of our times."

—Joseph Henrich, author of *The WEIRDest People in the World*

"Given their increased wealth, leisure time, and lifespan, modern Westerners should be the happiest people ever to have lived, and yet instead anxiety and depression appear to be on the rise. Heine, one of the pioneers of the psychology of meaning, argues that a root problem is a loss of identity and purpose. This book offers accounts of why this might happen as well as strategies for regaining our existential footing."
— Edward Slingerland, author of *Drunk*

"*Start Making Sense* should be a college read for all students and for anyone worrying about what counts as a meaningful life and how to live one. Heine is a preeminent social and cultural psychologist who brings the science to these timeless existential questions. He shows how variable the answers can be and how much they matter for health, happiness, and well-being. The result is a bold, accessible, and inspiring book."
— Hazel Markus, Stanford University

"Heine is a sage guide in a world that increasingly feels meaningless. *Start Making Sense* is essential reading for anyone seeking to understand the science behind our psychological need for purpose and meaning—and how these needs can be met through connectedness and cultural narratives. Through a rich tapestry of stories, studies, spirituality, and philosophy, Heine offers a clear and compelling vision for leading a meaningful life amid the complexities of the modern world."
— Michael Muthukrishna, London School of Economics

# start making sense

# start making sense

How Existential Psychology Can Help Us
Build Meaningful Lives in Absurd Times

## Steven J. Heine

BASIC BOOKS
New York

Cover design by Chin-Yee Lai
Cover images © Cagkan Sayin/Shutterstock.com;
© Honyojima/Shutterstock.com
Cover copyright © 2025 Hachette Book Group, Inc.

Basic Books
Hachette Book Group
1290 Avenue of the Americas, New York, NY 10104
www.basicbooks.com

Printed in the United States of America

First Edition: January 2025

Published by Basic Books, an imprint of Hachette Book Group, Inc. The Basic Books name and logo is a registered trademark of the Hachette Book Group.

The Hachette Speakers Bureau provides a wide range of authors for speaking events. To find out more, go to hachettespeakersbureau.com or email HachetteSpeakers@hbgusa.com.

Basic books may be purchased in bulk for business, educational, or promotional use. For more information, please contact your local bookseller or the Hachette Book Group Special Markets Department at special.markets@hbgusa.com.

The publisher is not responsible for websites (or their content) that are not owned by the publisher.

Print book interior design by Bart Dawson.

Library of Congress Cataloging-in-Publication Data
Names: Heine, Steven J., author.
Title: Start making sense : how existential psychology can help us build
    meaningful lives in absurd times / Steven J. Heine.
Description: First edition. | New York : Basic Books, 2025. | Includes
    bibliographical references and index.
Identifiers: LCCN 2024029140 | ISBN 9781541600812 (hardcover) |
    ISBN 9781541600829 (epub)
Subjects: LCSH: Existential psychology.
Classification: LCC BF204.5 .H45 2025 | DDC 150.19/2—dc23/eng/20241105
LC record available at https://lccn.loc.gov/2024029140

ISBNs: 9781541600812 (hardcover), 9781541600829 (ebook)

LSC-C

Printing 1, 2024

*To Christine,*
*Thanks for helping to make my own life*
*so much more meaningful.*

# contents

# start
# making
# sense

# Chapter 1

# The New Age of Anxiety

Man does not suffer so much from poverty today
as he suffers from the fact that he has become
a cog in a large machine, an automaton, that his life
has become empty and lost its meaning.

Erich Fromm, *Escape from Freedom*

Everyone seems on edge now. You've surely noticed it. It seems that everywhere one turns, people are awash with uncertainty and anxiety. So many people are struggling as they worry about the future. The world seems confusing, and people no longer seem to agree on the basic facts of what is happening around them. And it seems that every other young adult has been diagnosed with a mental health issue. These have been anxious times indeed.

People's anxieties surely got worse when the COVID pandemic upended their lives in countless ways. Making matters worse, climate change threatens to submerge cities along the coastlines while burning up the interior, artificial intelligence threatens to take over our jobs, social media makes people worry about how their lives compare with others, and increasing political polarization has gotten to the point that Thanksgiving dinner can feel about as tense as trying to defuse a bomb. The world feels far less stable and predictable than it did before.

The amount of uncertainty in our lives can be quantified, and in 1990 a group of economists set out to do precisely this by creating the World Uncertainty Index, which is largely based on how often words related to uncertainty appear in various publications. Over the first decade of its existence, the index hewed close to a score of around 10,000. After the 9/11 terrorist attacks in 2001, the index spiked up to reach 28,000. It jumped even higher, to 39,000, in 2012 during the debt crisis that threatened to break up the Eurozone. And then in 2020, during the early days of the COVID pandemic, the Black Lives Matter protests, and an extremely divisive American presidential election, it soared to its highest point yet of over 55,000—about twice as much uncertainty as came with the 9/11 terrorist attacks.[1]

Given that the uncertainty index, like the Dow Jones, has risen and fallen while trending ever upward, it wouldn't be surprising if your blood pressure has tracked a similar pattern over this same period. This is because we *just can't stand it* when things don't make sense. We have a psychological system that seeks to maintain a sense of meaning such that we can feel everything is stable and orderly and can predict and control what will happen to us. When people experience uncertainty, they don't know what is going to happen and they are unable to prepare themselves for it. Uncertainty makes people feel things are spinning out of control, leaving them helpless and worried.

The soaring levels of uncertainty that the world has been going through has left many people in a highly anxious state. Despite how uncertain things have been recently, we may be able to take some comfort in knowing that there have been previous eras of pronounced uncertainty and people somehow managed to get through those times. We can learn something about our current predicament by considering another time when the world also struggled with its collective anxieties. The last time the world made as little sense as it does now was during the middle of the twentieth century. People had recently struggled through the worst economic crisis in modern times only to face the most destructive war in human history, followed by the dawn of the Cold War and the realization that all of humanity could be destroyed in a nuclear Armageddon. It was a time of enormous upheaval, insecurity, and collective angst.

In 1947 the existentialist poet W. H. Auden wrote a book-length poem in which he pondered what it meant to live during such an anxious period. Auden believed that people were feeling scared, uncertain, and disillusioned as they suffered through a collective crisis of identity and purpose because the old certainties of the past had been shattered by the war and the challenges of modernity. Auden titled his poem about this period *The Age of Anxiety.*

The parallels between that turbulent age of anxiety with the nerve-racking times of the early twenty-first century are striking, as they were both periods in which people struggled to find a way to cope with feelings of stress and a lack of purpose in their lives. Some have called the current era that we're living through "the new age of anxiety," and I find that label to be especially appropriate. The early twenty-first century has been an exceptionally trying time, and it has created a rather chaotic culture in which people are struggling to find a way to lead their lives.

Why are people having such a difficult time during this new age of anxiety? To answer this question, we need to consider the role of a key psychological characteristic that helps people to successfully confront the difficulties of life—that is, *the sense that one is leading a meaningful life.* When people feel that they are leading a meaningful life, their lives make more sense to them. They have a sense of purpose that guides their behaviors. They feel that their lives really matter and that they're capable of making a difference in the world. Meaningful lives make people feel more existentially grounded—they know who they are and why they are doing what they're doing. When people feel that their lives are meaningful, they enjoy greater well-being and are less likely to suffer from the anxieties that come with uncertainty. The importance of living a meaningful life is a central focus of this book, and in the remaining chapters, we'll consider why we need meaningful lives, what they do for us, and how we can get them.

As important as it is to people's well-being to feel that their lives are meaningful, there are signs that meaningful lives are getting harder to come by. For example, every year since 1966 a representative sample of American freshmen college students has been asked about their most important life goals. Among the goals they were asked to rank was "developing a meaningful philosophy of life." In 1966, a full 88 percent of students selected it as their most important goal. However, fewer than half of college students in the twenty-first century saw having a meaningful philosophy of life to be a key goal in their lives—rather, the most highly ranked goal was to be very well off financially. Over this period college students became far less likely to see their lives as being guided by a meaningful philosophy of life. I think this change of attitudes can help to shed some light on why life in the twenty-first century has been so nerve-racking.[2]

Why might American students in the twenty-first century be feeling that they have less of a meaningful philosophy of life than before? To answer this, we need to consider what are the most reliable sources of meaning in people's lives. As we'll discuss throughout this book, the key ways that people derive a sense of meaning in their lives comes from the *connections* that they create between their lives and what happens around them. A life that is richly connected tends to be more meaningful. So what kinds of connections make life feel more meaningful?

First, people build a sense of meaning from the close interpersonal relationships that they have in their lives. When people feel supported by a tight network of relationships, their lives feel more meaningful: they can share anything that happens to them with their loved ones. These feelings of connection with others can also come from people's sense of community. When people feel that they belong to a community, this helps them build a sense of identity, and it contributes to the feeling of a meaningful life. People who have careers that provide them with a sense of identity, purpose, and mastery also feel their lives are more meaningful. In addition, the spiritual connections that people form between their lives and with what they believe transcends them are especially important in leading people to feel that their lives are meaningful. When people feel connected to something much larger than themselves, their lives feel more existentially grounded. All of these kinds of connections help people to feel better prepared to face the challenges of their lives, and we'll discuss each connection in this book.

With these bases of a meaningful life in mind, let's consider how we can better understand the turbulent times of this new age of anxiety. I'm a cultural psychologist, and I study how culture shapes people's minds. Our culture influences how we see the world, how we understand ourselves, and whether we feel that our lives are meaningful. But a challenge in studying cultures is that people have a difficult time appreciating their own culture because it is largely invisible to them, like the water that surrounds a fish. I've found that when we compare one culture to another, we gain a new perspective, which can shed some valuable light: we can better see aspects of our culture that are typically hidden from us. I think we stand to learn much about the tumultuous culture of the new age of anxiety by contrasting it with what the culture was like during the original age of anxiety. How have the lives of typical Americans changed between these two eras?

There are, of course, countless differences between the typical American's life from the mid-twentieth century compared to that of the early twenty-first century, but to understand what is contributing to people's tense feelings of angst, we need to focus on those aspects of the culture that contribute to people's sense of having a meaningful life. That is, we need to consider how well connected are Americans' lives between these two eras.

To begin, let's see how the typical American's interpersonal connections are compared to before. Unfortunately, people's connections seem to have weakened over time. First, people are spending far less time interacting with their family members than before. For example, one survey contrasted the habits of American families between the 1970s and the 1990s and found that, over that period, the time that families spent together vacationing, watching TV, or sitting and talking decreased, and the percentage of families who said that they usually ate dinner together dropped by about a third. By 2022, the average American reported only having about three dinners per week with their families. The picture doesn't get any better when we turn to people's romantic relationships, as married couples have been spending less time together than before, approximately nine hours per week less in 2003 than in 1975. Families are just not as connected now compared with a few decades ago.[3]

Americans' friendships have also been weakening. The amount of time that young people spend with their friends has dropped by about two-thirds in just the past couple of decades. And this recent trend built upon a sharp drop in sociability that was documented from the 1960s until 2000, which found that people were spending about 30 percent less time informally chatting with friends than they had in the 1960s, and they were about one-quarter less likely to spend time with their neighbors. In 2023, the US Surgeon General released a report entitled *Our Epidemic of Loneliness and Isolation*, which found that the number of Americans who reported having only three or fewer close friends has increased by over 80 percent in the past thirty years. Over the past several decades, Americans have become steadily less likely to spend time with their friends.[4]

Americans have also become far less engaged with their communities. In his classic book *Bowling Alone*, the political scientist Robert Putnam documented how much Americans have become detached from their communities compared with before. For example, Americans were more than twice as likely to belong to the PTA in the 1950s than they were four decades later. Likewise, far fewer people belong to civic groups than before. They are only about half as likely to belong to a union. They are far less likely to belong to service clubs, such as Rotary or Lions, and they are less likely to participate in community sports leagues. People no longer feel that they can turn to the community in times of need and are left having to figure out for themselves how to cope with the challenges that they face.[5]

People also derive much meaning from the connections that they create with their work, but these connections too have been increasingly undermined. For one, people change jobs more frequently than before, with millennials being considerably more likely to change jobs compared with those from previous generations. The twenty-first century has seen the rise of the gig economy, where people are often engaged in a number of temporary side hustles, such as driving for a car-share company or completing surveys online for pay. As the number of people working remotely has risen sharply, fewer have a workplace they can identify with or a set of colleagues with whom they regularly interact. The trend of people losing their jobs to automation has accelerated, and the specter of artificial intelligence taking over so many jobs has also placed people's future career identities under threat as well.[6]

Americans have been losing yet another kind of connection that is closely tied to a meaningful life—connections to a higher power. Since the 1950s, Americans have become about one-third less likely to attend church regularly. In 2020, for the first time in recorded history, fewer than half of Americans belonged to a house of worship. A full 30 percent of Americans say that they don't follow any religion, whereas in 1972 only 5 percent said this. Some people may see this as an encouraging development because of the intolerance that traditional religious beliefs can seem to foster. However, research on meaningful lives paints a more worrisome picture of this national trend. The potential cost of this secularization movement is that nonreligious people are far less likely than religious people to say that their lives are meaningful, and they show evidence of worse mental and physical well-being as well.[7]

These data on the ways that people are becoming disconnected from their families, friends, spouses, communities, careers, and religions are all from Americans. But the American experience is not unique, and there are parallels in many other countries around the globe. One clear trend around the world is that many countries are becoming steadily more individualistic over time. People are becoming more likely to prioritize their own personal interests ahead of those of their close relationships and groups. Research finds that people who live in more individualistic cultures tend to have less meaning in their lives. This trend suggests that people around the world are losing many of the traditional kinds of connections that form the foundation of a meaningful life.[8]

The existential psychiatrist Viktor Frankl described the kind of society that we're currently living in—one with fewer traditional bases of meaning—as an "existential vacuum." In an existential vacuum, people struggle with finding ways to see their lives as meaningful. Their lives are characterized by a state of boredom, emptiness, and apathy as they have difficulties in finding something in their lives that they can feel engaged with and can make their lives feel meaningful. In these contexts people are often searching for anything that can distract them from how pointless their lives feel. In an effort to fill this void, they may chase after superficial sources of gratification, such as excessive consumption or mindless entertainment, but these only serve to temporarily relieve their itch. Frankl thought that a key challenge for modern societies was that people did not have sufficient connections in their lives. He recognized that when people are struggling to find ways to lead a meaningful life, they are more vulnerable to developing anxiety and depression. The culture of twenty-first-century America shares much in common with an existential vacuum, and Frankl's concerns with the aimlessness of people's lives seems more relevant than ever.[9]

The challenges in this difficult era are quite evident to everyone. In a recent survey, Americans were asked how their lives compared to those of people like them from fifty years ago. A majority of them reported that life is *worse* today than it was fifty years ago, and most people expected that things would only continue to get worse in the future. When you look at the erosion of the key sources of meaning in people's lives, perhaps it isn't surprising that people say they are worse off now than before. It is difficult to feel fulfilled in a life that isn't well connected.[10]

But wait a minute. When you think more closely about this, the claim that life for Americans has become much worse than before is puzzling. It's puzzling because over this period of time, by many standards, so many things in the average American's life have gotten far *better* than they were before. To shed some light on the curious predicament of people's lives in the twenty-first century, let's consider some of the objective improvements in the quality of life that the average American now enjoys in contrast to the time of the original age of anxiety.

To begin, it would seem that average Americans are far wealthier now than they were before. In 1950 the median family income in the United States was $35,442. By 2017, controlling for inflation, it had more than doubled to $75,938. Much of the extra money that people have been receiving has gone toward the accumulation of more and more possessions, which they store in their houses, which have grown steadily over this time. In 1950, the average house size for a new single-family home in the United States was just under 1,000 square feet, yet in 2015 it had more than doubled to around 2,600 square feet. These are quite dramatic signs of economic improvements, although rising inequality means that many of these improvements have been more concentrated among the wealthy. It might be tempting to conclude that Americans' lives have become relatively more lavish because everyone is working harder now than before, but actually the opposite is true. In 2017, on average, Americans were working about 12 percent fewer hours than they did in 1950, so Americans have been experiencing an increase in leisure time compared to the past.

With the extra income they've been receiving, Americans are retiring earlier than they used to. In 1950, the average age of retirement was 70 years old; by 2010, this had dropped to 64 years old. Moreover, the amount of time that people spend in retirement has dramatically increased for the simple fact that people are living much longer now. In 1950, life expectancy in the United States was 68.1 years, which was less than the average retirement age then, meaning that typically Americans continued to work until their deaths. In contrast, life expectancy in 2021 was 79— about eleven additional years of life since 1950—and much of that increase is spent in retirement. People's lifespans have been increasing because of numerous medical advancements, among them vaccines that make people less likely to get sick and medical treatments that are able to treat, cure, and prevent many of the ailments that used to kill broad swaths of the population in the first half of the twentieth century. With such improvements in income, leisure, retirement, and health, the typical American's life would seem to be objectively better off than before. And these improvements in the quality of life are not just specific to Americans. As Steven Pinker argued in his book *Enlightenment Now,* since the mid-twenty-first century, life across the whole globe has been improving on almost all measurable metrics for centuries, with the notable exception of climate change. By these objective terms, it would seem that, for the most part, life has been getting easier.[11]

This contrast between the culture of Americans living through this new age of anxiety and those that lived through the original age of anxiety thus reveals two clear trends. On the one hand, life has been getting objectively better than before. It is easier for most people to have their basic physiological needs and desires satisfied than it was in the 1950s. On the other hand, however, people's existential needs are not being fulfilled as well now. The connections that provide the key foundations that underlie a meaningful life have been eroding over time. This leaves us in the ironic situation where, despite how much better our basic needs are being met, we're suffering more than we did before. The fact that life has become so much more challenging now, despite all of the material improvements, underscores just how important it is for people to have their existential needs met. We find it hard to thrive when our lives don't feel meaningful.

As people are struggling to find a sense of meaning in their lives in the new age of anxiety, they are bearing the consequences. The collective mental health of the world is not good right now. Many countries in the world have witnessed rapid growth in rates of anxiety, depression, and other psychopathologies. In particular, the so-called deaths of despair, which consist of deaths from alcoholic liver disease, suicide, and drug overdoses, have increased dramatically. These kinds of deaths await many who are unable to live meaningful and fulfilling lives. Since 1950, the rates of deaths of despair have tripled in the United States. Many of the struggles that people face have been increasing, particularly since around 2008, when rates of psychological distress, major depression, and suicide began to rise rather dramatically, with the increases being especially pronounced among the youth. These struggles with mental health spiked even more during the COVID pandemic, particularly with young people. As one large investigation of the rapid rise in mental illness among American young people concluded, these stark increases are happening because "American culture has increasingly valued extrinsic and self-centered goals such as money and status, while increasingly devaluing community, affiliation, and finding meaning in life." The difficulties of pursuing a meaningful life in the new age of anxiety have been taking a grim toll on people's mental health.[12]

## Learning from the Existentialists

As people struggle to find meaning in the existential vacuum of the new age of anxiety, many are desperate for some much-needed guidance. How can we cope with all of this uncertainty and go about leading a more meaningful life? Again, I think the original age of anxiety can provide us with much guidance to help us through these difficult times. It was during the original age of anxiety, while people were struggling with all of the angst of those uncertain times, that the world gave birth to a new philosophy. This new philosophy sought to spell out how people could embrace their freedoms and confront their anxieties in order to pursue a life that was rich in authenticity and meaning. As one of the founders of this new philosophy, Jean-Paul Sartre, put it, "Everything has been figured out, except how to live." This new philosophy sought to provide people with guidance for how they could live a more meaningful life. It was called existentialism.

The existentialists were a collection of largely European thinkers who first emerged during the chaotic times of the Second World War. They understood that many traditions from the past that people relied upon for guiding their lives could no longer be counted on in the rapidly changing environment of the modern era. The existentialists recognized that people can't look toward others to find out how to live a meaningful life—there was no one-size-fits-all approach that could work for everyone. Rather, they realized that people's lives unfolded as a direct product of their own choices and actions. They encouraged people to recognize that they were fundamentally free to decide how to chart their own life course.

In the aftermath of the Second World War, the ideas expressed by the existentialists couldn't have arrived at a more opportune time. An extremely uncertain and anxious world eagerly embraced their intoxicating ideas about freedom, authenticity, and the pursuit of a meaningful life. The existentialists were celebrities of their era: the press closely covered all that they had to say, and many of them spoke to packed audiences wherever they traveled. So popular were the existentialists that they did something that no other intellectual movement has ever done—they inspired their own fashion. Their devotees, who could often be found smoking cigarettes in cafés or jazz bars, had long straight hair and wore wire-rimmed glasses and black woolen turtlenecks. Let's briefly meet the key figures of the existential movement, who we'll encounter again throughout this book.

The existentialists included the charismatic French Algerian Albert Camus, who, aside from his influential contributions to philosophy, was also an actor, playwright, director, journalist, and novelist, as well as his university's soccer team's goalkeeper. His work was well recognized in his lifetime, earning him a medal for his efforts as editor-in-chief of the key underground newspaper of the French Resistance and the Nobel Prize in Literature. Camus was handsome, confident, and courageous and enjoyed much popularity. The journalist Adam Gopnik called him "the Don Draper of existentialism," as he had throngs of female fans and was famous for his many affairs.[13]

Camus saw people in a never-ending pursuit of a meaningful life, striving to form coherent connections among all of the different aspects of their lives. However, Camus recognized that finding meaning in life was a tall order, as he viewed the universe to be fundamentally meaningless, lacking any divine basis that people could turn to for guidance. He saw that humans were thus in a predicament of trying to create meaning out of a meaningless world. Sometimes people would become aware that the meanings in their own lives had been constructed like a house of cards—ready to collapse whenever they recognized the meaninglessness of their efforts. Camus called this experience of being aware of the inherent contradictions of life "the absurd," and when people were in the absurd, they would feel that nothing made sense anymore and would succumb to their existential anxieties. He felt that people needed to escape the absurd by doggedly continuing in their pursuit to construct a meaningful life. Camus remained an optimist and felt that we all can, and must, create a meaningful life for ourselves. His storied life came to an abrupt halt at the young age of forty-six, when his car crashed into a plane tree in central France.

One of Camus's closest friends, until a later falling out, was Jean-Paul Sartre. Sartre was an enormously influential thinker who passionately exhorted people to live their lives freely and authentically. The Frenchman saw that the ways that people's lives unfolded were all due to the choices that they made along the way. As he stated: "There is no traced-out path to lead man to his salvation; he must constantly invent his own path. But, to invent it, he is free, responsible, without excuse, and every hope lies within him." Sartre always practiced what he preached, and he showed the world what a life of freedom could look like. He famously led a polyamorous life together with his lifelong lover and fellow existentialist Simone de Beauvoir, with headlines calling them "the world's first modern couple." Although the freedoms of a polyamorous lifestyle have recently been growing in popularity, Sartre and Beauvoir were trailblazers and had to figure things out on their own. Sartre suggested they start their commitment by signing a two-year lease, but it continued for half a century until he died. They lived a bohemian lifestyle in Paris, and Sartre remained a freelance public intellectual throughout his long life, never taking a formal position at any university despite being one of the world's most celebrated philosophers.[14]

Simone de Beauvoir was a free-spirited philosopher who saw uncertainty and freedom to be at the core of people's existences. She felt that everyone should aspire to be in control of their own destinies, and this led her to play a key role in launching the modern feminist movement, arguing for the dismantling of the patriarchal structures that continued to oppress women. Always a champion of the downtrodden, Beauvoir embraced the diversity and complexity of the human experience and sought to liberate people from the injustices of society. Her life exemplified her many freedoms: she questioned societal traditions and enjoyed many affairs with both men and women alike, rejected all formal academic positions, and traveled the world.

Camus, Sartre, and Beauvoir had all been greatly influenced by the works of the dour German intellectual Martin Heidegger. Heidegger argued that people are inherently relational beings whose lives are inextricably intertwined with others, the particular contexts that they exist within, and are linked to how they understand their pasts and imagine their futures. He urged people to live authentically by embracing their freedoms and taking responsibility for their choices. But Heidegger's reputation ultimately suffered as he was unable to take responsibility for his own puzzling life's choices. He had been charmed by Hitler and joined the Nazi Party, which resulted in him betraying both his Jewish mentor, Edmund Husserl, and his Jewish lover, Hannah Arendt. In the subsequent decades, he tried to downplay this dark chapter of his life story, but he never apologized for his actions, nor how they had impacted those closest to him.

The existentialists also included a survivor of Auschwitz, the Austrian psychiatrist Viktor Frankl. It was while enduring the horrors of the concentration camps that Frankl identified how the inner decisions that people made regarding how they faced their adversities affected whether they lived or died. Frankl felt that people needed a sense of purpose to survive and that this laid the foundation for a meaningful life. His autobiographical account of his time in the concentration camps, *Man's Search for Meaning*, continues to be read in college courses around the world. Though it discloses the deep inhumanity of this time, it is surprisingly inspiring and helps people to confront their sufferings, live in the present moment, embrace their freedoms, and strive to lead a meaningful life.

The existentialists built upon the ideas of some nineteenth-century European thinkers, called the proto-existentialists. Just emerging from the Enlightenment, the traditional ways of the world were loosening, as was the authority of the church, and individuals were recognized as having more choices in their lives than before. Søren Kierkegaard, an anxious and melancholic Dane, was the first to identify how people were free to choose their life paths. He recognized that people could pursue an authentic existence by embracing their freedoms, yet at the same time he saw that it was those same freedoms that were at the root of their anxieties. Kierkegaard's ideas had much impact on the ever-suffering Russian novelist Fyodor Dostoevsky, who explored the alienation that some feel when struggling to follow their own life paths. His characters strived to live their lives authentically but suffered from the responsibilities of their choices.

Friedrich Nietzsche was quite accomplished in his youth, a young wunderkind professor of philology and an amateur composer. He became close friends with the composer Richard Wagner, and he counted the king of Bavaria as a fan of his works. But he was forced to give up his professorship at the young age of thirty-four because of health issues. From that point on, the stateless Nietzsche was supported by a small university pension, which allowed him to travel from country to country in search of a climate that could ease his persistent health problems. During these itinerant years, he would spend his days wandering along mountain paths, deep in thought, and later scribbling down his ideas. He would write in the voice of the prophet Zarathustra, urging his followers to strive to transcend the shackles of society and religion to become Übermenschen, overmen or supermen who embrace all of life's challenges, are authentic, and create their own life-affirming values. Nietzsche had rejected the idea of absolute truths, noting that we all experience the world through our own subjective lenses. Though few people read Nietzsche's philosophical musings during his lifetime, he became famous after his death and his ideas had a great impact on the existentialists.

The existentialists offered guidance for how people could best live their own lives, and we will revisit many of their ideas throughout this book. They emerged from the individualistic cultures of Western Europe where people were breaking free of the restrictive traditions of the past. The existentialists had largely abandoned formal religion, and they recognized that this meant that there were no longer any fundamental guidelines to dictate how people should lead their lives. People needed to discover the meaning in their own lives for themselves. When the existentialists abandoned religion, they also left behind the promise of an afterlife. They recognized that an awareness of the finitude of life brought forth a key source of existential dread: they questioned how one could find purpose in a life that was destined to become nothing but dust in the end. But the existentialists saw that confronting one's mortality could remind one of the urgency to live an authentic and meaningful life.

The existentialists all agreed on the key point that people's lives are ultimately what they make of them. There's no path that's been marked for people to follow; they need to blaze their own trails as they go along. The existentialists were captivated by the new freedoms that were available in the modern age and saw that people were free to choose how they approached their lives. They felt that people needed to use their freedoms to help them to live their lives authentically, making their life choices in ways that were consistent with their deepest values.

The freedoms that the existentialists preached about are exhilarating, and this was the primary attraction to so many of their ardent followers. But the existentialists recognized that our freedoms always come with a significant cost: if our destinies are up to ourselves, then we are ultimately responsible for our actions. Each choice that we make comes burdened with responsibilities that can weigh heavily on us, knowing that all of what happens to us is brought on by our own choices. The existentialists recognized that our freedom thus always comes bundled with much anxiety as we must contend with the possibility that we'll sometimes make the wrong choice. They saw that both freedom and anxiety were at the core of human existence.

The existentialists also recognized that the ways that people can chart the courses of their lives must always be done from their own subjective perspectives. Though we may feel that we are directly perceiving an objective reality, the existentialists realized that we are always experiencing the events in our lives through a story that we are telling as we go along. As Beauvoir put it, "One can never know oneself but only narrate oneself." The stories that we tell about ourselves and about our worlds determine how we make sense of our experiences, understand who we are, and direct our actions. Our life stories are guided by cultural values, and even though we are all unique individuals, each living a one-of-a-kind life, our stories share many common themes with those of others. As we'll see throughout this book, the ways that people tell their own life stories determines the meanings in their lives.[15]

## The Science of Existentialism

In the mid-twentieth century, existentialist ideas were enormously influential, and they were embraced around the world. However, these ideas were largely discussed and debated before there was really any scientific understanding around the issues that they raised. Their ideas were seductive and fun to ponder, but at the time there was no scientific basis to them. There was no scientific guidance available for how people could pursue a rich and meaningful life.

Recently, a new discipline of psychology has emerged that studies the kinds of questions that the existentialists originally raised but uses the tools of science. This field of existential psychology has sought to provide a scientific foundation for the pursuit of a meaningful life, and it offers a guide for how we can start making sense of our lives. As we'll see, this new science of existentialism has uncovered a lot of evidence in line with what the existentialists were arguing. It has explored such questions as: What aspects of people's lives lead them to feel the most meaningful? How do people come to narrate their life stories, and how might they tell their life stories in a more constructive way? How do people respond to having so much choice in their lives, and how can they come to live with their choices? How can people cope with the existential anxiety that comes with the awareness that their lives on this planet are so brief? How can people become more resilient when facing life's challenges? How do people respond when they find themselves stuck in the absurd? This book strives to provide some scientifically grounded answers to these kinds of questions, which are so central to our existences.

For the past couple of decades, my students and I have been conducting psychological experiments on these very kinds of questions. We have sought to understand how people come to make sense of their selves and their worlds. Our research has explored people's strategies for helping their lives to make sense, and the costs that people pay when their lives are incoherent. We have studied how people's cultures provide value and meaning in their lives, and how it shapes the ways that people understand themselves. We have investigated how people come to terms with the freedoms inherent in their lives. We have also considered the role that people's spiritual beliefs play within their pursuit of meaning. We've made much progress in being able to explain how people are able to lead meaningful lives.

One key question that we've investigated is what happens to people when their lives no longer make any sense—when they find themselves stuck in the absurd that Camus described. To study how people react when they feel meaningless, we designed a series of some highly unusual psychological experiments. We have probed people's responses to the absurd by having them confront the surreal films of David Lynch, watch an overly realistic humanoid robot, or be the unwitting participant in a magical trick where one person mysteriously transforms into another. In our efforts to investigate the absurd, we've had people play black-jack with reverse-colored cards and get immersed in the dream-like world of Kafka, and we've studied how people react when their closest relationships betray them. All of these studies point to some common strategies that people rely on to make their lives seem less absurd, as they struggle to move forward in their pursuit of a meaningful life.[16]

In the following chapters, we will consider how people can start making sense, even when everything may seem absurd around them. We'll explore why people need meaning in their lives in the first place, and how they go about trying to maintain it. And we'll discuss a number of strategies for how readers can better meet their existential needs, to help them lead more meaningful lives. These strategies can help prepare readers to live more effectively in this new age of anxiety.

# Chapter 2

# Becoming an Existential Ape

Lacking external enemies and obstacles, and forced
into the oppressive narrowness and conformity
of custom, man impatiently ripped himself apart,
persecuted himself, gnawed at himself, gave himself
no peace and abused himself, this animal who
battered himself raw on the bars of his cage
and who is supposed to be "tamed."

Friedrich Nietzsche, *On the Genealogy of Morality*

Albert Camus opened his famous book *The Myth of Sisyphus* with the statement: "There is but one truly serious philosophical problem, and that is suicide." It is indeed a vexing problem to understand how it can be that people may sometimes consider ending their own lives. And this disturbing fact points to a key question that this book will try to assess: Why is it that people can get so hobbled by their existential anxieties?[1]

People often get distressed when they try to make sense of the lives that they are leading, and this can lead to a great deal of existential angst, which can be a severe threat to people's well-being, leading to such problems as depression, anxiety, substance abuse, and suicide. But why people suffer from these kinds of existential anxieties is a puzzling question when you reflect upon it. Like all species, humans face challenges that we must surmount to survive. We are threatened by incapacitating disease, starvation, violence, and environmental disasters. But in addition to these external threats to our well-being, humans are also faced with some daunting internal challenges. We struggle in the face of our anxieties when we fail to feel that our lives are meaningful. Over the course of our time on earth, we will often consider how we are doing with our life projects. We may ask questions like: Does my life make sense? Am I doing a good job? What is my purpose? During our darkest moments, when we don't have satisfying answers to these questions, we may tumble into a pit of despair and even question what is the point of life.

Yet this particular philosophical problem becomes even more challenging to make sense of when we contrast the human situation with that of our species' closest relatives, for in many respects, our existential concerns are hard to find in other species. The psychologist Jesse Bering noted that "over the course of what amounts to centuries of meticulous observation by primatologists at hundreds of different sites, on no occasion has a distraught or ostracized ape ever been seen, for example, to climb to the highest branch it could find and jump. That's us. We're the ape that jumps."[2]

So how did humans become the ape uniquely cursed with this existential plight? How did our survival become dependent upon not just our abilities to confront the many external threats we face but also how we handle our own existential anxieties? How did we become an ape capable of torturing itself? When Camus attempted to address the problem of suicide, he stated: "I therefore conclude that the meaning of life is the most urgent of questions." I think Camus is right: the reason we're sometimes the ape that jumps is that we're the ape in pursuit of a meaningful life. Generally speaking, most people are not content to just live their lives however they may unfold; they're trying to figure out how they can lead a richer and more meaningful life and how they can avoid falling into existential despair. But before we can consider how we can best go about pursuing a meaningful life, we need to first understand why humans came to depend so much on meaning in the first place.[3]

## Living in Worlds of Meaning

One key factor that contributes to our struggles to live a meaningful life is that we are animals that exist within an *ecology of meaning*. Unlike other organisms, we don't just approach events in our environment in terms of their objective characteristics, such as whether something can provide opportunities for food, safety, or reproduction; we also consider what those events *mean* to us, and those meanings can vary quite widely across cultures and from individual to individual. Everything we encounter is wrapped up in layers of meanings, many of which are subjective and personal, and those meanings determine the ways that we make sense of our situations and the ways that we act. Moreover, our abilities to make sense of the meanings we encounter provide a key foundation for our pursuit of a meaningful life. I suggest our species could be renamed *Homo significativa*—meaningful man.[4]

To understand our existential needs for a meaningful life, we first need to consider how it is that humans became an animal that exists within an ecology of meaning. But what precisely is meaning? Meaning is one of those words that, well, can be hard to know exactly what it means. And this is because the word *meaning* commonly has two related but distinct definitions. When Camus declares that "the meaning of life is the most urgent of questions," he is referring to people's concerns with *existential meaning*. This kind of meaning reflects people's higher-order kinds of concerns, such as whether their life is connected to a sense of significance, coherence, and purpose. Existential meaning is what connects people's actions with concerns that transcend the here and now. These are the kinds of meanings that people are usually referring to when they talk about the meaning of life, and much of this book will focus on this kind of meaning.[5]

But there is a second, broader definition of meaning, which we'll explore more throughout this chapter. It's the kind of meaning that people consider when they ask questions such as: What does your hometown mean to you? Or what does our company's new policy on working from home mean? This second definition of *meaning* is something quite specific and simple: meaning is ultimately about *connections* between events, entities, and ideas. There are many kinds of connections that make up the meanings that we have in our lives. First, the connections we have with our closest relationships provide us with key sources of meanings and some of our most poignant feelings of meaning in our lives. But the connections that underlie meaning go far beyond our interpersonal relationships. We also get meanings from the connections that exist between us and events in the world and that link us and events in the world with ideas. Whenever we encounter something, the ideas that we expect to connect to that thing are what create a sense of meaning for us.

For example, consider what your job means to you. What are all of the ideas that you connect with your job? These may include the sense of pride you get when you do your job well, the fun conversations you have with your coworkers on your lunch break, the promotion that you're hoping to get, your most dreaded tasks that you have to do, your boss, your commute, your paycheck, and your company's main competitors. All of these ideas that you can connect to your job and more are what determine what your job means to you. We connect these ideas about our job into large, interrelated networks of ideas, which I call *meaning frameworks*. We develop these meaning frameworks across our lifetimes, and the particular meaning frameworks that we have shape how we interpret the events in our lives.

Psychologists have understood meaning frameworks to be the basis of how people understand the events in their lives, although psychologists tend to prefer more technical words to describe meaning frameworks, such as *schemas, paradigms, mental models,* and *worldviews*. But all of these terms capture the idea that when we understand something, we are basing that understanding on what ideas or events we expect to go together in predictable ways. The meanings that we create and share about our worlds are our simulations about what the world is actually like. We are motivated to understand the world, and we do the best we can to create meaning frameworks that accurately reflect it. When we encounter something new, we try to relate it to other things around us, and over time, with repeated experiences and discussions with others, we continue to add to and edit our meaning frameworks until they become better and better models of the worlds that we live in. These meaning frameworks allow us to understand our worlds and to feel that we are able to predict what will happen. However, the particular meaning frameworks that we embrace can vary widely among people.

Take the case of the COVID pandemic. What does the pandemic mean to you? In 2020, the COVID pandemic rapidly spread until it enveloped the entire globe, resulting in lockdowns in every country and several millions of deaths. Even those who avoided getting ill had their lives upended in countless ways as people were separated from their loved ones. They could no longer go to their workplaces, and everyone was left figuring out how to live their lives in social isolation. Though COVID was the result of a real virus, which followed the basic principles of viral transmission, people experienced the pandemic in very different ways. People's experiences varied so much, in part, because their meaning frameworks about the pandemic were vastly different from one another. Let's briefly reflect here on some of the ways that people's accounts of the pandemic differ.

Some people remained rather unfazed by the realization that the COVID virus was spreading around the world. Many saw COVID as a rather trivial disease, with the symptoms akin to those from a cold or the flu—a big "nothingburger" that shouldn't be any cause for alarm. In contrast, others saw COVID as the most severe health crisis of the past century, resulting in a sharp reduction in the average longevity of humans across the planet, and feared that the disease would continue to cause severe symptoms for many years after infection. Some people understood that masks were the key means for controlling the spread of the virus and urged the government to mandate masks in all public spaces, whereas others felt that masks were an afront to human dignity and any mandates for their use were evidence of a totalitarian government striving to take away people's basic freedoms. Likewise, when it came to COVID vaccines, some people claimed that the vaccines were hopelessly ineffective, if not dangerous, with the potential to alter people's DNA, make them sterile, or cause a host of serious diseases. In contrast, others celebrated the rapid development of highly effective vaccines as the pinnacle of scientific progress. They saw the vaccines as a necessary tool for bringing an end to the pandemic and something that should be required of everyone.

The sheer variety of accounts that people came up with to make sense of COVID is indeed rather stunning, and many meaning frameworks were not limited by plausibility, evidence, or reason. These divergent accounts of COVID remind us that people don't interact with reality directly; rather, people understand events in the world through the meanings that they connect with them. The different meaning frameworks that we have about COVID shaped how we understood the disease and how we experienced the pandemic.

As our competing accounts of the pandemic remind us, how we see events in the world is a product of the meanings that we relate to them: we understand and experience them through the lenses of the particular meaning frameworks that we hold. And the ways that we see things affect how we interact with our worlds and experience events. Friedrich Nietzsche emphasized the inherent subjectivity of the meaning frameworks that we construct about our worlds. He understood that everything people knew was based on the worldviews that they embraced. As he said: "There can be no facts, only interpretations." We understand each new piece of information by relating it to what we already know, and in so doing, we continue to add to our meaning frameworks, which may often be idiosyncratic and which we keep building upon throughout our lives.[6]

The connections that we make between ideas are what give them meaning to us, and this is true regardless of whether we're talking about simple events in our lives, such as our jobs, or the ideas associated with our grandest philosophical or spiritual pursuits. Thus, this more general definition of meaning as connection is broader than and encompasses the more specific definition of existential meanings that give our lives meaning. Existential meaning is also based upon connections, with the key difference being that these connections link our lives to ultimate sources of value, significance, and purpose, which help us to transcend our mortal existences. Our lives have many connections, including connections to our interpersonal relationships, our communities, our culture's values, our work, our sense of purpose, and our religions. All of these connections help to give our lives meaning.

The notion that meaning comes from connection is not esoteric; it is the most basic description about how our brains process information. When we learn something new, we form associations between it and other events and things. Our brains form associations between everything that we encounter, and these get represented in vast knowledge networks. We learn that hammers go with nails, dark clouds lead to rain, and the weekend brings a respite from work. Forming meanings is not just the way that human brains operate but the way that the brains of all species work. Even simple creatures, such as worms, learn things by forming associations between events in their environments. But humans rely on meanings to a far greater extent than other species. To get a better appreciation of how humans came to be so dependent upon meanings in their lives, let's compare the cognitive abilities of humans with those of our closest animal relative, the chimpanzee.

Chimpanzees share a lot in common with humans as we both descend from a shared ancestor that lived around seven to ten million years ago. Like humans, chimpanzees have very large brains—the largest among all species of nonhuman primates. And, accordingly, chimpanzees are an extremely intelligent species. Indeed, it can be quite humbling to see just how advanced their capabilities are. In certain respects, chimpanzee intelligence even exceeds that of humans. For example, chimpanzees have a remarkably good working memory, which is the ability to hold a number of different thoughts simultaneously in mind. One study pitted a group of chimpanzees against a group of university students on a working-memory task, and the champion of the contest emerged from team chimpanzee. Moreover, chimpanzees have quite incredible strategic skills, their ability to optimize their behavior in a competition with others. Researchers once trained chimpanzees to play a strategic competitive game that required them to attend to a series of events and to fluctuating changes in various payoffs in exchange for apple cubes. The chimpanzees competed against a group of university students who were playing the same game. It was no contest: the chimpanzees clearly outperformed the university students. On some cognitive tasks, humans are entirely outclassed by chimpanzees.[7]

A key reason that chimpanzees have such remarkable intellectual skills is because of the cognitive demands that their challenging social lives present to them. Chimpanzees live in complex hierarchical groups, the largest among nonhuman primates—although they frequently break off to travel and feed in smaller subgroups, whose membership varies considerably. An individual's relative position within these groups determines who gets access to valuable resources, such as desired food and mating privileges. Sitting at the top of the pyramid, and enjoying all the perks that come with it, is the alpha male. It isn't easy to become the alpha male. One has to compete against all the other males for this coveted position. Tellingly, the alpha male isn't necessarily the strongest male in the community. His position is maintained not so much by his brute strength but by the political alliances that he is shrewd enough to maintain with others. Other chimpanzees that he is allied with can usually be counted on to side with him in his conflicts with others; however, these alliances change regularly, depending on who the individuals are around in a given situation and their past history with one another. In addition to depending on their alliances, contests for dominance among aspiring males may sometimes rest on the role of a mediator, often served by one of the higher-ranking females. The mediator, who has relations with each of the conflicting males, serves to lower the hostilities among them. Rising in a chimpanzee hierarchy, then, can be seen as a matter of skilled politics: it requires one to understand and exploit the relations among the other chimpanzees.[8]

The political skills of chimpanzees are formidable. Former Speaker of the US House of Representatives, Newt Gingrich, has described how much his own political acumen was influenced by a book by primatologist Frans de Waal, titled *Chimpanzee Politics*. Apparently, the ways that chimpanzees form coalitions and rivalries serve as a good model for the operation of Congress, which, upon reflection, makes a whole lot of sense.[9]

For certain kinds of cognitive skills, such as their working memory, chimpanzees might just be the smartest species on the planet. But just because chimpanzees have some impressive cognitive skills does not mean that they are equally brilliant in other ways of thinking. In particular, there is one key cognitive skill for which chimpanzees just can't hold a candle to humans. This ability is an integral skill to being human, and it's a talent that you clearly possess yet may not even recognize that you have.

Simply, when you interact with another person, you synchronize your attention and goals with them so that you're both paying attention to the same topic. If you tell someone, "Look at that cat in the tree," you will both be attending to the cat in the tree. If you ask someone what they think about the government's new proposed tax increase, you and your conversation partner will simultaneously be thinking about the new proposed tax increase. If you ask someone to help you to carry a bookcase through a doorway, you will both synchronize your goals and actions in a way to make sure that you are able to get the bookcase through the door without damaging it. This skill seems so basic and simplistic that you have probably not given much thought to it. When individuals are attending to the same thoughts and have their goals aligned with each other, they have achieved a state of *common ground*. This state allows for a merging of people's minds. When people have achieved common ground, they are in sync with each other and are in a position to communicate and cooperate with each other. When humans interact, they effortlessly create common ground between each other, as they automatically attend to what those around them are doing and they synchronize their attention and goals. Even young children can create this common ground, and they work toward maintaining it with each other. Being able to reach a state of common ground is what allows people to be able to share meanings with each other.

In contrast, chimpanzees rarely achieve common ground. They usually can't synchronize their attention and goals because they just aren't motivated enough to engage with the perspectives of those around them; instead, they largely focus on their own goals. Without being able to achieve common ground, they are rarely able to merge their minds in the ways necessary to cooperate with each other. As the primatologist Michael Tomasello has noted: "It is inconceivable that you would ever see two chimpanzees carrying a log together." Such a simple act of cooperation as carrying a log requires that two individuals look at the same scene, recognize that they are both attending to the same scene, and communicate with each other what their goals are and how they each should act. Chimpanzees just seem too preoccupied with their own thoughts to be able to take on the perspective of others.[10]

Some of the most startling findings that emerge from primate cognition studies are those that show how remarkably uninterested chimpanzees can be with each other. They really don't seem to be thinking about each other much at all. We can observe this lack of interest in just how selfish chimpanzees can be, particularly when there is food available to share. Indeed, sharing among chimpanzees is hard to find. Even mothers can't always be relied upon to share with their infants. Sometimes, when their infants have desirable foods, chimpanzee mothers may snatch the food directly out of their mouths so they can eat it themselves. The extent of chimpanzees' disinterest in others was dramatically demonstrated in one lab experiment that investigated how motivated chimpanzees were to cooperate with their group mates. The lab apparatus was set up such that a chimpanzee could choose between one of two ropes to pull in order to get some food: they could either select a rope that would deliver food only to themselves, or they could select a rope that would deliver food both to themselves and to one of their group mates sitting across from them in a separate enclosure. There was zero cost for the chimpanzee to choose the option that would also give their group mate a meal: they received the same amount of food themselves regardless. But the chimpanzee showed no preference to choose the rope that would grant the other chimpanzee a treat. And they didn't do this despite how much screaming and begging the other chimpanzee did. They seemed to have no interest in the outcome of the other chimpanzee.[11]

So what is perhaps the most consequential difference between humans and chimpanzees is our deep and unrelenting interest in each others' minds. Humans are quite fascinated by what's going on in the minds of others. We want to know what others are thinking, and we want others to know what we ourselves are thinking. Humans want to share their experiences with others, and this helps them to create a sense of common ground with each other. When given a choice, studies find that young children would rather work collaboratively with others than work alone. In stark contrast, chimpanzees prefer to work on tasks by themselves. As we'll see below, it is our desires and abilities for connection that underlies humans' capacity for meaning.[12]

This key difference between humans and chimpanzees in terms of their interest in sharing their mental experiences with each other is the product of some biological adaptations that have occurred over the past few million years. One reason chimpanzees are less interested in each others' mental experiences is that it's harder for them to see each others' gazes. The sclera, the part of the eye that surrounds the iris, is dark for chimpanzees, so it's much more difficult for them to attend to each others' gazes—it's hard to tell where the iris ends and the sclera begins. When you can identify someone's gaze, you can tell what they're looking at, and this is hugely informative as to what they may be thinking about. With dark sclera, it is more challenging to identify where one's gaze is directed, and perhaps not surprisingly, chimpanzees rarely make eye contact with each other. There just isn't that much information that they can pick up.

Actually, it's difficult to see the sclera of all other species of primates too, more than two hundred different species. Since the time that we last shared a common ancestor with chimpanzees, our eyes have evolved to highlight our gaze. Over that time, our sclera became white, and the shape of our exposed eyes changed such that a greater proportion of our sclera became visible. This suggests that it must have been adaptive for our ancestors to be able to have their gaze identified by others. Those of our ancestors who had whiter and more visible sclera were better able to have their minds read and understood by others, and this ultimately led them to be more likely to survive and pass their genes to the next generation. It allowed our ancestors to communicate their thoughts more effectively to others. The physical nature of our bodies has evolved to help our minds communicate more effectively with each other.[13]

Our meaning-sharing abilities got another enormous boost after our hominid ancestors started to create an entirely new kind of meaning: *symbolic* meaning. We learned how to connect certain sounds to meanings and came to understand that sounds can stand for something else—that is, we developed language. This ability to rely on and communicate with linguistic symbols was a game-changing adaptation, which resulted from several interrelated adaptations. Various genetic mutations led to our larynx dropping lower in our throats and neural circuits being rewired, and we gained more precise control over hundreds of muscles that regulate our chests, tongue, lips, and face. These adaptations allowed us to create a far greater range of sounds in comparison to chimpanzees. It provided us with a system that was much more effective for delivering meanings and keeping us connected to one another. To begin with, language facilitated our ability to reach a sense of common ground: it allowed us to direct the attention of others to concerns that we have. Having language provided a means for us to communicate our desires more successfully and to influence the mental states of others. Moreover, having a language greatly expanded the kinds of thoughts we could entertain. It allowed us to consider thoughts beyond the immediate present. For example, one person could communicate to others to be careful around certain mushrooms because they had heard someone got sick after eating them, or they could communicate that a waterhole would likely dry up as it had in the past.

Because these symbolic meanings that we share can be endlessly combined, they enable us to contemplate much larger and more complex ideas than we could otherwise ever even consider. For example, imagine trying to explain to someone how the United States elects a new president without using any words: it's impossible to even conceive of, let alone communicate, such complicated ideas as that without language. We can build such vast and complex meaning frameworks because of our abilities to share and combine symbolic meanings with others.

A third adaptation that prompted humans to share meanings is our neural system, which evolved to reward us when we share information with others. The pleasure that we get from sharing information can be seen in an experiment where participants were given a number of tasks to talk about while their brains were being scanned. The experiment found that when people were discussing information about themselves, the reward centers of their brain showed more activation. Humans share so much about their inner worlds with others because it *feels good* to do so. And, in general, when things feel good to us, it's nature's way of encouraging us to engage in those behaviors more because they were adaptive in the ancestral environment, such as having sex or eating food that is rich in calories. The pleasure that we feel from sharing our experiences suggests that it was adaptive for us to share meanings with each other, and because of this, we have a rather irrepressible urge to tell others what is going on in our minds, and likewise, we are interested to learn what others are thinking about as well. One doesn't have to look far to find evidence for our relentless desire to share our thoughts with others. Analyses of conversations reveal that approximately 30 to 40 percent of everyday speech involves people sharing their private experiences or personal relationships. For most of human history, experiences were shared primarily through conversations and storytelling. More recently, we have developed social media technologies, which we primarily use for sharing our experiences. For example, one study found that up to 80 percent of posts on X (formerly known as Twitter) were announcements about people's personal experiences. This need to share is also why people post pictures of themselves on Instagram or Snapchat and send reaction gifs to each other. We want to let other people know how we're experiencing the world: what has happened to us, how we feel about it, what we want, what we're going to do about it, who we're having relationships with, and, ultimately, who we are.[14]

This sharing of experiences that so typifies human interactions has an enormous consequence. It means that we are not confined to living in our own individual psychological worlds. We live in a collectively experienced psychological world, based on meanings that we have shared with each other, and we are probably the only species that lives in such a rich shared reality. When we tell each other how we feel, what we think is right, what we find unacceptable, and so on, we end up collectively contributing to a shared reality that is built up from shared meanings. This shared reality did not begin with us but has rather been growing and changing for countless generations before us, as our ancestors were also sharing their experiences and weaving together a shared fabric of ideas. This shared reality far exceeds what any individual mind can conceive of and exists among our collective minds, which stretch back through time. We were all born into such systems of shared meanings, and we spend our lives contributing to them and shaping them in our own idiosyncratic ways.

The shared reality that we live in is critical for creating the foundation for us to become an existential ape in pursuit of a meaningful life. As we'll explore more below, having a shared reality with others ultimately provides us with the basis of standards and norms that gives meanings to our behaviors. These shared standards and norms provide us with a way of considering whether what we are doing is appropriate, whether we are acting in ways that are valued, and, ultimately, whether we are leading a good life. The meanings that we share with each other that make up our shared reality ultimately come to constitute our cultures.

## Being a Cultural Animal

Humans are a cultural animal in that the worlds that we live in are made up of shared cultural meanings, and it is our cultural nature that underpins our pursuit of a meaningful life. Our cultures are large encompassing frameworks of shared meanings that influence every aspect of our lives. These shared meanings with others in our social network provide us with a rich set of norms, which guides our behavior and is largely unique in the animal kingdom. We don't just act in ways that we independently decide are appropriate; rather, we are surrounded by a shared reality that dictates what kinds of behavior are valued, shunned, tolerated, or encouraged. Through our interactions we learn, for example, what kinds of food are appropriate to eat and what kinds we should avoid. Every society has food prohibitions. For example, as a Canadian of German descent, I would never dare to eat some foods that are delicacies in other cultures, such as fermented shark from Iceland, deep-fried tarantulas from Cambodia, or maggot cheese from Sardinia. I've spent much of my adult life trying to avoid *natto*, the smelly, slimy fermented soy beans from Japan. The norms that we learn from our cultures also dictate who it is OK for us to marry, with some cultures allowing a man to marry multiple women or a woman, multiple men. Other cultures allow children, first cousins, and people of the same gender to marry. The norms we learn dictate how we should dress for a formal occasion, how we should greet someone when we meet, what time we should show up to a scheduled meeting, what kinds of jokes are funny, and what we should do to celebrate our holidays. Each culture establishes norms around ways to earn a living and what amount to be paid for work, using a currency that the group has collectively determined has a particular value. We learn from others what are appropriate ways to raise our children, who we can turn to as our leaders, which gods we should worship, and how we can live a life that will earn us respect and status from others. These kinds of cultural meanings, which we learn from our interactions with others, sustain all of our activities—there really aren't any domains of our life that take place in a culture-free space. And, as we'll see below, these cultural meanings undergird our quest to lead meaningful lives.[15]

The cultures that we inhabit are maintained by the interactions among all of the individuals that live in them. Each new member to a culture is either born into it or migrates to it, and everyone, whether native born or immigrant, needs to learn the local cultural meanings to function well. Because every member of a culture is obligated to learn the local cultural meanings, each individual ultimately helps to perpetuate that culture, and so the shared realities of a culture can remain remarkably persistent and stable across time. Italy provides a stark example of cultural persistence. In the thirteenth century in medieval Italy, the northern regions of the country had a number of egalitarian institutions such as guilds and neighborhood associations, which facilitated the development of commerce and strong government throughout the region. In contrast, the southern regions did not have these institutions but were instead governed by autocratic Norman kings, which resulted in much corruption and lower levels of trust among families. The modern nation of Italy was unified in the 1870s, and the same laws and reforms were applied across the whole country. Yet to this day, the governance of the country retains the same divisions that it had in the medieval era. The northern Italian regions continue to have powerful and effective regional government organizations, greater social capital, and higher average incomes, whereas the southern regions continue to struggle with problems of governance, corruption, distrust, and lower incomes. More than eight centuries later, the cultural divide between northern and southern Italy persists, as each new member of those two regions learns the local ways of doing things and ultimately contributes to perpetuating those local norms. This cultural persistence is a reason why historical events that happened long ago can still be recognized in culturally specific themes that persist to this day.[16]

Cultures are interesting entities because, on the one hand, they have this remarkably stubborn habit of persisting across time, as in the Italian case. However, at the same time, aspects of cultures can change quite rapidly. Recall from Chapter 1 how much the culture of the United States has changed between the two ages of anxiety. Likewise, we can see how fluid cultures can be when we consider just how quickly new cultures can begin to form. New cultures are poised to be born whenever a group of individuals regularly interacts with one another and, in doing so, share meanings. As soon as people are sharing a regular conversation space, they begin to influence one another, and new cultural norms can emerge quite quickly.

One study investigated the formation of new cultures among students at the University of Northern Iowa. The researchers took advantage of the fact that students at that university are randomly assigned to live in particular college residence houses, a total of thirty-two different houses. This set the stage for testing how new cultures form by exploring what happens to a group of new individuals, with few preexisting ties, who come to live together in environments where they would be forming a shared interaction space. At the beginning of the term, when the students had just moved in, they completed a set of questionnaires asking about their attitudes toward a long list of various issues, such as whether the United States should use military force in Iraq or whether it was OK for a man to have sex with a woman who was drunk. Then, a few months later—after the students had dined in the same dining halls every evening, watched movies and played ping-pong together in the recreation rooms, and had countless late-night conversations on all kinds of topics—the students were asked to complete the same set of attitude questions again. When the researchers analyzed the results, they identified a striking trend. After spending a term living together and interacting and sharing meanings, the students tended to agree more with the others in their dormitories on these various issues than they did with students living in the other dormitories. Each dormitory had a distinctive way of looking at these topics, and these ways were shaped by all of their interactions with their dorm-mates over this time. After just a few months, they had created new dormitory-specific cultures of people with somewhat similar views on the world. Of course, these dorm-specific cultures are considerably more tenuous than many other kinds of cultures that we belong to, as the students were only together for a few months and they interacted with a lot of people from outside their dorms over this time too. But, still, the difference between these kinds of transient dorm cultures and other more enduring kinds of cultures, such as Japanese culture, are differences of degree rather than of kind.[17]

Because cultures emerge from the meanings that we share with others, we end up living in multiple, overlapping cultural worlds that are based on the different circles of interactions that we have. At the broadest level, we can identify some shared interaction space that transcends national boundaries, so we can talk, for example, of Western culture, which encompasses meanings that have been shared among people living in countries in Europe and the places that have been colonized by Europeans. Western culture includes some shared ideas about religions, institutions, values such as individual rights and freedoms, and preferences for certain kinds of art, music, and cuisine. One step down from here, we can also talk about national cultures, such as Italian culture, in which people usually share a common history and language, artistic styles, media, food, traditional celebrations, and government. We can also talk about regional cultures, such as those found in the US South, Sicily, or Kyushu, Japan, which are distinct from the other regional cultures in their respective countries. But culture extends beyond mere geography, as within any particular region we are likely to interact with some people more than with others, and the various social networks that we belong to can also beget cultures. Almost any social network that we regularly participate with will create its own specific culture. We can talk about particular corporate cultures, such as Microsoft culture; there is also Black culture, LGBTQ culture, Catholic culture, Wall Street culture, hockey culture, Republican culture, and cosplay culture. These cultures emerge whenever people share a regular communication space and are exchanging ideas with each other, which provide the basis of norms, practices, beliefs, and values.

We all belong to a unique set of overlapping cultures that has shaped our personal history through our participation in various groups and social networks, and these experiences provide us with distinctive sets of cultural meanings, which guide our behaviors and give our lives meaning. But though we are all influenced by our respective cultures, we are also individuals, and not everyone responds to these shared meanings in uniform ways. Some individuals might embrace some of those cultural meanings, others may be indifferent to them, and some might actively rebel against them. Although the ways we interpret and respond to these cultural meanings can vary among individuals, the meanings themselves are widely shared within a cultural context and come to be known by most members of each culture. However, because people in different cultures are interacting with different groups of people, cultural meanings can vary tremendously from culture to culture.

To get an idea of how cultural meanings can vary across cultural contexts, consider the example of meanings associated with rather trivial behaviors, such as having salmon for dinner. What does it mean to eat salmon? Well, in my household, it's part of a regular rotational menu, so if we're eating salmon, it's probably Tuesday. In a different context, someone eating salmon might signify that it's Lent, and their salmon dinner affirms their Catholic identity. For another person, eating salmon one night might demonstrate their decision to stop eating meat and to take on a new pescatarian identity. For a Brahman Indian widow, eating salmon could be seen as a moral failing because fish is believed to heighten one's sexual appetite, which would jeopardize the spiritual devotion she is expected to show her deceased husband. The exact same behavior—having a salmon dinner—can have starkly different meanings across cultural contexts. And to a large extent, it's the meanings of our behaviors that determine their consequences to us.[18]

Cultural meanings come to shape pretty much all of our behaviors: we are always acting in culturally guided ways. Our species relies on cultural meanings far more than any other animal—really, there's no comparison. In stark contrast to the vastly complex shared worlds that we live in, chimpanzees, for the most part, live in their own individual worlds, which are rather tenuously linked with those of others. They rarely exchange information with others because they are largely uninterested in what others are doing. As a result, chimpanzees form few shared ideas regarding what is appropriate behavior or how they can learn from each other. The most comprehensive analysis of chimpanzee culture has identified only seven habitual behaviors that reliably distinguish different populations of chimpanzees and another thirty-two behaviors, which are only occasionally observed by some members of each population. For the most part, chimpanzee culture has remained rather static across time and is largely similar among different groups of chimpanzees—their technologies rarely change, nor do the few customs that distinguish one group of chimpanzees from another. Their cultural world, which has likely stayed fairly constant for millions of years, is so steady and unchanging because chimpanzees are not sufficiently interested in exchanging information with each other.[19]

The shared realities that humans live in are so much richer in meanings than they are for chimpanzees or any other species. But at our core, humans are just like other animals and are in a Darwinian struggle to survive and reproduce. The efforts that we make throughout our lives are directed toward satisfying a set of fundamental needs that are largely the same as those of many other species of animals. Like other species, we have some basic physiological needs, which include our need for resources to survive and to protect ourselves by avoiding threats that may harm us. We are also an ultrasocial species, meaning we have a pronounced need to belong: our survival is enhanced by our ability to have a set of allies who we can count on to help us in times of need. As in other species, we also need to attract mates to reproduce. Humans are a pair-bonding species, which means that after we have mated we need to retain our mates, to entice them to stay with us. It's important for us to keep our mates because, unlike other species, our offspring remain dependent on us for a long time and require many resources from us. Especially in the ancestral environment, having two devoted parents ensured the offspring's survival. We also must ensure that our children have the best opportunities to survive and find mates so that they can pass on their own genes. We also need to protect and enhance our status because status tends to bring us access to more resources, more helpful alliances, and better mating opportunities for us and our offspring. These basic human needs aren't all that different from the needs that chimpanzees have, with the exception that chimpanzees don't pair-bond; they don't try to retain mates, and fathers don't contribute much to the parenting. The key difference between us and chimpanzees, though, is that because of our cultural nature, the ways that we can go about satisfying these basic needs is by mastering particular cultural meanings, which can vary tremendously across cultures.[20]

Humans are unique in the animal kingdom in that we pursue all of our basic needs in culturally packaged ways—ways that can differ tremendously from one culture to another, with very different meaning frameworks. Whatever those cross-cultural differences, all people everywhere depend on the meaning framework of their particular culture to satisfy the same basic needs of resources, protection, status, belongingness, acquiring and retaining a mate, and raising children. The key challenge for humans is that they need to learn and master cultural meanings to enhance their status, obtain sufficient resources, and attract a mate and to prepare their children to do so as well. From a Darwinian perspective, those people who are best able to learn and utilize cultural meanings are better able to satisfy their basic needs and will be more likely to have surviving offspring.

In this way we can see how humans are cultural animals: we are dependent upon our cultural meanings in order to survive and to thrive. We are born into this world remarkably helpless and with largely the same cognitive equipment as humans everywhere, and this equipment is dedicated to acquiring the cultural meanings from our environment. Those meanings that we acquire serve to determine how we live our lives, create our identities, and imbue our lives with value and purpose.

The meaning frameworks that humans rely on have been growing more and more complex since our hominid ancestors first started to share meanings with each other so many eons ago. Over this time, those meanings have grown so vast that our individual brains can no longer contain them. We have come to be dependent on much knowledge that we don't necessarily have for ourselves. For example, our health is dependent upon the wealth of medical knowledge that has accumulated over the centuries, and many of our jobs are dependent on complex technologies, such as computers, jet engines, and the internet. No individual has all of the information that these technologies are based on in their own brain. Rather, this knowledge resides in our collective knowledge base, which is part of our extended cultures.[21]

Unlike other species, humans have, from the beginning, operated in an environment that is both physical and saturated in meanings. Humans have always had to consider cultural norms and evaluate their behavior and lives according to how well they measured up to those standards. The unique challenge for humans as a species is that for us to thrive and live lives rich in purpose and meaning, we needed to navigate a vast and growing network of cultural meanings. But for us to do this effectively, we needed an additional adaptation to guide how we operate within that cultural matrix. Our abilities to function well within a matrix of meanings required us to evolve something else that is largely unmatched in the animal kingdom: we needed to evolve a self.

## How Cultures Make Selves

Over the past few million years, as humans evolved to be more and more motivated to share meanings with each other, they began to live in an ecology of shared meanings that emerged from the collective interactions of others from their culture. What makes our situation unique is that our survival is contingent on us being able to understand the meanings that make up this shared reality and to use them to pursue our basic needs. Our self is what helps us to do this. Our selves are shaped by the meanings of the cultures that we live in, and our selves consolidate those cultural meanings, organize them, and make them more accessible to us so that we can readily use our cultural meanings to pursue our basic needs. We each carry a copy of our cultures' meanings inside of us so they are always at hand. By internalizing and organizing cultural meanings, this ensures that our default reactions to events in the world will largely be aligned with cultural standards. The array of behaviors that we'll be tempted to engage in, more often than not, will be ones that are deemed appropriate and valued within our cultural contexts, and, hence, will help us to lead lives that feel meaningful. The function of our self is to connect our bodies to the meaning frameworks that make up our shared reality, in order to allow us to operate most effectively within it.[22]

The foundational premise of the field of cultural psychology is that you can't separate the self from its culture—their meanings are inextricably tied together, such that our cultures and selves ultimately serve to make each other up. To understand the self, we need to understand the cultural context that it exists within.

I first became aware of how fundamentally culture shaped the self when I worked for a couple of years as an English teacher at a junior high school in a small town in Japan after I had graduated from university. It was a memorable life-transforming experience that ultimately led me on the path to becoming a cultural psychologist. During my time working at a school in Japan, I encountered so many practices that were strikingly at odds with my own experiences several years earlier when I had been a student at a Canadian junior high school. It became clear that these different cultural practices that I encountered in the school reflected the different kinds of selves that were cultivated in the two countries.

One of the first things that became readily apparent to me upon teaching in Japan was how much of behavior there was collectively shared. For example, in class I would go up and down the row and have each student take turns answering the same question in English: "What day is it today?" Much of the time when I asked a student this question, they didn't answer me but instead turned to their friend to ask them how to say it. This was really puzzling and bothersome to me. I tried to emphasize to the students that I was asking them to try and answer the question themselves, and I didn't want their friends to help them. But the Japanese teacher who I cotaught with let me know that the students' behaviors were totally normal and acceptable, and I saw it regularly in all the classes I taught. Getting to the correct answer was often a group effort, and students were expected to get help from their friends when they were not sure themselves.

The collective nature of my students' behavior was also evident each day in the afternoon during cleanup time. I was surprised to learn that there were no janitors at the school. The students were responsible for cleaning up the entire school and its grounds, which they did with remarkable gusto over a twenty-minute period each afternoon. They cleaned the blackboards, swept up the floors, put away any mess, emptied the garbage cans, wiped down the tables, and, quite remarkably, scrubbed the floors of the entire school by pushing wet rags along the floor. I had assumed that it would be difficult to get all of the students to participate, but they appeared to recognize that the cleanliness of the school was their shared responsibility, and it seemed that everyone embraced the task.

I was also quite struck by how the class went about governing itself. At the end of the day, the students from the whole class would have a meeting, no teachers involved, where they made several key decisions, such as what the class would do for the upcoming culture festival. They might assign the students to different jobs for preparing all of the sets for a drama performance, or they would practice a group dance they would perform together in unison. Most of the students would actively participate in the meetings, and I was amazed at how many different opinions they would first generate, before quickly working toward a group consensus. The faculty meetings that I regularly have to attend at my university could benefit if they all saw how smoothly these students would make group decisions.

The students were responsible for enforcing the norms of fitting in, and one unfortunate way they accomplished this was through bullying each other. Bullying continues to be a real problem at

Japanese schools—considerably more prevalent than at Western schools—and it's something that is often found in the workplace in Japan as well. It seemed that almost every class had a couple of kids who were bullied relentlessly for acting differently, whether those differences seemed problematic or praiseworthy. The expectation was that everyone toed the line, and you risked the wrath of your peers if you ever tried to do things differently.

These various traditions to build a sense of group identity that I encountered in a junior high school in Japan are not that unlike the kinds of traditions that one finds in other collectivist societies from around the world. In collectivistic societies people come to learn from their experiences that they are to prioritize the groups they belong to and to act in ways that benefit the group, even if sometimes this requires some sacrifice on the individual's part. In such societies people learn that selfish behaviors, which may compromise the harmony of the group, are not to be tolerated. A great example of this tradeoff between an individual's self-interest and that of the group can be seen in the COVID pandemic. While the pandemic was devastating everywhere, it caused far fewer deaths on a per capita basis among countries in East Asia—cultures that prioritize the group and have little tolerance for those that deviate from the culture's norms—than it did elsewhere. In collectivist cultures, people are more willing to accept the idea that certain individual freedoms, such as whether to wear a mask, get vaccinated, or avoid interpersonal contact with others, should be trumped by concerns for the well-being of their group. Places that have historically had higher levels of contagious diseases tend to become more collectivistic over time, as coordinating group efforts has proven to be effective against the spread of contagious diseases. And, of course, the daily practices that are more common in collectivist cultures extend far beyond reducing disease transmission; they also emphasize achieving a sense of belongingness, contributing toward the collective good, trying to fit in with others, and sharing a group consciousness.[23]

The daily cultural practices that people regularly engage in, such as whether teachers allow students to turn to their friends for answers, don't exist separate from them. Rather, people's selves adjust to these regular behaviors, and they come to share the values that these daily practices convey. When someone is raised in a collectivistic society, it is likely that they will come to care about the value of fitting in with others, they will come to identify with their groups, and they will judge themselves and others in terms of how much they are contributing toward collective goals. The self comes to be shaped by one's culture.

Many hundreds of psychological experiments have demonstrated how the nature of the self differs among cultures on the basis of the daily practices that are common there. People in collectivistic cultures are likely to develop an *interdependent self*—a self based largely on the groups and relationships the individual has. This is especially evident if you ask people from collectivistic cultures, such as Japan, to describe the kind of person they are. Typically, when describing themselves, people from these cultures usually refer to the key relationships they have, the groups they belong to, and the roles they have within those groups—they think of themselves primarily in terms of how they are connected with others.[24]

In contrast, when you ask people from more individualistic cultures to describe themselves, such as from the United States, they typically do so in a starkly different way. These people exemplify the *independent self.* Rather than focusing on how they connect with others around them, people with independent selves instead focus inward and conceive of their self as built upon a unique configuration of internal psychological characteristics. They describe themselves in terms of their personality traits, such as whether they are outgoing, open-minded, or punctual, and tend to focus a lot on their abilities, such as whether they believe they're a good cook or have an especially good memory. People with independent selves also focus on their personal attitudes, such as whether they are against vaccinations or are in support of legal abortions. These inner psychological characteristics of our personalities, attitudes, and abilities, form the basis for how people see themselves as unique from others. I'm imagining that this description of independent selves may seem somewhat familiar to most of the readers of this book, as I suspect that most of you live in an individualistic culture. Joseph Henrich, Ara Norenzayan, and I have called people with independent selves WEIRD (Western, Educated, Industrialized, Rich, and Democratic) people, and they are the most studied population in the behavioral sciences. However, in the context of all the cultures in the world, WEIRD people are highly psychologically unusual, and the independent selves that they tend to have are rarely found in most other societies.[25]

These differences in the self-concepts of people from different cultures are not just hypothetical. People with different kinds of self-concepts have been found to differ in many aspects of their psychology, such as how they reason, how they are motivated, what they feel, what their moral values are, how they work with others, how they perceive the world around them, and what bases provide their lives with meaning. For people with more interdependent selves, the key goals that they aspire to on a regular basis include achieving a sense of belongingness with others, fulfilling their interpersonal obligations, and attending to their relationships. In contrast, the key goals that those with more independent selves aspire toward are to feel that one is unique, self-sufficient, trustworthy, and competent. Research continues to find just how profoundly people's cultures shape their self-concepts. And the kinds of self-concepts that we maintain influence the ways that we go about trying to lead a meaningful life.[26]

We are now in a better position to answer the questions that I raised at the beginning of this chapter: Why are we the ape that jumps? Why do we feel this urgent need to make sense of our lives and to conclude that we are leading a meaningful existence? And why are we at risk to be burdened by existential angst if we fail to do so?

I suggest that an answer to these questions comes from the recognition that humans are creatures that live in an ecology that is made up of meanings—we could be called *Homo significativa*. These meanings emerge from our shared interactions with others, and they ultimately come to form a shared reality that we live in—a shared reality that is the basis of our cultures. These cultural meanings get woven into everything that we do, and they shape the kinds of lives that we live.

Our self-concepts are shaped by the cultural meanings around us, which provide us with norms and standards for what entails good and appropriate behaviors and what are the bases for leading a meaningful life. We are always comparing ourselves to these cultural standards to evaluate how we are doing in our lives. These standards serve to make our actions more meaningful, but our worries about whether or not we are doing a good job at meeting those standards put us at risk for developing existential angst. When we pursue a meaningful life, we are pursuing a life that meets the collectively shared standards and values of our culture.[27]

But, of course, meeting those cultural standards is not always so easily achieved, and often we may feel that our lives aren't as valued or as coherent as we would like. How can we go about ensuring that our own lives feel meaningful when we realize that they might not make all that much sense?

# Chapter 3

# Understanding Ourselves and Our Worlds Through Stories

Every man carries with him through life a mirror,
as unique and impossible to get rid of as his shadow.

W. H. Auden, *The Dyer's Hand and Other Essays*

The chaos and uncertainty of the new age of anxiety has made life more challenging because people have a basic psychological need to believe they can predict and control what is happening to them. When the world feels uncertain and doesn't make sense, people no longer feel able to predict or control what will happen to them, and this leads to a lot of discomfort and angst. Albert Camus called this state where people are unable to make sense of what is happening around them "the absurd."

As Camus saw it, the human folly is that people are always struggling to make sense out of a world that has no sense to offer.

As an atheist, he felt that, at root, the universe was inherently meaningless. Camus believed that everything that happened in the world was nothing but the unfolding of natural laws that had no consideration for anyone's life nor what that life might possibly mean. But people's lives generally do feel meaningful, and it's of great importance that they do—when people feel that their lives are meaningless they are at risk of slipping into depression, anxiety, and boredom. Camus felt that people could create a sense of meaning and purpose in their lives through their actions and the choices that they made. He felt that people need to find a sense of purpose underlying what they do to be able to rise to the challenges they face in life and to keep going forward, even when times are difficult.

But Camus felt that every now and then people would be reminded of the inherent meaninglessness of the universe and of their own lives, and in those moments, they would end up in the absurd, and their existential anxieties would be sparked. They would recognize the contradictions in their own lives and how nothing seemed to really make sense anymore. People want to feel that they can clearly understand their lives and their place within the world, as it's only when people's lives make sense that they can feel meaningful. But the key challenge people face is that, in many ways, their lives often really don't seem to make much sense at all.[1]

Consider how we might make sense of the life of Camus. Camus had a remarkably successful career from a young age, and he quickly settled in Paris where he enjoyed a comfortable life as a famed public intellectual. He enjoyed much celebrity, he traveled internationally where he was always received by huge crowds, and he spent many evenings surrounded by some of the world's leading thinkers at cafés and salons. But the tremendous success that Camus achieved as an adult couldn't be further removed from his childhood in Algeria. Camus was raised by a single mother, who was widowed before his first birthday. She was illiterate, and Camus struggled to communicate with her because of her hearing and speech impediments. Camus's mother was barely able to make ends meet by working as a housekeeper in a poor suburb of Algiers. Their house had no radio, newspapers, or books. Camus's life seems to be sharply divided between his impoverished and challenging childhood and the great success that he enjoyed as an adult.

Camus has to be the most likeable of the existentialists: he was a real mensch who was always generous to those around him and was deeply loyal to his many friends. Despite leaving Algeria at a young age, he continued to remain close to his childhood friends throughout his life and was always ready to loan them money. When Camus was awarded the Nobel Prize in Literature, he dedicated the award to his fifth-grade teacher, who he remained close to until his death. Even after achieving his remarkable fame, Camus continued for years to write for the newsletter of his university's soccer team where he used to play goalkeeper. He was especially doting toward his mother, taking care of her throughout his life, and he remained deeply committed to his family. We can easily see the intense loyalty Camus had for his close relationships. On the other hand, Camus was never loyal to his wife. He was famous for his infidelities and had several mistresses throughout his marriage. Camus's philandering caused his wife much anguish and was thought to be the key source of her long-standing suicidal depression. When faced with the question, "Was Camus a loyal person?," we'd reach dramatically different conclusions depending on who his loyalty was directed toward.

Camus's own views were hobbled with inconsistencies. His name is synonymous with existentialism, and he has always been recognized as one of the most influential of the existentialists. Yet Camus continually denied that he was an existentialist, each time offering a different puzzling explanation for why he rejected the label. His works continue to be taught in philosophy classes around the world, and it is in this field that he made his greatest contributions. But he also refused to identify as a philosopher. Camus was always a champion for the oppressed—in particular, he was an advocate for those who faced injustices from colonialism—and urged people to rebel against their colonial overlords. Yet when it came to the independence movement in his own country, Algeria, he refused to participate and famously sat on the sidelines. Camus instead focused on the plight of his mother who was still living there. In contrast to how he preached against the injustices of colonialism everywhere else, for Algeria he instead stated: "I believe in justice, but I'll defend my mother before justice."[2]

In many ways, Camus's life would seem to be rife with inconsistencies. But, then again, so probably is your own. We often aren't very consistent, and there are times when our lives don't really seem to make a whole lot of sense. For example, we may seem like quite different people when we're in different situations. We might find that when we're with our parents, we act sullen. When we're with our friends from college, we may act silly, while we may be ambitious and responsible at work. When we're on our daily commute, we may be short-tempered and scream obscenities toward other drivers, but when we're with our children, we may be caring and doting. Which one of these different personas is the real self? Our inherent inconsistencies are further on display when we try to corral our competing urges. One day we might feel committed to going on a diet and getting in shape but then find ourselves the next day in front of the TV having just eaten an entire pint of Häagen-Dazs. Which part of our self is in charge?

And when we look back at our past, we may struggle to identify a common thread that connects the different chapters of our lives. For example, we might realize that the person we were in high school seems to share little in common with the way we think of ourselves now. How is it possible that back then we had those friends, those interests, those ambitions, and whatever led us to want that hairstyle? How can we continue to be the same self across time when we grow and change so much? Indeed, we can be so different across situations and times that it can feel like our self is a collection of Jekylls and Hydes all battling it out in our brains.

How should we respond when we notice that the many aspects of our selves seem to be clashing with each other? Walt Whitman, for one, didn't seem to be particularly bothered by his own inconsistencies: "Do I contradict myself? Very well then . . . I contradict myself; I am large . . . I contain multitudes." Perhaps we would fare well if we followed Whitman's advice and just accepted the fact that we're contradictory and get on with our lives. But as Camus saw it, we can't usually be so cavalier about our inconsistencies. For Camus, the ultimate human quest entailed trying to integrate everything we encountered about our selves and our worlds. Camus proposed that we have a "nostalgia for unity"—that is, we have a strong impulse to take everything in our lives and to weave it all together into one seamlessly integrated whole that is spared from contradictions. This impulse can often lead us to perform all sorts of psychological contortions. For example, if someone works in the oil industry, they may be more likely to come to question the science behind climate change, as otherwise they'd be left with the troublesome inconsistency that their chosen occupation is damaging the planet. Or if someone had an abortion in college but later joined a church that is staunchly pro-life, they may come to view their earlier abortion as something that they had been coerced into doing and had never really wanted for themselves. Our desire for a unified and integrated self often leads us to alter some of our beliefs to dispel the inevitable inconsistencies that we discover about ourselves.[3]

Camus viewed that it was inevitable that we'd stumble across inconsistencies in our lives and trip into the absurd. He felt that people have "an appetite for clarity," which compels us to try to understand everything around us, and we do this by aspiring to convince ourselves that everything we know fits together well, into one integrated and unified whole. We're motivated to feel that our view of the world corresponds with reality, so we continually search for more information, connecting it with what we already know, in an effort to confirm that our understanding of events is correct. But he also saw that this drive to keep trying to add to our worldviews with everything we came across would ultimately take us to the edge of our meaning frameworks: at some point we will realize that what we think we know just really doesn't make much sense at all. In our efforts to think deeply and to connect everything that we encounter, we will inevitably notice a tear in the matrix and end up stuck in the absurd. As Camus put it, "Beginning to think is beginning to be undermined."[4]

In our efforts to understand all of the events around us, we want, most importantly, for our *selves* to make sense—we want to feel that we are interacting with our worlds with a consistent self that organizes all of our experiences, values, beliefs, and social relationships into one coherent and unified entity. We want to reflect upon our selves and the experiences we're having and conclude that everything about us adds up. Although it may feel sometimes that we have a chaotic chorus of different identities, Camus's challenge for us is that we need to find a way for them all to converge and speak as one. We wish for a clear and consistent sense of who we are. If we're able to understand ourselves well, we're in a better position to make sensible choices in our lives and to pursue a meaningful and authentic life. To feel otherwise, as Camus saw it, would leave us stuck in the middle of the absurd.

My own research has been focused on trying to figure out how people make sense of themselves. The ways that people come to understand their lives certainly isn't always a straightforward process. We have found that some people really strain to figure out who they are. Jennifer Campbell, Paul Trapnell, Ilana Katz, Lorraine Lavallee, Darrin Lehman, and I created a personality measure that assesses what we called one's *self-concept clarity*—that is, how much a person feels that the contents of their self are clearly understood and remain largely the same across time, without contradictory elements. This measure included items such as "On one day I might have one opinion of myself and on another day I might have a different opinion," or "I spend a lot of time wondering about what kind of person I really am." We found that people who agree with these items tend to struggle to make sense of their selves. Reflecting on their selves doesn't bring a feeling of clear identity to them but rather makes them feel confused and alienated—trapped in the absurd.[5]

This feeling that one's self is not so easily made sense of has some real pronounced costs. People with lower self-concept clarity generally aren't faring as well as those who have a clearer sense of who they are. Those who have this feeling that their self just doesn't make much sense often suffer from low self-esteem and depression, and they are less likely to view their lives as meaningful. Having a self that feels like it's a bunch of warring factions can make a rather ordinary day feel like a series of assaults on one's mental well-being. At its worst, this feeling of having an absurd self makes one more at risk for hurting oneself or even considering suicide.[6]

## Building a Self Through Our Stories

Ultimately, then, the root of our existential project—to understand who we are and to make sense of the life that we're living—really matters. We risk a lot if we're unable to weave all the different threads of our self together. And as we grow and change across our lives, exploring different facets of ourselves and finding ourselves in new situations, it is by no means a simple and straightforward task to try to integrate all of the occasionally contradictory aspects of our selves. But humans have arrived at a solution for escaping the absurdity of ourselves and finding a way to unify everything together: quite simply, *we tell stories about ourselves.* We create stories about going on a journey where we confront all of the experiences and challenges in our lives. These stories help us to organize all of the meanings about our lives and the world and our place within the world. And the stories that we tell about ourselves can help us to pursue Camus's quest. Our stories can help to keep us out of the absurd and to unify all of the apparent contradictions and inconsistencies. This ongoing narrative—the story about who we are, what we are doing, and why we are doing it—lays the foundation of our selves.

To better understand how our stories lie at the heart of who we are, we first need to consider why humans are so attracted to telling stories in the first place. As the world happens to us, we tend to make sense of it through the ongoing stories we create. In many ways our learning is facilitated through stories: their narrative nature helps to communicate ideas, guides how we interpret them, organizes them across time, identifies a perceived sense of cause and effect, and aids us in remembering them. Teachers rely on stories to better educate their students, marketers rely on stories to connect consumers with their products, and lawyers rely on stories to argue for a defendant's guilt or innocence. Stories are one of the more effective ways that we can ensure an idea gets understood and remembered.[7]

It is no coincidence that our grandest ideas, about who we are as a people and where we come from, are usually communicated through stories—through oral traditions or written down for posterity in religious texts. Our penchant to tell stories is found in all cultural traditions and is especially evident in those cultures that don't have a written language. It is common in many small-scale societies around the world for people to sit around a fire and share stories that provide an entertaining way of sharing key information about how people are supposed to behave—conveying what kinds of behaviors are valued or shunned—together with an understanding of how their current lives have been shaped by the past. People living in modern industrialized societies also tell a lot of stories, typically rather brief ones, as they go about their day. For example, one study recorded American mothers' conversations with their young children and found that mothers were telling stories at the rate of about one every seven minutes. And, of course, if you look at how people in modern industrialized societies have been living so much of their lives in front of a screen in an era of peak TV, you can appreciate just how much of our lives are spent in a narrative mind-set.[8]

Our drive to tell stories is automatic and can happen even when we aren't aware that we are doing it. We seamlessly integrate the events that are happening around us into a narrative with characters, a setting, and a plot that unfolds across time. Because we rely so much on stories to understand the world, we are often in a position where we can't readily distinguish between our own stories and reality—they have fused into one. As Jean-Paul Sartre noted: "This is what fools people: a man is always a teller of tales, he lives surrounded by his stories and the stories of others, he sees every-thing that happens to him through them; and he tries to live his life as if he were telling a story." We live in a world of stories, and most of what we understand is happening around us is limited to the information that fits with those stories. And, most strikingly, we're usually not even aware that we're telling them.[9]

It may seem surprising to say that you understand the events in your life in terms of a story you're not even aware you're telling yourself. I know it certainly doesn't feel that way. It usually feels that we are in direct contact with the events that are happening to us, and that our experiences are aligned with reality—what we see is what we get. But we can start to see evidence for our relentless and largely invisible storytelling compulsion when we encounter stories told by others that we can recognize as being somewhat disconnected from reality. In particular, we can see how people's stories can be detached from reality when we consider people's memories. Our minds are full of memories of our life events, and it can seem to us that our brains store these memories much like a video recorder, providing an archival record of the events of our lives. However, memories really aren't stored in any way like a video recorder, and researchers have found that they are able to create completely false memories in the minds of study partici-pants with relative ease.

For example, researchers interviewed participants' family members about what the participants had experienced between the ages of four and six. They then met with each participant and described three true events and one false event from the partici-pant's past, thus planting the seed of an event the participant had never experienced. Later, when researchers asked participants to recall some details that they had learned from the earlier meet-ing, people would relate false memories of made-up events, such as getting lost while shopping with their parents as a child, being the victim of an animal attack, being taken to the hospital because their hand had gotten caught in a mousetrap, or getting in trouble at school for putting Slime into a teacher's desk. Participants in these studies were able to seamlessly weave together a rich narrative that connected snippets of relevant memories they had with the entirely false ideas that were planted in them. When they were asked to recall these fictitious events, the participants created narratives on the fly that connected and organized what they thought must have happened with whatever information they had at hand, and they were typically completely unaware that what they were recalling was fabricated. At the end of these studies, participants were truthfully informed that these events had never actually happened to them. They frequently protested that this couldn't be the case, given how clear their memories felt to them.[10]

The ways that people can so easily create false memories reveals how urgent is our need to feel that we are making sense of our worlds. When we encounter things that don't fit with our expectations, such as our memories for events that never happened, we usually don't sit and ponder about this conflicting information. Rather, we rapidly and seamlessly make up a story so that everything seems to fall back in order again. This is the key virtue of our storytelling penchant. Our stories take the often conflicting information that we encounter and organize it in ways that provide us with a sense of coherence, of cause and effect. The stories fill in the gaps to hide the contradictory information, and for the most part, we remain entirely unaware that we have made up these stories or that these stories are in any way different from reality.

This ability of our storytelling penchant to erect a convincing Potemkin village to conceal the absurd landscape that surrounds us is nowhere more important than for the most fundamental stories that we tell: the stories about ourselves. These stories don't just serve to patch up the disconnected parts of ourselves; they create the very foundations of them. When we reflect on who we are, we're typically considering our lives as a narrative that unfolds across time—all of our relationships, the events that we've experienced, how we've grown over time, and where we see ourselves heading in the future. As the psychologist Dan McAdams has noted, our "identity itself takes the form of a story, complete with setting, scenes, character, plot, and theme." Our life stories are essential in helping us weave together the impression that our lives are coherent, valuable, and undergirded by a strong sense of purpose.[11]

Starting in adolescence, we begin to link the experiences in our lives by telling an autobiographical story about ourselves. Many of us experience our first existential crisis at this time, trying to figure out who we are and deciding the life we're going to live. In this first draft of our life story, we begin to note the events in our life that have shaped who we are, and we organize them around our goals, personality traits, and values. Once we have started this journey of telling stories to make sense of ourselves, we never stop, and we continue to add new episodes to our life story. We tell stories about our childhood, how we fell in love, how we came to pursue the career that we did, about those occasions when we did something comically stupid and the moments when we were the hero. We are the protagonist in our stories, and in them we confront many different situations, challenges, and relationships, which we link together in narrative form. Typically, the stories that we tell are not perfectly truthful accounts of what has happened but are an improvised telling that makes our life feel more sensible. Our stories are able to integrate all of those disparate facets of ourselves because at any given moment we are able to focus on particular episodes of our life and edit out the parts that don't quite fit in. When we tell our stories well, they serve to keep us out of the absurd and to provide us with the feeling that our life is coherent and sensible.[12]

While each story that we tell about ourselves is unique in certain respects, it often shares a number of features in common with those told by others. Many stories share common themes, such as a theme of redemption, which highlights how we conquered some challenge from the past, or a theme of contamination, which recounts how our life suddenly got worse. The stories we tell often contain similar content, as many people have similar key challenges and experiences. For example, everyone who has a romantic partner has a story about how they first met—a story they may have jointly created with their partner and embellished over the many times they have told it.[13]

As unique as our lives are, people from the same culture face similar challenges and share many common meanings, so it is quite natural that the stories we tell have so much in common with the stories of others. In particular, our stories about our lives often rest upon quite simple, but extremely important, premises that are also often shared in other people's stories. For example, our stories might be built around key premises such as *I am good, The world is so,* or *People get what they deserve.* We rarely question these premises; we accept them as a given as they are so commonly encountered in our culture. But we can be so committed to these premises that they serve as a lens through which we see how our life unfolds.

## The Struggle to Stay Good

What does it mean for someone to tell their life story around a premise, such as *I am good*? Consider the example of Paul

Frampton. He was facing trial for his alleged crimes and was housed in the notorious Villa Devoto prison in Buenos Aires. He shared a squalid cell there with over eighty prisoners, many of whom were violent members of drug cartels. Frampton had witnessed a fellow prisoner get murdered just a few feet in front of him. His new situation was difficult for him to process, as nothing from his earlier life had prepared him for any of this.

At the time, Frampton was a sixty-eight-year-old British professor of theoretical particle physics who had been working at the University of North Carolina in Chapel Hill for the previous thirty years. He was a widely published scientist who was very active in the physics community. He was not by any means a thrill seeker, and he had never used drugs before. But the story of how this accomplished scientist ended up in an Argentinian prison, ultimately receiving a sentence of four years and eight months for smuggling drugs, reveals just how powerful people's desires can be to tell their life story around the premise *I am good.*

Frampton had been a lonely man. His work dominated his life, and he never had much success with women. But Frampton wanted to find a partner and have a family, and he turned to some dating apps. One day, he got a message from someone named Denise Milani, and they started to text regularly. Milani told Frampton that she wanted to settle down, get married with him, and start a family together. She told him, "You're the best thing that's happened in my cursed life." Frampton was thrilled to finally get to pursue his dream of starting a family. But the whole situation was preposterous. You may want to google Denise Milani to see why. Milani is a famous swimsuit model—the winner of Miss Bikini World—whose physique resembles that of a real-life Jessica Rabbit. Indeed, the person that Frampton had been texting with was not the real Denise Milani but a drug dealer who convinced him to carry some luggage across international borders that purportedly belonged to Milani but was actually a bag packed full of cocaine.

When Frampton showed pictures of Milani to his friends and told them that they planned to get married, it was obvious to them that he was being conned, and they told him so. This is how Frampton's situation appeared to everyone else. But note that we experience the events in our lives through the lenses of our life stories, and the lens that Frampton was looking through was rather distorted. "I have been accused," said Frampton, "of having a huge ego." For example, he had seen himself as destined to some-day receive a Nobel Prize, although no one else seemed to think this was likely, and as a child he had seen himself as "cleverer than Newton." When Frampton was awaiting his trial in jail, he was determined to leave his defense to a public defender to save money because he was certain he could convince a judge of his innocence. And Frampton thought it was perfectly reasonable that the stun-ning Denise Milani, who he had never met or even spoken to on the phone, had reached out to him with the intention of marry-ing him—a man thirty-three years her senior and who by his own admission worked about eighty-four hours each week. However unlikely this situation may appear to everyone else, it fit in well with Frampton's extremely positive self-views. As he put it, "It seemed plausible at the time."[14]

In Frampton's case, his own positive self-views would seem to be rather delusional. Two psychologists who evaluated him for his trial concluded that he likely had narcissistic disorder. People with narcissism tend to have a deep sense of entitlement and are committed to the belief that they deserve special treatment: they feel they are so deserving because they are convinced that they are so much better than everyone else. While Frampton's positive self-views are excessive, his example reflects how deeply committed most people are to the belief that they are good. Of all the premises that form the structure of our life stories, the premise *I am good* arguably plays the most central role. Simply put, people usually tell their life stories in such a way that they regularly remember and present themselves as good, talented, moral, and sensible. How does this key premise *I am good* shape how we experience our lives?

To explore this question, let's first start off with an example of how you think about yourself. Consider some ways that you might evaluate your own abilities. For the next set of questions, please choose one of these three responses as you answer them: A: above average, B: average, and C: below average.

How would you rate your ability to get along with others?

How good of a driver are you?

How creative are you?

How considerate are you?

How dependable are you?

How much street smarts do you have?

How good of a friend are you?

So what do your answers to these questions look like? Did you answer "above average" for most of these? Or maybe even for *all* of these? Most people do think that they're better than average for these abilities. Now, while it is possible for some people to be better than average across all of these abilities, the laws of statistics would predict that, on average, the typical person should be about average. But when you look at people's self-ratings of their abilities, you can see that their ratings rarely line up with the laws of statistics. For example, one study asked a sample of American college professors to evaluate how good they were at being a professor. A full 94 percent rated themselves as better than average! I suspect Paul

Frampton would too. Another survey asked American high school students how good they were at getting along with others. One of the response options was "I'm in the top 1 percent of people"—but this option was chosen by a full 25 percent of the students! When we see such a split between people's views of themselves and the laws of statistics, it's clear evidence of a bias in people's thinking. The bias that people are showing here is how strongly they embrace the premise *I am good*, and this distorts their views about themselves. On average, most people think they are better than they really are.[15]

When people are telling stories about their individual selves, they are usually building them around the premise *I am good*. However, when we are reflecting on our life stories, we often go far beyond just thinking about ourselves as individuals. Much research has found that the self is quite imperial and has claimed territories that are far removed from our own bodies. Just as we are motivated to believe that our individual self is good, we are motivated to believe that all that is connected to us is also good. For example, when most people reflect upon their country, they usually view it in especially patriotic and undeniably positive terms—clearly better than most other countries. Likewise, when people consider the members of their family, they are also likely to view their family members as better than average too. Any groups that people belong to, or relationships that they have, tend to be seen in a positive light. And when people think about their possessions, they come to think about those in ways similar to how they think about themselves—as better than average. This tendency for people's possessions to get cast in the same warm glow as their selves can create some challenges. People may wish to sell their goods, say on Craigslist, and their positively distorted view of their possessions often leads them to ask for a price that is considerably higher than what others think it's worth. They demand such a high price because they're viewing their stuff through the same rose-colored lenses that they view the rest of themselves—a phenomenon that is termed the *endowment effect*. Anything that reflects upon oneself is usually thought of in ways that cohere with the premise *I am good*.[16]

While most people have strong desires to build their life stories around the premise *I am good*, this is not at all a straightforward task. It can be fraught because the world often presents itself in ways that seem completely at odds with this premise, as people sometimes don't look very good at all. Their romantic interests may reject them. They might fail an important exam. They might get fired from their job. How can people tell a life story about how they are good when their life is presenting them with evidence that is clearly at odds with this?

When bad things happen to people, the experience not only hurts their feelings, but it can also completely upend how they understand themselves. The premises in people's narratives about themselves provide the basic structure to their life stories, so people are strongly motivated to defend those premises. People rely upon an arsenal of psychological defenses to ensure that their life stories never stray too far from these premises. It is important to remember that people don't experience their lives veridically; they view the events in their lives through the lenses provided by their life stories. Just like Paul Frampton, the stories that people tell about their lives typically involve some fabrications and embellishments to ensure that they are better aligned with these key premises, such as *I am good*.[17]

Much research in social psychology has documented some of the key tactics that people rely upon in defending the premise *I am good*. For example, when people perform poorly at something, they tend to trivialize their failures. This trivialization disarms those failures and prevents them from overwriting their life stories. Imagine, say, that someone fails a calculus test. A common defensive response is to conclude that this test was just not that important to them. They may say to themselves, "Who cares about calculus anyway. I'm not going to become a mathematician." In stark contrast, people will typically show the precise opposite pattern for their successes and will interpret those events as being of outsize importance. So if someone aces a calculus test, they may think to themselves about how crucial calculus is for their future career success and how it's key to getting into graduate school or getting a coveted job as an engineer or a financial analyst. By titrating how importantly people view their successes and failures, they can shape their emotional reactions to these events in a way that enables them to tell a more convincing story that *I am good.*[18]

A second common strategy for defending the premise *I am good* is that people will often turn to different kinds of explanations to make sense of their successes and failures. Imagine a person who just started dating someone who they really like, only to get ghosted by their date the next day. In an effort to defend their life story and self-image, that person would identify the problem as lying *outside* themselves. They would conclude that something isn't right with their date—perhaps their date is dealing with a lot of their own emotional baggage, may be afraid to pursue a new relationship, or is so mixed up they couldn't appreciate all of the charms that this individual clearly has. On the other hand, when things work out well for someone, they are likely to interpret it in an entirely different way. If their date is going swimmingly, they are likely to conclude that it's because they are an attractive and desirable person. People will commonly take personal credit for their successes, but blame their failures on circumstances beyond their control, and they usually feel better for doing so. This biased way of explaining successes and failures enables people to see their successes as key evidence that they are good, while their failures are largely irrelevant to the *I am good* premise because they're the product of external uncontrollable forces.[19]

The urgency with which people defend the premise *I am good* is starkly revealed in a costly psychological defense that people sometimes turn to. Imagine that a student is facing an examination in a course that they are not well prepared for. They recognize that there's a good chance they'll fail the exam, which could be seen as evidence that they are a poor student or just aren't very bright. How can they deflect this looming threat? An especially anxious student might engage in self-handicapping and actively sabotage their own performance. On the eve of their exam, rather than heading to the library to make a last-minute attempt to study, they might instead decide to go out to celebrate a friend's birthday party. This decision will almost certainly guarantee that they'll do poorly on the exam, but it offers a handy excuse for their bad performance. Their self-handicapping allows them to explain to themselves, and to anyone else who knows about their exam performance, that they failed the test not because they weren't smart enough but because they didn't get the chance to study: they were such a devoted friend they had to spend the entire evening at their friend's birthday celebration instead of preparing for the exam. These kinds of dramatic psychological defenses reveal the extent that people are sometimes willing to go, including sabotaging their own performance, just to come up with a plausible way to convince themselves that they are still good.[20]

When people tell their life stories they often align them with a particular version of the premise *I am good*—that is, they are defending their self-esteem. Self-esteem reflects how positively a person evaluates themselves—what they think their intrinsic worth is. People who have higher self-esteem are more likely to think that they have many desirable traits. They usually think that they are talented, smart, funny, a good friend, and a moral person. They are more likely to feel secure in their relationships as they believe that they are a desirable partner and to expect that their efforts will ultimately lead to success. These people are able to maintain their high level of self-esteem precisely by relying on the various kinds of defenses we've discussed earlier to ensure that their life story hews close to the premise *I am good.*[21]

Curiously, while the premise *I am good* shapes the life stories of most people, this premise guides people's life stories differently across cultures. In the West, people make efforts to build their self-esteem, whereas in East Asia, people strive to be good by maintaining face. In contrast to the self-deceptive strategies that Westerners use to convince themselves that they're doing well (think of Paul Frampton, for example), East Asians aspire to convince *others* that they're doing well. One way to do this is by owning luxury brands such as Cartier or Chanel. Everyone recognizes that these brands are incredibly expensive, and that's really the key point with luxury items: they signal that the person has spent a lot of money, which helps convey the impression that they must *have* a lot of money. They can convince others to see them in ways that can help boost their self-respect and status. This is a key reason why top luxury brands, such as Louis Vuitton, Gucci, and Remy Martin, are so popular in East Asia and receive the bulk of their income there. Alternatively, people can strive to maintain face by remaining vigilant and identifying where they might be coming up short and are at risk of losing face. This strategy involves individuals being especially sensitive to any information that telegraphs they may not be doing well. Then the individual can work hard toward correcting whatever shortcomings they might find. This self-improving strategy, which is common among East Asians, provides an alternative way to tell life stories around the premise *I am good.*[22]

## I Am Not Very Good at All

While most people write their life stories around the premise *I am good,* there are some people, a minority in most contexts, who don't embrace this premise. Not everyone really believes they're good; rather, some people's stories are written around the premise *I am not very good at all.* People who have low self-esteem interpret the events in their lives with the expectation that things are just not going to work out very well. Such people tend to have rather pessimistic expectations for themselves. They often go about their lives expecting that, sooner or later, those who love them will ultimately reject them. They usually focus more on how things can go wrong rather than on how things can get better, and they're typically expecting the worst. In contrast to most people, individuals with low self-esteem don't usually see themselves as more talented than others, and this dark stain about how they view themselves usually spreads to include their extended selves as well. People with low self-esteem also don't think as positively about their romantic partners or their friends as do other people. Their pessimistic views extend even to how they think about their possessions. When they are selling their possessions, people who have negative thoughts about themselves will ask for less money for their stuff in comparison with other people. Their life story gets told around the premise *I am not very good at all.*[23]

But, regardless of whether someone is committed to the belief *I am good* or *I am not very good at all*, everyone still needs to feel that they have an accurate understanding of themselves—otherwise people remain stuck in the absurd. One of people's more fundamental psychological needs is to feel that their lives make sense, and this need guides the stories that people tell about themselves, regardless of how positively they think of themselves. A key way people evaluate whether their understanding of themselves is correct is by confirming that the social world validates their views. People tend to see themselves as a mirror of how others view them, and this means that if someone is committed to the belief that *I am good*, then they'll have a strong preference to see that the social world confirms that they are good. Such people prefer it when others say nice things to them or offer them positive feedback. The positive expressions of others confirm that one is correct in concluding that *I am good.*

Curiously, this same search for social validation of people's understanding about themselves also holds true for people who embrace the premise *I am not very good at all*. People with low self-esteem will have their understanding of themselves proven correct when others say critical things to them or belittle them. When others are mean to people with low self-esteem, this can actually confirm to them that their negative self-views are accurate. Quite remarkably, much psychological research finds that people with negative self-views can actually *prefer* to associate with people who say negative things about them. For example, one study examined married couples to investigate how people's self-views predicted the intimacy of their relationship. For those people who embraced the premise *I am good*, their results were rather straightforward: the more their partners had nice things to say about them, the more intimacy they felt with their partners. Simple enough. But among those people with low self-esteem, they reported more intimacy in their marriages when their partners were *critical* of them. Their desire for the social world to reflect their negative self-views is so strong that they have more love for a partner who regularly reminds them that they aren't very good at all.[24]

People's desires to have others confirm their views that *I am not very good at all* can have some interesting consequences. Together with Eric Mercadante and Karl Aquino, I conducted a series of studies to investigate the kinds of bosses that people prefer to work for. Not surprisingly, we found that those people with positive self-views liked to work for a boss who gave them autonomy and treated them fairly. However, it was a very different situation for people who viewed themselves negatively. Strikingly, we found that people with low self-esteem didn't seem to mind as much having a boss who would bully them—having a boss who was domineering and would belittle them was consistent with how they viewed themselves. This is how they thought leaders should behave. For example, in one study, we showed American adults videos of a couple of celebrity chefs and had the participants rate the chefs' leadership qualities. One chef, Curtis Stone, acted encouraging and respectful toward the other cooks, whereas the other chef, Gordon Ramsay, went on a rampage in the kitchen, cursing at and threatening to fire the other cooks and throwing food when it wasn't cooked to his standards. Curiously, people with low self-esteem judged Ramsay to be a much better leader than did the other participants. His behavior toward his employees seemed to match what they expected from a boss. On the other hand, the participants with high self-esteem thought Ramsay was a horrible boss, and they had a strong preference for the other chef. When people embrace the premise *I am not very good at all*, they prefer to live in a world where sometimes their negative self-views are confirmed, as this at least provides the assurance that they know who they are.[25]

These kinds of studies reveal that the premises that guide our life stories serve as a lens through which we observe the events of our lives. These premises don't just determine how we view ourselves; they also influence how we make sense of the behaviors of others around us. Whether one's life story is told around the premise *I am good* or *I am not very good at all* determines much about how we experience the world around us.

## Understanding the World Through Our Stories

Our life stories shape how we understand ourselves, but we also rely on stories to understand our worlds. For example, the story that people told about the COVID pandemic shaped whether they viewed the pandemic as a terrible threat to the planet's health or as a trivial matter that tyrannical governments used as an excuse to restrict people's freedoms. And, like our life stories, our stories about the world are also told around some key premises.

Simone de Beauvoir earned worldwide fame with the publication of her 1949 magnum opus *The Second Sex*, which has been called "the single most influential work ever to come out of the existentialist movement." The book provides a far-ranging and extremely insightful analysis of women's oppression across cultures and history and is widely seen as launching the second wave of feminism. It is somewhat surprising that it was in this most influential of feminist treatises that Beauvoir made the controversial argument that women were, in part, complicit in maintaining their subordinate status. She noted that "men encounter more complicity in their woman companions than the oppressor usually finds in the oppressed" and even provocatively suggested that a woman "chooses to want her enslavement." Her key question— "Why do women not contest male sovereignty?"—is a puzzling one, and it continues to spark much discussion to this day.[26]

Beauvoir's efforts to provide an answer to this question presage the discovery of a key psychological defense that people rely on for making sense of their worlds. As Beauvoir noted, women had historically been part of a situation in which they were subordinate to and dependent upon men. Women were born into this situation, and it constrained their possible reactions to it. As Beauvoir saw it, women had not been free to walk away from the constrictions of a male-dominated world as it was the only world they had ever known. Growing up in a world that had told them that they had fewer capabilities and opportunities than men, women came to accept this hierarchical view of society, which had been imposed upon them, even though this view imprisoned them. They were part of a patriarchal society that had historically viewed men as powerful and women as powerless, and these understandings had shaped their identity. There was no easy way to escape this situation because it seemed that all of society understood the world to be this way—their oppression was the status quo. So, as Beauvoir argued, most women came to naturally accept these terms as this was the way the world was presented to them, and by accepting these terms, women played a role in perpetuating this unjust system. Beauvoir recognized that women, of course, wished to improve their status: their desire to be treated fairly was obvious. But she recognized that women possessed a competing psychological motivation that ran afoul with their desires for equality. They had a desire to see the world as they believed it to be.[27]

Beauvoir focused on the case of women's oppression, but in many ways, a similar story could be told about the oppression of other disadvantaged groups throughout history. Disadvantaged people find themselves part of a system that is oppressing them, and because they have less power and fewer resources than their oppressors, there is often little they can do about it. One possible solution is that the disadvantaged could rebel against the system and force the system to make changes. But, curiously, this rarely happens. As the historian Howard Zinn noted, "Rebellion is only an occasional reaction to suffering in human history; we have infinitely more instances of forbearance to exploitation, and submission to authority, than we have examples of revolt." More often than not, it seems that the oppressed act in ways that support the system that subjugates them.[28]

Members of disadvantaged groups not only participate in an oppressive system, but even more perplexing, they also often act in ways that contribute to their disadvantage. For example, why would so many poor Americans vote for a party that promises to prevent the government from subsidizing their health care? It is the poor who would benefit most from public health insurance, yet often one hears poor Americans arguing against such a benefit. In recent elections it has been high-school-educated whites who have been among the most reliable voters for the Republican Party and their platform to keep health insurance privatized. As film director Michael Moore put it in his documentary *Fahrenheit 9/11*: "I've always been amazed that the very people forced to live in the worst parts of the town, go to the worst schools, and who have it the hardest are always the first to step up to defend that very system." Curiously, disadvantaged individuals often seem quite willing to tolerate a system that exploits them, rather than using their large numbers to force governments to prioritize their interests.[29]

A key reason that people will so often accept a social system that subjugates them is that there can be some curious psychological benefits from maintaining the status quo. The status quo typically provides some people, usually straight white men in the case of Western societies, with more power and opportunities than others. This arrangement has, of course, been oppressive, and many people rightfully wish to change the existing hierarchy. But efforts to change the system are often bogged down by some psychological inertia. A challenge that people face in trying to change the present circumstances is that the status quo has the psychological advantage of being *familiar*. And we tend not to fully appreciate the power that familiarity has on our judgments. The existing social hierarchy, unfair as it is, can provide people with a sense of order, even to those at the bottom, because it is familiar, and this can help to quell people's existential anxieties. In our efforts to work toward reducing the unfairness in the world, we need to confront the psychological biases that are blocking the way.

We can gain a better understanding for why people seem attracted to the status quo if we consider that people live in a shared reality with others from their cultures. This shared reality provides them with norms and standards that guide their behaviors, informing them of what is valued, shunned, or encouraged. People need to understand these norms so that they can work toward getting ahead. This collective understanding of a shared reality is maintained by people telling each other a shared story for what the world is like, which includes many details, such as how people are supposed to act, what are the consequences for breaking these norms, and who in society has the advantages and who has the disadvantages. Because people need to feel that they understand the shared story that they have about the world, people have motivations to defend that story, even if they'd rather the world was otherwise. Thinking *the world is so* provides them with the sense that they understand their worlds: they know the rules of the game and are prepared to play accordingly. When the current system is challenged, especially when change is occurring rapidly, it can undermine people's feelings of certainty, making them less sure how they are to act, which can lead to feeling that things are spinning out of control.

The unconscious desire that people have to preserve the status quo is what social psychologist John Jost calls "system justification." This theory has spawned hundreds of experiments that have revealed that people will engage in a variety of curious psychological defenses that help to protect the status quo. By accepting that *the world is so*, people are able to feel that their current system is fair and legitimate, and they are more certain that their understanding of the world is correct. People tend to assume that the way things are is the way things *ought* to be, which results in the perpetuation of the status quo, even when it is blatantly unjust and oppressive.[30]

For example, in recent decades, economic inequality has increased in most nations of the world. The situation of the rich has improved dramatically, yet the situation of everyone else has largely stagnated or gotten worse. For the vast majority of people, higher economic inequality is a bad thing, as most people are relatively worse off in unequal countries compared to more equal ones, and there is a long list of societal and psychological problems that go hand in hand with inequality, such as reduced life expectancy, lower school achievement, increased crime, and lower levels of trust. Yet, paradoxically, it is precisely in those places where economic inequality is the highest that people are the least bothered by inequality. People who live in more unequal contexts are more likely to say that vast income differences between people are justified because the rich must be working harder and they must have more talent, whereas in more equal places people tend to find inequality to be far more problematic. The nature of inequality in one's own country shapes one's attitudes toward that inequality, such that people are usually likely to conclude that the status quo is just fine.[31]

People also justify the status quo by maintaining complementary stereotypes about groups in society—stereotypes that simultaneously emphasize contrasting positive and negative elements. For example, think about what are some common stereotypes about the rich and the poor. In Charles Dickens's *A Christmas Carol*, the fabulously wealthy Ebenezer Scrooge was portrayed as miserable, bitter, and cruel—hardly a perspective that makes being rich seem very desirable. In contrast, Dickens described the destitute Cratchit family as "happy, grateful, pleased with one another and contented with the time." This complementary stereotype of the happy poor in contrast to the sad and lonely rich is commonplace throughout society. But surveys of happiness never find that the poor are, on average, happier than the rich; rather, surveys of happiness typically find that happiness goes up alongside wealth, although the boost in happiness that comes with increased wealth gets weaker the wealthier one becomes. This false stereotype that the poor are happier with their lives helps to justify the system we live in. By thinking of the poor as content with their lot, it is no longer so problematic if the social system continues to leave some people in poverty. This false stereotype that poverty has its rewards helps to justify that *the world is so*—if people think of the poor as happy, there should be less desire to try to change their circumstances. Research finds that when people are presented with descriptions of individuals being poor but happy, they are then more likely to agree with statements such as "Society is set up so that people usually get what they deserve." These complementary stereotypes help people to justify the status quo.[32]

Of course, this desire to maintain the status quo, to view *the world is so*, is not the only motivation that people have, and their other motivations are often in conflict with their desire to maintain the status quo. People also have motivations to achieve status, power, and freedom, and for the oppressed, these other motivations are in stark conflict with people's motivations to view *the world is so*. But despite these other competing motivations that people have, accepting that *the world is so* and believing that the current system is there for a reason serves to help people view the world as an orderly place, even among those who are oppressed by the status quo. People's preferences for familiarity remain as stubborn obstacles for achieving social justice goals.

Another premise that guides people's stories about the world is *people get what they deserve*. Simply put, people tend to think that good things happen to good people, and bad things happen to bad people. But the news is full of stories of horrible and senseless tragedies, of innocent victims meeting dreadful ends. These stories potentially undermine this premise. The existence of innocent victims suggests that the world may not be so just after all and that there is a disturbing randomness to the world, where tragedies can occur without rhyme or reason. And if events in the world sometimes happen in unpredictable ways, then, of course, this means that it's also possible that such horrible things might someday befall us, no matter how careful we may try to be.

The notion that there is an inherent randomness to the world can be acutely psychologically threatening, so to combat this, people do their best to impose a sense of justice such that *people get what they deserve*. For example, when faced with a news story about someone killed in a car crash, you may find yourself especially attentive to details that suggest the victim may have contributed to their unfortunate fate—perhaps the driver wasn't wearing

a seat belt, or had been driving back from the bar, or had been texting. This is a common reaction when people learn of tragedies.
Dozens of psychological studies have found that when people hear
of someone being treated unjustly, they show an unconscious tendency to view that person more negatively. By putting down the
victim, people can change their perception of how the world is
unfolding. It's no longer the case of bad things happening to innocent victims, but bad things happening to someone who maybe
wasn't so innocent after all. This reaction can help the world feel
less random and less threatening.[33]

Rape victims often have to endure people questioning them
about what they may have done that could have contributed to
their rape. Nancy Raine wrote a moving book titled *After Silence*
about her own experience rebuilding her life after having survived a horrific rape by a stranger who had snuck into her apartment when she had stepped outside to take out some garbage.
As she described the experience, several people, even her close
friends, told her that she was partly to blame. One suggested that
her overall negative attitude may have attracted more negativity
from others around her, and another suggested that she should
have been more careful in choosing which neighborhood to live
in. People often show similar kinds of seemingly callous reactions
when they hear about people who have contracted dreadful diseases, such as AIDS or cancer. They often search for ways that the
person's lifestyle may have contributed to them getting sick.[34]

The sheer power of the premise *people get what they deserve*
may be most directly evident when people come to interpret the
misfortunes that have occurred in their *own* lives. In the aftermath
of a rape, rape victims are often living in abject fear of their rapist
and are terrified that they may be raped again. Their whole worldview has been upended, and they find themselves now living in

a world that no longer seems safe or under control. But if a rape victim can feel that she may have acted in a way that may have contributed to her attack, while knowing that her actions can be changed in the future, she may feel a little more in control of her life. If she can think "I shouldn't have walked alone," or "I should have made sure to lock the windows," she can regain a sense that her life is under control and can feel a little safer knowing that she can act in a way that will help her to avoid a future tragedy. These kinds of self-blaming responses are common among rape victims. One study of rape crisis centers found that approximately three-quarters of women who had been raped blamed themselves at least somewhat for what had happened to them. Likewise, another study found that accident victims who blamed themselves for their accidents fared better in their recovery than those who did not. Despite not being responsible for the terrible fates that they suffered, imagining that their actions may have contributed to their traumatic events can help to provide people with a sense of control and prepare them to get on with their lives. If people can direct some unwarranted blame toward themselves, the world may feel a little less random to them and they can at least feel that they can do something to avoid future tragedies.[35]

The stories that we tell about ourselves and our worlds are built around these key premises, and this influences how we experience the events in our lives. We observe what happens through the lenses of our stories, and this provides the foundation from which we can pursue a meaningful life. We depend a great deal on a variety of psychological defenses to ensure that the world continues to match the stories we tell about it.

Chapter 4

# How Our Brains Ensure
# Our Lives Make Sense

Humans are creatures, who spent their lives

trying to convince themselves,

that their existence is not absurd.

Albert Camus

A s an existential ape, we have a need to feel that our lives are meaningful, and we stand to suffer whenever we feel they are not. But how do our brains enable us to do this? How are our brains able to recognize when we have stumbled into the absurd, and we are no longer able to derive meaning from what is happening around us?

As I'll describe below, our brains have evolved what I term a *sense-making system*, which ensures that we feel what we are doing is meaningful and makes good sense. This system is triggered whenever we slip into the absurd and encounter something we're unable to make any sense of. Our brains then alert us that there is a problem so that we can strive to regain our footing and try to make sense of things all over again. This sense-making system serves to ensure that our lives are feeling meaningful and directs us to make efforts to correct matters whenever it senses anything that no longer makes sense. We'll discuss how this sense-making system is able to help us to maintain meaning in our lives by first considering two examples of ways that we're able to repair our sense of meaning and connections when they are threatened. We'll first explore the role that nostalgia plays in helping us maintain a sense of meaning in our lives, and then we'll discuss how our brains help to ensure that we're able to maintain our interpersonal connections with others. These examples will illustrate how our sense-making system is able to help us to extricate ourselves from the absurd.

## Maintaining Meaning Through Nostalgia

If someone from the 1980s got into a time machine and traveled to the present, they would surely be in for some surprises. While they may be disappointed to learn that there are still no flying cars, they likely would be struck by the many new technological innovations such as the internet, smartphones, and electric cars. They may also be taken aback by how many more people are now sporting tattoos and body piercings and that openly gay couples and transgender individuals are a far more common sight. But what these time travelers probably couldn't have foreseen about the present is just how uncannily familiar the popular culture is around them.

The early twenty-first century is awash in nostalgia and retro designs. As Simon Reynolds, author of *Retromania*, puts it: "There has never been a society in human history so obsessed with the cultural artifacts of its own immediate past." The movie theaters are playing remakes of films that were created just a few decades before, such as *Ghostbusters, Dune, A Star Is Born,* or *Charlie's Angels*. New television series set in previous decades are discussed as much for their plots as they are for the way they nailed the décor, fashion, and music of those times. Consumer products are sometimes sold in ways that harken to the past, with Pepsi selling their sodas in cans with their design from the 1960s and Cheerios offering their cereal in a box reminiscent of how it was sold during the Second World War. Companies are releasing new high-tech products that are designed to resemble their low-tech forebears from decades earlier, such as Bluetooth radios, digital cameras, or toasters that look as though they came from your great-grandmother's house. One can find boutique shops selling overpriced soaps or chocolate bars in packaging that looks as though it were taken straight off the shelves of a frontier general store. Facebook has also gotten in on the nostalgia game by promoting "Throwback Thursday," where people post old photos and comment on events surrounding particular memories. It seems that everywhere one looks, there are signs from our pasts.[1]

CNN declared 2011 as the year of nostalgia, and the trend has not shown any signs of slowing down. It seemed to spike even more during the COVID pandemic, and everywhere one looks, we see reminders of days gone by. Is it a coincidence that such a notable characteristic of the new age of anxiety is just how much people seem stuck in the past?[2]

Fyodor Dostoevsky was well aware of the deep allure of our nostalgic memories. He stated that "you must know that there is nothing higher and stronger and more wholesome and good for life in the future than some good memory, especially a memory of childhood, of home. . . . If a man carries many such memories with him into life, he is safe to the end of his days." When we reflect upon our pasts, we bring up a host of warm feelings as we relive many of the earlier chapters of our life stories. One reason that we encounter so many nostalgic reminders in the marketplace is because the irresistible appeal of nostalgia has not been lost on advertisers. Advertisers often aspire to link their products with nostalgic connections with the audience's past in order to exploit the warm feelings that they so reliably elicit. Coca-Cola gets placed in the hands of a Santa Claus right out of a Norman Rockwell painting, McDonald's commercials show their food being eaten by kids playing old video games alongside a 1980s Cyndi Lauper soundtrack, and Walmart commercials feature their customers arriving in vehicles made famous from *Knight Rider, Scooby Doo*, and other popular Gen X shows. In a deft stroke, the warm feelings that people have of their imagined pasts get linked with the products on the screen.[3]

This broad appeal of the past, and the warmth that our nostalgic memories bring, raises the question of why we might be so attracted to nostalgia in the first place. When we look back at the past, why don't we usually think, "Wow, those days sure stunk!," or when we see a retro product, conclude, "The new ones just look so much better"? We rarely cast a critical eye toward the past; instead we have a robust tendency to celebrate it. This tendency is all the more curious because, when you really think about it, the past was rife with its own problems. War and violence were more common in the past, people were poorer, lifespans were shorter, and racism, sexism, and homophobia were even more formally entrenched than they are today.

But this is not how most people remember things; rather, it is an almost universal reaction to romanticize the past as a simpler and better time. I think the past is seen so fondly because those moments become imbued with the nostalgic sense of how past events have paved the way to who we are in the present. The past is the setting of the early chapters of our life stories, and it provides richness and context to our understanding of the life we have lived and the person we have become. That people seem to enjoy their nostalgic reflections so much suggests that they might be serving an important function, and much psychological research shows that they are. Our feelings of nostalgia provide us with key existential benefits; they can ground us with important bases for leading a meaningful life.

Not all memories of the past are tinged with nostalgic feelings. We can gain an appreciation for how nostalgia bolsters our sense of meaning when we consider the kinds of memories that people tend to feel are most nostalgic. When people are asked to recall a memory that they feel was especially nostalgic, they tend to focus on events that share a few essential similarities. First, our most nostalgic memories are almost always social in nature. We recall being with others, especially with our closest relationships. We also tend to focus on some key momentous events, such as weddings or graduations, or major family events, such as past celebrations of Christmas or early childhood vacations. In our most nostalgic memories we're usually playing a central role. It's the time that we went to the prom or when we first jumped off the high diving board, rather than us sitting on the sidelines observing others. Our nostalgic memories are also more likely to share a redemptive theme—we feel nostalgic when we remember how we stood up to that bully, threw away our last pack of cigarettes, or got accepted into college. In sum, our most nostalgic memories are ones that chronicle our most important relationships and some of the key moments of our lives. They're the greatest hits album of how we came to be who we are.[4]

Importantly, our nostalgic reflections provide us with a richer sense of identity. They connect our lives of the present with the fateful events of our past, providing us with a sense of self-continuity across time. When we look back at our pasts, and remember how we were then, we can gain a better appreciation for how we came to be the person we are now. When people reflect on their past, it throws their true self into relief—the person they feel they really are—and it boosts their feelings of authenticity. And in these moments of a heightened awareness of who we are, our actions tend to feel as though they are guided by a sense of purpose, and we feel ready to pursue the most important goals in our lives.[5]

In sum, our nostalgic feelings make our lives feel more *meaningful*. Our memories of our past ground us with all of these key sources of meaning in our lives, and they are part of the stories we tell about ourselves. By exploring *when* people are most likely to be reflecting on their pasts, psychological research can reveal the existential benefits of nostalgia and how it reflects upon our sense-making system. People are not equally likely to wax nostalgically at any point in their lives. Rather, we are most likely to drift off in a nostalgic reverie precisely at those times when we feel that our life is presently unsatisfyingly low in meaning. There are many occasions when our lives feel relatively meaningless, for example, when we are feeling particularly lonely and disconnected from others, or when we are bored and are struggling to find anything fulfilling in our actions. During these times when a sense of meaning is especially hard to come by, people are eager to find ways to give their lives a nice boost in meaning. And it is at exactly those moments when our sense of meaning has drifted away that we are most likely to turn to memories from our past in an effort to regain our existential footing.[6]

We can readily see the meaning-boosting functions of nostalgia in a psychology experiment that social psychologist Clay Routledge and his colleagues conducted. In this study, British university students were asked to read an essay that argued that, in the grand scheme of things, their lives were rather trivial and meaningless. They were reminded that the earth was close to five billion years old and that more than eight billion people were living on the planet, and in this context, any individual's relatively brief life really doesn't amount to much at all. The students who read this bleak essay were compared to another group who read an entirely different essay. This other essay didn't touch upon anything about meaning in life and was instead a control essay of a similar length describing how computers operate. The students were then asked to complete some items about their feelings of nostalgia: for example, they were asked how much they agreed with the statement "I feel nostalgic at the moment." And, indeed, those students who had read the meaning-threatening essay reported feeling more nostalgic than those who had read about computers. The experience of having the wind of meaning knocked out of them led people to reflect more nostalgically, in an apparent effort to regain a sense of meaning all over again. These kinds of efforts to rebuild a sense of meaning precisely when it is hard to come by provide us with a glimpse of how humans have a true need to feel their lives are meaningful. When we notice that a sense of meaning in our lives is lacking, we engage in strategies to try to get it back.[7]

We can understand our nostalgic memories as akin to a bank account for our sense of meaning in life. As we live our lives and have key experiences that make us who we are, we deposit these memories into a vault, locked away for later withdrawals. And then when we catch ourselves in a moment of existential despair, when we're questioning why things are feeling so meaningless, we can make a withdrawal from the nostalgia bank. We can play some songs from the soundtrack of our youth, flip through a photo album, or watch a rerun of a favorite childhood show to again appreciate the people we're connected with and how we've come to be who we are. Our nostalgia serves the important function of imbuing our lives with a sense of meaning.

Research on nostalgia highlights the somewhat homeostatic nature of meaning in our lives and provides an example of how our sense-making system operates. Our sense of meaning can rise and fall depending on circumstances, and we have various means at our disposal, such as nostalgic reflections, to attempt to regain a sense of meaningfulness when it feels insufficient. On the other hand, when people experience their lives as especially rich in meaning, they are less likely to search for other ways to make their lives feel more meaningful. This homeostatic nature of meaning serves to help people to keep their levels of meaning in balance. People tend only to work toward regaining a sense of meaning in their lives when they feel that it is scarce.

When we consider that people turn to nostalgic reflections to help them to prop up a sense of meaning when they're running short of it, it's no longer a puzzle that the new age of anxiety is so replete with everything nostalgic and retro. So many of the sources of meaning that we depend on are not so readily available in the existential vacuum of the early twenty-first century. But our need for meaning remains unabated, and in such times, we deal with this lack of meaning by turning to our past, to reexperience events from earlier chapters of our life story.

As a meaningful species, *Homo significativa*, we live and pursue all of our basic needs within an ecology of meaning. We do this by connecting our bodies to this cultural matrix of meaning via ourselves, and we strive to work toward a meaningful life.

However, this pursuit is jeopardized whenever we feel that we are no longer existentially grounded. We need to ensure that we are not alienated and that we're not left detached from key sources of meaning. Our feelings of nostalgia can serve as a tool we can rely on to regain a sense that our lives are meaningful whenever we feel that our sense of meaning is threatened. These feelings help to provide a sense of continuity across the course of our life; they help us to reflect on our interpersonal connections, give us a sense of purpose, and bolster us with a sense of meaning.

Our ability to feel nostalgia and orient ourselves toward a more meaningful life is one example of a way that we respond to threats to our sense of meaning. Our nostalgic feelings provide a glimpse into the functioning of our sense-making system, which operates to help us to notice whenever our lives feel short of meaning by prompting us to strive to regain that meaning all over again. But nostalgic memories are just one of many ways that we can maintain meaning in our lives when we are feeling meaningless. Let's now consider how neural mechanisms in the brain enable us to protect and maintain our interpersonal connections by alerting us when our sense of meaning is threatened.

## Maintaining Our Interpersonal Relationships

We can gain a better appreciation for the ways that humans maintain meaning in their lives if we first step back and consider meaning more broadly. As we discussed earlier, ultimately meaning is a matter of connections—things that connect to each other, such as snow being cold and someone believing that they are a good person. We also get meaning through our close interpersonal relations. These relations serve to connect us with others and bring meaning to our lives through those social connections. Just as we have a desire to protect the connections that underlie our sense of meaning, we have a similar desire to protect our interpersonal connections.

Humans are an ultrasocial species, and we are especially dependent on our relationships to thrive. We can see the extent of this dependence by how much we tend to suffer when our relationship needs aren't being satisfied. Quite frankly, when people aren't getting their relationship needs met, they can really struggle. We all know how unpleasant it can be to feel lonely or rejected. The sad and alienated feelings that come with feeling disconnected from others are not trivial and can make us at greater risk for depression and other kinds of mental illnesses. But the costs of feeling disconnected from others extend far beyond the psychological toll. It is only relatively recently that researchers have learned just how pronounced the dangers are to people's physical health when they are not sufficiently connected with others. For example, research finds that people who are more socially isolated are less likely to survive a heart attack or stroke. Because they lack social support, it is more difficult for them to recover from these kinds of medical emergencies. Having one's relationship needs unmet can even weaken the immune system. One study found that American university students who had a smaller social network tended to show a weaker immune response to getting the flu vaccine in contrast to those with closer connections. The full extent of the critical necessity of social connectedness was revealed in one large-scale investigation that summarized the findings from 148 separate studies that explored the links between people's relationships and mortality. The results showed that people who had a strong network of social relationships were 50 percent more likely to survive over the next several years than those who felt more isolated. The enormity of this risk factor is just starting to be appreciated: having insufficient social support was found to be a larger risk factor for dying than drinking more than six drinks a day, being obese, or not exercising. Indeed, the only single behavior that contributed more to an individual's mortality risk than the quality of their social relationships was whether they were a regular smoker. The link between feeling lonely and poor physical health is so strong that researchers have identified a dose-dependent effect—each extra episode of feeling lonely is associated with a slightly worse health outcome. The many ways that physical health is associated with relationships shows how important it is for an ultrasocial species like us to be well grounded in a web of close relationships.[8]

The links between our relationships and our health suggest that it's vital for people to attend to their belongingness. Psychologists have demonstrated that our desires for belongingness form a full-fledged need for humans, akin to our need for food and protection. When we're deprived of food, our body signals this to us with pangs of hunger, which impel us to replenish our nutrients to stave off death by starvation. Likewise, when we're cut off from our important relationships, our body signals us with specific feelings that motivate us to replenish our belongingness tanks. When we're feeling isolated from others, we feel lonely, and this prompts us to make more efforts to seek out some kind of social connection. We might reach out to call a friend that we haven't seen in a long while, start a conversation with a stranger, or make plans to join a singles network. Our lonely feelings sound the alarm that our belongingness needs are not being met, and we stand to suffer if that trend continues.[9]

We can see more evidence for the human need to belong whenever people move to a new situation where they don't have existing relationships with others, such as when they move to a new city, start a new job, change schools, or join a workshop that's full of strangers. In these situations, people typically interact with others with a different mind-set than they do when they're already embedded in a tight social network—they are more outgoing, make more efforts to find common interests, and strive to form new relationships. People have a drive to form connections, to ensure that they're tethered to a rich network of relationships, and they make more efforts to do so whenever they're feeling that their current set of relationships is not adequate.

This drive to form new relationships, however, is much reduced when people feel that their current relationship needs are satisfied. People who are in satisfying romantic relationships or have a network of friends that they regularly see are akin to a person who has just finished a large meal. Their relationship needs are fully sated, and they are less likely to make efforts to form new relationships. For example, when people form a new romantic relationship or get married, one very reliable prediction is that they will be spending less time with their old friends. One researcher quantified this cost of friendships in people's marriages and concluded that "falling in love will cost you two friendships." An individual's marriage is meeting a larger proportion of their relationship needs so they benefit less than otherwise from their other friendships. Likewise, people in large extended families tend to have fewer friends than those who are from smaller families—either our families or our friends can help to provide us with the social support we need. When we are in the state where our relationship needs feel sated, we are typically not suffering pangs of loneliness, which would prompt us to form new relationships.[10]

Further evidence that our desire for relationships serves a deep-seated need is that, to a certain extent, people readily substitute relationships that have ended with new people. Though we have close relationships with *specific* others, who we can care for very much, rather than with people in general, when an existing relationship dissolves, we will often seek a new relationship to replace it. When people enter college, they typically see their high school friends less, as those friendships get largely replaced with new ones. The evolutionary psychologist David Buss refers to a common human mating strategy as brachiating: just as a gibbon moves through the jungle by swinging from branch to branch, always holding on to something, a common mating strategy for many people is to not leave a romantic relationship until they have a new relationship ready to replace it. But people don't always swap one romantic relationship for another: other kinds of relationships can help fulfill their belonging needs. When people get divorced, they often will spend more time with their friends and family than they did before. Responding to a damaged relationship by replacing it with a new one further highlights our need for belongingness. If people fail to form a new relationship after losing an existing one, they are vulnerable to the many kinds of mental and physical health issues that plague the lonely.[11]

As members of an ultrasocial species, we depend upon a system that will ensure our basic relationship needs are being met. This system for maintaining our sense of belongingness with others shares much in common with how we maintain a sense of meaning in our lives. Recall that people are more likely to turn to nostalgic reflections when they sense that their life is rather meaningless, and their memories help to boost their sense of meaning higher, bringing it back up to an equilibrium point. Similarly, people strive to rebuild their sense of belongingness when it feels threatened. The system is triggered whenever someone feels that their relationships are inadequate, such as when they feel lonely, which leads them to marshal efforts to regain a sense of belongingness. In this way, people can act to bolster their feelings of belongingness whenever it feels threatened and bring it back into balance.

Loneliness is one feeling that signals that people's belongingness needs aren't being met. But people also need to be vigilant to whenever their existing relationships may be vulnerable, and one clear signal that highlights this is the sting that comes with interpersonal rejection. When people feel the pain of being rejected, they become excruciatingly aware that their current relationships might be in jeopardy. Rejection has been called "the mother of all fears," and few things cause more psychological distress than being excluded. One researcher found that many people offered that they would rather be physically hit than be ostracized. Think of occasions in your own life when you have been excluded. Perhaps you weren't invited to a social event that many of your friends had attended, and the pictures on Instagram of everyone's happy faces only reminded you that you'd been excluded. Or you might have been picked last in gym class, as no one wanted you on their team. Or perhaps—what can hurt most of all—you were dumped by a loved one. We can all readily imagine or remember the sting of these rejections.[12]

When one's heart is broken, the feeling is so distinct and overpowering that it's hard to think about anything else. It just really *hurts* when a close relationship has ended. It's not a coincidence that we discuss the feelings of interpersonal rejection with the same words we use to describe physical pain. Indeed, across many different languages, the words used to describe interpersonal rejection and physical pain are similar. A broken heart is really hurtful because of the way both interpersonal rejection and physical pain are experienced in the brain—they rely on much of the same neural circuitry.[13]

When you put your hand on a hot stove, your brain very quickly alerts you to the pain that you're experiencing. In particular, there are two distinct regions of your brain that become activated in such a situation. First, burning your hand activates a region near the center of your brain in the anterior cingulate cortex (ACC), which immediately communicates the distressing part of your pain. It's like an alarm system telling you to immediately focus your attention on the problem. The back part of your brain called the somatosensory cortex is also activated; this part communicates to you both the location and intensity of the pain. This very rapid circuit lets you immediately respond by pulling your hand off the stove before you cause even more damage to it. This system for detecting physical pain is vital for us to avoid doing injurious damage to our bodies.[14]

The overlap in the ways that our brains respond to physical pain and interpersonal rejection was clearly demonstrated in a famous neuroscience experiment by Naomi Eisenberger, Matthew Lieberman, and Kip Williams. American college students were placed in a brain scanner while they watched an avatar of themselves playing catch with two other avatars in a computer game called *Cyberball.* The participants were falsely informed that the other two avatars were controlled by two other participants who were also lying in brain scanners. In actuality, the other avatars were controlled by a computer program. When the ball was thrown to the participant's avatar, they would catch it, and then they could choose which of the two avatars to throw it back to. The game proceeded normally for a while, until the participant noticed that the other two avatars had suddenly stopped playing with them. Without any warning, this three-person game of catch had unexpectedly become a two-person game, and the participant was soon sitting on the sidelines for the rest of the game, waiting in vain for the ball to be thrown back to them. The researchers studied the participants' brain activity following this moment of interpersonal exclusion and identified a clear pattern. Their ACC showed an increased pattern of activation, just like when someone is experiencing physical pain. Their neural alarm had been tripped, signaling that there was a problem that needed their immediate attention. Those participants who later reported that their feelings were hurt the most by the rejection were also the ones who showed the greatest level of activation in their ACC. On the other hand, there was no increased activation in the participants' somatosensory cortex following the exclusion, indicating that there was no physical sensation of pain. This shows that when people sense that they are being rejected, they are alerted by the neural alarm in the ACC. They recognize that their belongingness needs are at risk, and they are now ready to act accordingly. The same alarm that tells us when to take our hand off the stove also warns us when our relationship needs are being threatened. And as we'll see below, this same alarm system alerts us to other meaning threats that we may experience.[15]

That this neural alarm system signals both physical pain and interpersonal rejection has some interesting consequences. Consider what happens when we take painkilling medication, such as the Tylenol brand of acetaminophen (which also goes by the name paracetamol). Typically, people take a Tylenol when they're feeling some physical pain, and the drug reliably diminishes the pain. How acetaminophen actually reduces people's sense of pain continues to be debated, although it is clear that the drug passes the blood-brain barrier and enters the central nervous system. Given the shared alarm system that underlies physical pain and interpersonal rejection, we might wonder whether acetamino-phen could also affect our feelings of belongingness with others. The social psychologist C. Nathan DeWall led a team of research-ers who explored this question by giving American college stu-dents one of two pills to take. For half of the participants, the pills contained 1,000 mg of acetaminophen, whereas for the other half, the pills contained a placebo. The participants weren't informed which version of the pill they had received. The participants were then put in a brain scanner to play the same *Cyberball* game described earlier, where they found themselves unexpectedly excluded by the other two avatars. When the researchers analyzed the results, they found that the participants who had taken the placebo showed the same pattern of brain activation as the study described earlier: that is, after they were excluded from the game of catch, they showed increased activation in the ACC. In stark contrast, though, those participants who had received the acet-aminophen showed no increased activation in the ACC follow-ing their rejection. The acetaminophen appeared to dampen their neural alarm. In a second study, the same researchers gave pills to another sample of American college students and had them take the pills each day over a period of three weeks. Again, half of the participants had received acetaminophen, whereas the other half had received a placebo. Over the course of the three weeks, the participants were asked to complete a brief scale each evening that assessed how often they had felt excluded and suffered from hurt feelings over the day. Quite remarkably, over the course of the study, those participants who had taken acetaminophen reported fewer instances of hurt feelings than did those who had taken the placebo. The acetaminophen seemed to dull the pain of their hurt feelings.[16]

## An All-Purpose Neural Alarm

This neural alarm that's localized in the ACC gets triggered when-ever we experience either physical or interpersonal pain, and it serves to alert us that these events require our immediate atten-tion. However, this alarm system appears to be triggered by a much wider array of problems than just ones that involve physical or interpersonal pain—in particular, it seems to be triggered by the kinds of events that elicit existential angst. For example, one study put participants in a brain scanner and had them contemplate their mortality and that one day their existence would come to an end. While reflecting on these existential concerns, participants showed a spike of activation in their ACC. Likewise, another study explored what patterns of brain activation were associated with something called *cognitive dissonance*. We'll return to talk more about cognitive dissonance in Chapter 6, but, in a nutshell, this is the disturbing feeling that people get when they realize their lives aren't making any sense. And where in the brain does this disso-nance appear to be experienced? It also appears to be localized in the ACC. Actually, the ACC seems to be triggered by a broad range of different experiences. It's also more active whenever people experience something that violates their expectations. For exam-ple, even when people make the most trivial kinds of errors, such as accidentally hitting the space bar on a computer when they were trying not to, it elicits a very reliable and clear signal in the ACC. This neural alarm seems to be triggered by a wide variety of events that require our attention.[17]

While there is still much ongoing debate among neuroscien-tists about the particular functions that different brain regions serve, an emerging perspective is that it's more informative to look at particular networks of brain regions that are connected to each other. Individual brain regions are not activated in isolation; rather, patterns of activation are spread across different pathways in the brain connecting various brain regions. And the ACC appears to be part of a very important neural network that connects the ACC to some other parts of the brain, including the anterior insula, the ventrolateral prefrontal cortex, the amygdala, the ventral striatum, and some other regions. This network has been called the *salience network*, and it seems that any event that stands out to us triggers it. As our brain processes the constant stream of sensory information, the salience network serves to alert us to any troubling information that requires further processing. It's as though a flag is waved in front of our faces alerting us that our attention is required. When this salience network is triggered, it signals that a problem has been detected, and our brain shifts from its default mode network to a vigilant state as it strives to address the problem.[18]

One way that we can see evidence that our brain depends on a common signal to alert it to different kinds of problems is by again exploring the effects that painkillers have on various kinds of psychological threats. While it certainly isn't something that most consumers are aware of, and it's somewhat worrisome to consider, a growing field of research has found that consuming acetaminophen tends to blunt people's emotional responses to a wide variety of events. For example, when people have consumed acetaminophen they seem to be more willing to take risks, are less bothered by decisions they have made, are less distrustful of others, and are less able to empathize with another's pain. My students Daniel Randles and Nathan Santos and I even found in an experiment that taking acetaminophen dulled people's existential anxieties when they reflected upon the fact that someday they were going to die. When we take something to numb our physical pain, it may also be numbing our emotional reactions to other kinds of events.[19]

Acetaminophen may have these broad effects on how we react to troubling events because it appears to dampen the neural alarm in the ACC. We found some evidence for this effect of acetaminophen on our brains in an experiment I conducted with Daniel Randles, Julia Kam, Michael Inzlicht, and Todd Handy. We wanted to explore whether acetaminophen affects the ways that the brain responds to simple cognitive errors that people make, and we did this by measuring the electrical activity that was centered around the ACC in our participants, using an electroencephalogram (EEG). We gave Canadian university students a very straightforward task to complete on the computer while they were wearing a cap that was fitted with several electrodes to measure the patterns of electrical activity in their brains. The participants were instructed to hit the space bar whenever they saw the letter *E* and to refrain from hitting the space bar whenever they saw the letter *F*. Simple enough. But as easy as the task was, because it was repeated a few hundred times and participants were encouraged to go very quickly, everyone sometimes made errors. Occasionally, participants saw the *F* to signal that they should refrain from pushing the space bar, but they ended up typing the space bar by mistake. People would typically react by saying something like *doh!* as they caught themselves making this simple error. We were interested in what the electrical signal that was centered around the ACC looked like when people made those errors depending on whether they had consumed acetaminophen or not. About an hour before participants completed this simple cognitive task, we had given each participant a pill. As in other studies, half the participants consumed a pill containing 1,000 mg of acetaminophen, whereas the other half were given a placebo. Interestingly, when we looked at the results, there were clear differences in the electrical signal that people's brains made when they made an error. For the participants who received the placebo, the electrical signal that was centered around the ACC looked a lot like that found in other related research. There was a clear pattern indicating that people were consciously aware of their error, signaling a *doh!*-like response. In contrast, the electrical signal among those participants who had consumed acetaminophen didn't show as much of a *doh!* response, and they seemed less aware that they had made an error in the first place. The painkiller seemed to dampen people's response to having made an error.[20]

I suspect that the psychological effects we and others have found after people have taken acetaminophen are surprising to you, as, aside from dulling physical pain, we certainly don't seem to feel psychologically different when we take acetaminophen. In all of the experiments that my lab conducted using acetaminophen, we asked our participants at the end of the study whether they thought they had consumed the pill that contained acetaminophen or the placebo. We found that participants were never able to guess this correctly beyond chance level performance—they simply couldn't tell—which tells us that the psychological effects of acetaminophen are largely invisible to people. We don't seem to be able to sense the broad kinds of effects that have been found to be associated with acetaminophen. On the other hand, despite the growing evidence for the ways that acetaminophen impacts our feelings, it is far too premature to recommend self-medicating your existential anxieties with painkillers. The various studies that I've discussed above about the effects of acetaminophen were all conducted in the lab with a relatively small number of participants, so it will be important for more research to try to replicate these findings to see how reliable they are. Moreover, one should keep in mind that acetaminophen is one of the most abused over-the-counter medications, and there are clear health risks with it. The range of a safe and effective dosage is relatively narrow, and one doesn't have to exceed the daily recommended maximum dosage by that much before one is at risk for serious liver damage. In fact, acetaminophen is the leading cause of liver transplantation in the United States, and most cases of people who overdose on the drug do so accidentally. But with these caveats in mind, the consistent pattern of findings across these various studies exploring the psychological effects of acetaminophen suggests that many of our anxieties and emotional reactions share something in common with the experience of physical pain. This is further evidence that a common alarm signal, which appears grounded in the salience network, is alerting us whenever we encounter something that is of emotional significance to us.

But to say that various different experiences are all signaled through a common neural alarm system does not mean that they all feel subjectively the same to us. Physical pain simply does not feel the same as emotional pain. We never wonder if that pain in our chest is heartburn or a broken heart—they really feel different to us. And that's the same for when we're contemplating our deepest existential anxieties. It doesn't physically hurt when we feel our life doesn't make sense, and that feeling in turn is not the same as being rejected by someone. But if all of these experiences do involve this ringing of the same neural alarm, we can see that these are associated with a few different kinds of feelings. We feel physical pain when we hurt ourselves, and we feel lonely or have hurt feelings when we're rejected. But how should we describe the feelings that come when our neural alarm has alerted us that our lives no longer make any sense and that we've stumbled into the absurd?

## Uncanny Feelings

The question of what it feels like to be in the absurd attracted the attention of Sigmund Freud. Freud was fascinated by the unsettling feelings that people get when they are in situations that they can't quite make sense of. In an essay that he wrote more than a century ago, Freud pondered the kinds of circumstances that were most likely to elicit a particular kind of creepy and uneasy feeling in people. For example, he suggested that these uncomfortable feelings might arise whenever people experience the paranormal, such as when they imagine that someone is able to read another's mind, or when someone is given the "evil eye." Freud thought these same unsettling feelings would also arise whenever we encountered anything to do with death, such as when we looked at a cadaver or wondered whether a ghost was present. And, in perhaps his most Freudian example, he described how he personally had felt this same strange and alienating feeling while walking through a red-light district in Italy. As he put it,

Strolling one hot summer afternoon through the empty and to me unfamiliar streets of a small Italian town, I found myself in a district about whose character I could not long remain in doubt. Only heavily made-up women were to be seen at the windows of the little houses, and I hastily left the narrow street at the next turning. However, after wandering about for some time without asking the way, I suddenly found myself back in the same street, where my presence began to attract attention. Once more I hurried away only to return there again by a different route. I was now seized by a feeling that I can only describe as *uncanny*.[21]

In his essay, Freud identified the uncanny as the common feeling that people have in the many example situations that he offered. He offered a rich description and explanation of the uncanny that still guides research on this topic to this day. Freud recognized that uncanny feelings don't necessarily arise just because one is experiencing something that is unfamiliar. Being in a new situation or encountering something new—such as starting at a new school or seeing someone fly a drone for the first time—doesn't really seem to elicit any uncanny feelings. Rather, he noted that we feel the uncanny when we have unfamiliar experiences in a familiar setting. It is precisely when a situation that is largely familiar and sensible to us is juxtaposed alongside something that just does not fit that our uncanny feelings are most likely to be elicited. It's the contrast between the feeling that everything is normal and going as expected with the addition of something that seems deeply abnormal. Freud called this the "unfamiliar familiar" and noted that this was the setting in which we feel the uncanny.

It is somewhat challenging to describe what the uncanny feels like. It has few physical sensations, and as Freud had noted, it's not a particularly strong feeling and one needs to be in the proper mind-set to experience it. Rachele Benjamin and I created a psychological measure to get a better sense of what uncanny feelings are like. We found that the uncanny is best captured by two kinds of sensations that can be described as feeling unnerved and feeling disoriented. The unnerving feelings of the uncanny are associated with unsettling and creepy sensations that make one feel a little uncomfortable. In contrast, the disorienting aspects of the uncanny reflect how we feel we are not fully in control of what is happening around us. I think that these are the feelings people experience when they're in the absurd.[22]

However, this description of the uncanny as consisting of unnerving and disoriented feelings still probably doesn't do enough justice to describe the sensation. Perhaps some of you are still struggling to imagine what the uncanny feels like. In our research, we find that people vary quite a bit in how much they feel the uncanny. People who tend to be a little more neurotic and to see the world as a threatening place are especially likely to feel it. But others who are far less attuned to it may still not quite get what I'm referring to when I talk about our uncanny feelings.

To get a better sense of what the uncanny feels like, try to imagine as well as you can what it feels like when you're in the following kinds of situations: Have you ever experienced déjà vu? You know you're experiencing something for the first time, but you're having the distinct sensation that the precise same moment has happened before. The feeling that comes with this state is the uncanny. You also likely felt the uncanny during the first COVID pandemic lockdown in April 2020. Suddenly, the familiarity of your hometown was deeply unfamiliar. The normally bustling streets were strangely silent—traffic jams blessedly vanished for a short while, and the shops were largely closed. Your hometown probably felt a lot like a ghost town, as everyone was stuck in their houses.

You can also experience the uncanny when you ponder big existential questions such as whether you existed before you were born, or what is going to happen to you after you die. You can also sense it when you're staring at the Milky Way and reflecting on the mind-boggling fact that there are billions of those galaxies, each containing billions of stars, and there may even be an infinite number of universes. In our own research, the situation that prompted the strongest feelings of the uncanny was to have our participants watch a clip from a surreal David Lynch film called

*Rabbits.* You can probably find the film on YouTube and experience these uncanny feelings yourself.[23]

Masahiro Mori, a Japanese roboticist, felt these same feelings when he attended the 1970 World Expo in Osaka. One of the robots on display there had been fitted with twenty-nine artificial muscles in its face to allow it to make humanlike emotional expressions. One might expect that it would be fun and engaging to interact with such a realistic robot, but to Mori and many other people who attended the Expo, the robot made them feel profoundly creepy. This experience led Mori to propose the notion of "the uncanny valley." In general, he noted that when robots, avatars, and animations get more realistic, we tend to like them more. However, once they approach a point where they become too similar to humans, a spotlight is shone on whatever nonrealistic elements that remain, and this elicits a deep, disturbing sense of the uncanny that makes our skin crawl.[24]

Take Disney's film *The Polar Express.* It seemed destined to be a successful feel-good movie, as it was an animated holiday special starring one of the most popular actors of our time, Tom Hanks. Disney invested a lot in producing that film, particularly in developing a new kind of computer-generated imagery that is known as performance capture, and *The Polar Express* was the first film to be entirely created with this technique. This resulted in the most realistic animated film ever produced up until that point. But this realism didn't translate into greater love and affection for the film. Quite the opposite. When CNN reviewed the film they noted that "those human characters in the film come across as downright . . . well, creepy . . . *The Polar Express* is at best disconcerting, and at worst, a wee bit horrifying." The key problem with the film is that Tom Hanks's character looks just like Tom Hanks . . . well, almost. And it's the "almost" that's the problem. A live-action Tom Hanks is not creepy, nor is an unrealistic Tom Hanks, as in his character, Woody, from *Toy Story*. But the Tom Hanks in *The Polar Express* is largely familiar with a few unfamiliar elements, which elicits the uncanny.[25]

Until recently, the uncanny valley was only an issue for hyper-realistic animated films, wax museums, and robot displays at scientific expos. But as technology continues to infiltrate more aspects of our lives in the twenty-first century, it's creating new kinds of problems. The uncanny valley presents a particular challenge for life in the metaverse, where people are promised a world where their avatars can interact with others in a highly realistic situation. Even more challenging, perhaps, is the huge hurdle that the uncanny valley presents for the incipient sex robot industry. The key challenge for the industry remains how to make a robot sexually desirable when the more realistic they make it, the more disturbing are the uncanny feelings that it elicits.

While there are many different kinds of experiences that elicit the bothersome feelings of the uncanny, I think that the uncanny is another sensation associated with the triggering of the salience network, along with feelings of physical pain or interpersonal rejection. People feel the uncanny when things just don't make sense anymore and they're stuck in the absurd. In general, our feelings serve to steer us toward more adaptive actions. We feel fear when we're in danger, we feel disgust when we see something that is contaminated, we feel lustful when we have opportunities to reproduce, and we feel lonely when we're insufficiently relationally attached. Likewise, I think we feel the uncanny when we recognize that things are no longer making any sense. These feelings signal to us that something is not right, and we need to figure out what the problem is. Our uncanny feelings prompt us to try to get out of the absurd and regain a sense of meaning.

## A Sense-Making System

I propose that our brains have a sense-making system that operates to ensure that our lives continue to make sense. When everything seems sensible and fits with our expectations, we are able to function effectively, as the world tends to match our understanding of it. But our sense-making system alerts us whenever we encounter events that we're unable to make sense of. This sense-making system is built upon a salience network that rings our neural alarm whenever it senses that something needs our attention. It is triggered in those occasions when things just don't make sense anymore, leading us to tumble into the absurd and feel that things seem meaningless. It can be set off by a broad range of different kinds of existential threats that often are accompanied by feelings of the uncanny, such as when we contemplate that we are going to die someday, ponder how our lives don't make sense, or even when we are in the uncanny valley and are trying to make sense of the unfamiliar familiar. Over the next few chapters, we'll consider the many different kinds of meaning threats we can experience that can make our lives feel meaningless, and how our sense-making system responds to orient us back to a situation where we can feel that all is well again.

I think that humans evolved this sense-making system because of the challenges of living a life as a meaningful species. Humans live in ecologies of shared cultural meanings, and their selves and life stories have been shaped by those very meanings. We depend upon these meanings to survive. We are trying our best to understand our world and our place within it. When these meanings get threatened, we are in a vulnerable position and are at a loss for how we can continue to effectively function in our worlds. We need to feel that our understanding of the world coheres with reality, and thus we have a need to defend the meanings that we rely on, to ensure that they're intact. Our sense-making system serves this key role of signaling when we need to defend our meaning frameworks, and it's activated anytime we trip into the absurd. It alerts us with uncanny feelings that something isn't right, and this marshals our efforts to try to regain a sense of meaning and to dispel those bothersome feelings. We want to return to the state where we are feeling that everything makes sense and our lives are existentially grounded again.

This sense-making system reveals how we have a drive to maintain the sense that our lives have sufficient meaning. Whenever we experience that things don't make sense or are without meaning, we are alerted to try to work to regain a sense of meaning all over again, to bring it back into balance. As we already discussed, one example of this is that when people feel that there isn't sufficient meaning in their lives, they are more likely to engage in nostalgic reflections, which helps them to regain the sense that their lives are meaningful and brings them back to equilibrium. A similar pattern can be seen in how people respond to feelings of loneliness and interpersonal rejection. These feelings signal that their belongingness needs are threatened and their full attention is required to try to find new ways to regain a sense of interpersonal connection again. Our sense-making system operates in a homeostatic way to keep us feeling that everything makes sense and feels meaningful.

But once our sense-making system has alerted us that something is insufficiently meaningful, we need to act in an appropriate manner to regain a sense of meaning. How can we best do that? What are the different ways that people can respond to rebuild a sense of meaning when they feel that it's threatened? To answer this, we need to consider the basic cognitive-building capacities that underlie our feelings of meaning.

# Chapter 5

# Maintaining Meaning in Our Lives

Life has no meaning *a priori*. . . .
It's up to you to give it a meaning, and value
is nothing but the meaning that you choose.

Jean-Paul Sartre, *Existentialism Is a Humanism*

M other died today. Or maybe yesterday, I don't know." With these words, spoken by the protagonist, Meursault, Albert Camus opens his classic novel *The Stranger*. The character of Meursault is unable to find any meaning in his life. He has no concern for conventional values or social norms, and he remains indifferent to everything that others care deeply about. He lives in a state of existential alienation where nothing he does serves any purpose or is linked to any underlying values—the events in his life remain entirely bereft of meaning. Things simply happen to Meursault, and while these events elicit feelings at the time, these feelings fade as soon as they pass over him. He never reflects upon them later or integrates them into his life story. In the novel Meursault kills a man while he is on a beach, but he has no idea why he does it—he tells the judge that it was because the sun was bright. He pursues everything in his life without any engagement at all. When Meursault's ostensible girlfriend asks him if he loves her, he replies that the question "doesn't mean anything, but I don't think so." And when his mother dies, he fails to have any lasting emotional reactions and only registers it in the way one would describe yesterday's weather. Nothing that Meursault does is a concern outside the present moment that he is in. He is unable to weave the threads of his life into any semblance of a meaningful life, and he remains but a shell of a person.

Meursault stands as a cautionary character—he leads a meaningless life that none of us could ever want for ourselves. Camus suggests that if we don't make efforts to pursue a meaningful life, our lives could end up as empty as Meursault's. But how is it exactly that we do this? How do people go about finding meaning in their lives?

To go about understanding how people pursue meaning in their lives, we need to consider the basic cognitive capacities that humans possess that enable them to find meaning and make sense of their worlds. We are surrounded by people, objects, and events, but by themselves, these things are all meaningless. They only become meaningful to us when we begin to connect these things with other aspects of the world and with our lives. When events in our lives happen, they do not just wash over us as they do with Meursault, but we engage in some efforts that serve to construct a sense of meaning in what occurs. But how people are able to connect the events that happen to them in a way that is meaningful is not a simple or straightforward process; it requires much cognitive effort and some basic human meaning-making capacities.

## Faking and Making Meaning

The challenges for creating a sense of meaning are most evident in young children as they are born without an understanding of what is meaningful in their worlds. Everything that happens to young children is at first brand new to them—they do not yet have any built-in meaning frameworks to make sense of what is taking place around them. In the words of William James, when a baby first interacts with their world it "feels it all as one great blooming, buzzing confusion." For young children, almost everything seems new and unfamiliar, and they're constantly encountering things that they can't make sense of. In many ways, young children would seem to be stuck in the absurd because they haven't yet acquired the meaning frameworks to help them to make sense of their lives. So we can learn the basic ways that people learn to make meanings by considering how young children come to understand what is happening around them.[1]

The ways that people are able to make meanings was a topic that fascinated Jean Piaget, a Swiss child psychologist who conducted pioneering research in the early twentieth century on how children go about making sense of their worlds. He reasoned that, unlike adults, children did not yet have much experience, so they have few meaning frameworks to rely on. And without any of these meaning frameworks, whatever they encountered must feel rather meaningless to them. But even though they didn't have access to any existing meaning frameworks, Piaget saw that young children were prepared to make meanings as they went about trying to live in an unfamiliar world. They are constantly encountering new events and experiences, and they need to build new meaning frameworks in order to understand what is happening. As they interact with their worlds, they come to learn that the dog is OK to pet but not the raccoon; they discover that strangers will give them candy on Halloween; they recognize that Grandma is someone they can always count on; and they ultimately come to understand who they are. With each new experience, they are faced with the rather daunting challenge of having to learn precisely what it means.

Piaget was interested in how children responded when they encountered something new and unfamiliar to them. At the time of their first encounter, they aren't able to relate this new event to anything that they know, so it starts off as something largely without any meaning to them. They need to figure out a way to impose meaning onto something that originally seems meaningless. For example, imagine that a young child is told that they are going to their aunt's graduation. The child has never heard of a graduation before: What could this possibly mean? In this kind of situation, in which the child has encountered something that remains meaningless to them, Piaget saw that the child had two different possible ways of responding. The first response is something that I term *faking meaning* (Piaget called this assimilation). The child would try to understand what a graduation is by relating it to other kinds of things they already know about. The child searches for any possible existing meaning frameworks that this new event could fit into. For example, the child might see that Mom is dressing up like she does when she goes to church. So maybe graduation is like going to church? Then the child sees that their aunt is wearing a long, flowing black gown that looks like the kind that wizards wear. So maybe a graduation involves wizards? Later, the child sees there is a party and a cake, so maybe a graduation is like a birthday? By trying to fit this new experience into existing meaning frameworks, the child is faking a sense of meaning—the child wants to fit the graduation into meaning frameworks they already have.

These efforts to fake meaning can initially feel satisfying, as they provide the child with the sense that they are able to see meaning in something that had earlier been meaningless. However, this strategy of faking meaning has its limits. The child can only go on for so long thinking that a graduation is something like wizards, birthday parties, and going to church before the child recognizes that they had it all wrong. The child will then be back to feeling that a graduation is meaningless. Faking meaning is a temporary solution that can only get you so far.[2]

Piaget saw that the child's other possible response is something I term *making meaning* (Piaget called this accommodation). Upon realizing that a graduation is something different from wizards, church, and a birthday, the child needs to turn away from those other meaning frameworks that they have been relying on and create a new meaning framework that can best explain what a graduation really is. At some point, probably after asking more questions, noticing other details, and experiencing other examples of graduations, the child will ultimately have created a more accurate meaning framework by which to understand graduations.

This is the ultimate goal that we're always aspiring to when we encounter things that don't make sense. We have a strong motivation to accurately understand our worlds, and it is adaptive for us to be able to do so. We are driven to create an accurate simulation of the world we live in and our role living within it. The better our meaning frameworks match with reality, the more likely we'll be able to successfully navigate our worlds. Making meaning is what we depend on for our survival. However, there are significant downsides to our efforts to make meaning. First, it's rarely easy to do. Making meaning can require a lot of effort, interrogation, and personal research and can often take years to accomplish. There is nothing simple about creating new meaning frameworks. A second downside is that it often comes at the expense of disrupting our current understanding of the world. Our new meaning frameworks often stand in opposition to our previously acquired ones, and this can be problematic. We realize that our previous understanding of the world is not as we had assumed it to be, and this can be destabilizing.

Piaget's discovery of these two responses to the unfamiliar—faking meaning and making meaning—are not just observed in young children. The influential philosopher of science, Thomas Kuhn, saw scientists facing a similar problem as children, and this helps to illuminate people's struggles to find meaning in the world. Like children, scientists are trying to figure out that which they don't yet understand. They are often encountering new phenomena that do not fit well into any of their existing meaning frameworks. In his classic book *The Structure of Scientific Revolutions*, Kuhn tried to capture how scientists go about making discoveries. Kuhn importantly recognized that scientists do not just see new phenomena directly as they are. They always see them through the lenses of their meaning frameworks, which Kuhn called "paradigms." These meaning frameworks provide the basis for all scientific understanding. Scientists are trying to create meaning frameworks to explain the world, and they are aspiring for these to be accurate reflections of reality. But science is ultimately a process, and many of the meaning frameworks that scientists have relied on in the past have been discarded in favor of newer ones.

Take the example of the scientific understanding of our universe. In 150 CE, the classical Greek astronomer Ptolemy proposed that the earth was fixed and was the center of the universe. The stars, planets, and the sun all revolved around it. This scientific paradigm had a lot going for it. It was consistent with people's experiences of the earth as stable and flat, as well as with people's observations of everything in space moving across the sky above them. It also had the advantage of being aligned with what was written in the Bible; for example, the Ptolemaic view fits with the biblical account of God stopping the sun and the moon so that Joshua could continue to avenge his enemies in daylight. But over time, astronomers were noting a number of observations that just didn't fit with the Ptolemaic paradigm. For example, Mercury and Venus were never spotted being far away from the sun, the moon would change shape over the course of the month, and the planets didn't appear to move across the sky in straight lines. But for centuries, astronomers insisted that these kinds of anomalies could be made to fit into the Ptolemaic paradigm. They just had to keep adding various small modifications to the theory, such as proposing that the planets were spinning in their own epicycles as they moved across the night sky. That is, Kuhn was essentially arguing that previous astronomers first engaged in faking meaning, by forcing these anomalous observations to fit into the existing Ptolemaic paradigm, even if the paradigm needed to be regularly tinkered with to be able to contain them.

Kuhn argued that this way of faking meaning could only get scientists so far. Typically, the number of anomalies continued to grow as science progressed, and it became increasingly apparent that the old framework was no longer really functioning and a new framework needed to be made. At this point, Kuhn argued that scientists would go through a *paradigm shift* as they created a brand-new meaning framework. These paradigm shifts do not unfold gradually over time, but rather, as Kuhn put it, "the new paradigm . . . emerges all at once, sometimes in the middle of the night, in the mind of a man [sic] deeply immersed in crisis." In the case of astronomy, this came when Nicolaus Copernicus proposed that Ptolemy had it all backward. In 1543, on his death-bed, he published a book arguing that the earth was neither fixed nor the center of the universe but was like the other planets, which all revolved around the sun. As is typically the case with making meaning, though, scientists did not rush to embrace the new Copernican paradigm. Most astronomers remained commit-ted to the Ptolemaic view. It wasn't until ninety years later that Galileo, aided by an improved telescope, confirmed that Coperni-cus's theory was correct, and then most astronomers finally came to reject the Ptolemaic paradigm in favor of the Copernican one. As Kuhn argues, science doesn't advance so much from the sheer accumulation of facts and observations; it advances when one meaning framework is replaced by a better one. The succession of improved meaning frameworks is what accounts for scientific progress.[3]

Looking at the competing paradigms of Ptolemy and Coperni-cus, it may seem surprising that it took ninety years before astron-omers could be convinced by the Copernican paradigm—after all, it could explain the motion of celestial objects so much better than the Ptolemaic one. But it often really is not easy to alter our own meaning frameworks, especially for ones that we are so depen-dent upon. As the physicist Max Planck noted, "a new scientific truth does not triumph by convincing its opponents and making them see the light, but rather because its opponents eventually die, and a new generation grows up that is familiar with it." Planck's cynical observation that science progresses one funeral at a time shows how committed scientists typically are to their favorite theories. They have relied on their theories to make sense of their observations over their entire career. It is often just too difficult to drop them in favor of new and better theories, as they have only ever understood their research through the lens of their particular paradigm. Making meaning can be so challenging that scientists often end up dying before they are able to accept that their preferred meaning framework was wrong.[4]

Both young children and scientists rely on these two strategies of faking and making meaning when they encounter events that they can't make sense of, and so, too, do the rest of us. Much research finds that these are two common ways by which people try to get out of the absurd when they can no longer make sense of things. When we step into the absurd, our first response is to try to fake meaning and to convince ourselves that everything makes sense and that our current meaning frameworks are working just fine. We can see an example of how people go about faking meaning in a classic psychological experiment that was conducted by Jerome Bruner, together with Leo Postman, in 1949. Bruner had been interested in how people depend on meaning frameworks in their lives to understand the events that happen to them. He thought it was crucial for psychologists to understand the mind in terms of what events *mean* to people. We expect there to be certain patterns in the world, as we develop expectations for what is happening around us, and we have strong desires for these patterns to be coherent and stable. Often the patterns that we notice are richly complex, such as how a stock trader expects the stock market to react to the results of an election. But many of the patterns that we encounter are remarkably simple and trivial. Yet, regardless of their complexity, as Bruner shows us, we still expect all of the patterns we encounter to be coherent and stable.

Bruner sought to mess with the simplest of people's meaning frameworks: the ones they rely on when they play cards. As anyone who plays cards knows, there are a few straightforward patterns in a deck of cards. There are thirteen cards in each suit, and four suits in a deck: hearts, clubs, spades, and diamonds. We know that hearts and diamonds are red, whereas spades and clubs are black, and we fully expect to see these color associations every time we play cards. But Bruner wanted to see what would happen if he breached this simple yet basic expectation in his participants, who were American university students. He took a deck of cards and painstakingly painted over the cards to change the red cards to black, and the black cards to red. Then, in his experiment, he sat in front of a participant, flashed them a card, one at a time, and asked the participants to say out loud what cards they had seen. Quite strikingly, he found that most people typically "saw" the doctored cards just as they had imagined them to be. When he would show them a red six of spades, they usually didn't see it as a red six of spades. Rather, some would respond by saying they saw a six of hearts, whereas others would see a black six of spades. These responses are examples of faking meaning. When people encounter something that doesn't make sense, they often do not even consciously notice that they've encountered anything problematic. Typically, our first response is to see what we're expecting to see.

But this faking meaning is never completely convincing, and with enough time, people start to sense that something's wrong. In Bruner's study, he found that, as he continued to show his participants cards, most of them started to get curiously *anxious*. They seemed to sense that something was wrong, but many of them were unable to recognize what it was they were anxious about. After all, the participants were only being asked to tell the experimenter what card they saw—why should that create any anxiety? But many participants seemed distinctly bothered by the experience. Bruner termed these kinds of reactions to anomalies *disruptions*— participants were experiencing a collapse of their meaning frameworks for playing cards. For example, upon being shown a card with a red spade, one of the participants was quoted as reacting this way: "I can't make the suit out, whatever it is. It didn't even look like a card that time. I don't know what color it is now or whether it's a spade or heart. I'm not even sure what a spade looks like! My God!" When we realize that our attempts to fake meaning are no longer panning out, we recognize that the meaning framework we're depending on has been torn asunder, and this can be very unsettling. As we'll later see, this reaction is not limited to perceptual anomalies, such as seeing a red six of spades. We can have the same kind of disrupting reactions when we recognize that the life story that we've been telling ourselves isn't making as much sense as it should. The breakdown of our meaning frameworks can leave us smack in the absurd, and it is often accompanied by much anguish.[5]

When people are in the absurd and are unable to fake their way out of it, they will attempt to make meaning instead. We can see some evidence for people's efforts to make meaning in a curious phenomenon that is found in various groups and organizations around the world. Many organizations have elaborate initiation rituals that new members must endure before being admitted. We can see these kinds of rituals in various cults, religions, the military, sports teams, and some companies. In particular, the idea of harsh initiation rites is often associated with fraternities, which often require new pledges to engage in a series of humiliating, painful, and sometimes dangerous hazing rituals before they are admitted to the fraternity. Sadly, this practice can often get out of control, especially when heavy drinking is involved, and the rituals can be so dangerous that they have sometimes resulted in the tragic deaths of new pledges. But all of this raises the question of why would so many different kinds of organizations impose these kinds of costly initiation rituals in the first place? It would seem like a counterproductive thing to do. If you wanted people to feel dedicated to your organization, shouldn't you treat them kindly, rather than make them endure humiliation and pain? It would seem that if new members associated the organization with the unpleasant hazing rituals they endured, they would come to like the organization *less*. This at least would seem to be the rational response. But when it comes to our struggles to make meaning in our lives, people are often anything but rational.

The social psychologists Elliot Aronson and Judson Mills have long been interested in how people make meaning out of absurd situations. They were interested in the peculiar appeal that organizations with harsh initiations seem to have, and they suspected that these brutal kinds of initiations might actually cause people to like the organizations *more* than those with milder forms of initiations for some reasons that we'll explore below. In their classic experiment, conducted in the 1950s, they recruited female students from Stanford, who volunteered to participate in a study of group discussions. The students were told they would only be able to join the group if they first went through an initial task that served as the initiation. Half the students were randomly assigned to be in the "severe initiation" condition, in which they were made to feel uncomfortable and embarrassed. While the experimenter observed and evaluated them, the students were asked to read into a microphone a series of obscene words that you still can't say on television today. In the 1950s, saying such words out loud in public was a bigger faux pas and was considerably more embarrassing than it would be today. The other half were assigned to the "mild initiation" condition. They were also asked to read some words into the microphone, but their list didn't include any embarrassing words. Then the participants listened to a recording of a discussion by the group: they all heard the exact same discussion. And after listening to this discussion, the participants were given the opportunity to join this group if they liked, and they all rated how appealing they thought the group was. Those women who had been assigned to the more humiliating task of reading the obscene words rated the group as more desirable than did those participants who had been given the milder, inoffensive list of words to read. As other studies have since found, harsher initiation rituals really do appear to cause people to be more interested in joining the group.[6]

So why should harsh initiations have this curious appeal? We can understand this from the perspective of making meaning. Imagine the unfortunate participant who was assigned to the severe initiation condition in the study above. She was given the opportunity to join a group, but it first required her to endure something really uncomfortable and embarrassing. In trying to make sense of why she was willing to put up with this embarrassing task, the participant appeared to engage in some meaning making. She ultimately decided that the group's discussions were really quite interesting and the group was worth joining. By thinking of the group as inherently desirable, she is providing a justification for why she was willing to put up with the unpleasant initiation. Those experiences of suffering lead to thoughts that the group must really be worth it; it would have to be a really desirable group if she was willing to put up with all that humiliation to join it. In contrast, the participant in the mild initiation condition didn't have to endure anything unpleasant, so she didn't need to come up with any justifications for her behavior. By making meaning, those participants who received the more severe initiation ultimately came to change the way they saw the discussion group. In the context of actual fraternities, when pledges try to justify why they were willing to endure such unpleasant hazing rituals, they can end up having more positive attitudes toward their fraternities, which may continue to shape a lot of their college experiences and their later memories of them. When people justify their behaviors, they create whole new meanings about the fraternity they want to join. They have revamped their meaning framework about fraternities.

This is a rather simple kind of meaning that people are making in this study—convincing themselves that a group is more desirable because of what they were willing to put up with to get in there. But in many other contexts, it isn't straightforward how to make new meanings out of our lives. Sometimes we encounter things that we can't understand, and we aren't able to fake our way through it. We are often just like the old scientists who hold on to their discredited theories until they've died because we are just unable to make any sense of things. What happens when we're in the absurd and the world seems meaningless, but we can't fake or make any meanings to help us get back to feeling that the world makes sense again?

## Meaning Maintenance

This question of how we make meaning out of a situation that seems meaningless is one that I had been struggling with for some time until I met Travis Proulx, who was then a graduate student at the University of British Columbia. Travis was a frenetic whirlwind of ideas, was remarkably creative, and had a deep obsession with the existentialists—he often even dressed in a way that would have looked right at home at a Parisian café in the 1950s. Travis saw the world through an existentialist lens, and he recognized that the psychological questions I was interested in were similar to those considered by Søren Kierkegaard, Martin Heidegger, and Albert Camus. Just as the existentialists saw it, I was trying to understand how people go about leading a meaningful life and recognized that, when things don't go according to plans, people may end up stuck in the absurd. We shared an interest in trying to figure out how people can get on with their lives when things just no longer seem to make any sense.

Together with Kathleen Vohs, Travis and I wrote a paper in which we reinterpreted the results of many other psychological theories by looking at them through an existentialist lens. We proposed that there is a commonality to people's reactions when they experience a threat to their meaning frameworks and stumble into the absurd. A wide variety of different kinds of psychological experiences—such as when people observe themselves acting in unexplainable ways, feel rejected by others, endure a blow to their self-esteem, or reflect upon their own mortality—share some elements of people being stuck in the absurd because all of these experiences are meaning threats that violate people's expectations. We expected that all these different psychological phenomena should lead people to respond in similar ways in their efforts to regain a sense of meaning and were specific examples of people's defensive reactions to meaning threats in what we called a *meaning maintenance model.*[7]

But the ways that people were responding to these various kinds of psychological threats did not seem to fit well with either of the two known responses to encounters with something that is meaningless—that is, faking and making meaning. They seemed to reflect a very different kind of reaction. We reasoned that these other psychological phenomena could be seen as revealing a *third* strategy by which people respond to the feeling that they are in the absurd. In that moment when people feel unable to find a way to make any sense of what is happening, they need a way to escape the absurd and return to a state where life seems to make sense again.

We proposed that people do this by *regrounding* themselves whenever they encounter the absurd. When people feel that life doesn't make sense, they turn to, and more strongly embrace, the other sources of meaning in their lives. They exaggerate whatever meaning frameworks they rely on, and this serves to dispel those alienating and uncanny feelings that characterize our feelings in the absurd. They become even more committed to their other beliefs and become an exaggerated version of themselves. Religious people will become more religious, patriotic people will become more patriotic, and liberals and conservatives will become even more polarized as they become more committed to their political views. It seems that people will come to embrace more strongly any of the key premises that make up their life stories, such as beliefs that *I am good* or that *people get what they deserve.*

Once people have gotten rid of that disorienting sense that comes with feeling meaningless, they are then back in a position where they can move forward and reflect on any meaningless experiences from a more grounded and less anxious position. These efforts to reground themselves into their other meaning frameworks do not solve the original problem of what threatened their meaning in the first place, but they do help to allay their existential anxieties for the time being. It removes them from the absurd so that they can get back to their lives unimpeded again.

We thought that our account that people reground themselves when they face meaning threats could integrate much of the psychological literature by identifying a common response across so many different kinds of theoretical paradigms. But in order to be convincing to our critics, Travis and I recognized that we would need to demonstrate this regrounding response in entirely new kinds of situations that fell outside the scope of other competing psychological theories. That is, we needed to find novel means of getting people into the absurd so that we could see whether they would respond by trying to reground themselves. But to be able to study this, we needed to discover ways that we could take people out of their normal state where everything seemed to be making sense and drop them suddenly into a situation where things felt meaningless. Moreover, Travis and I reasoned that in order for us to build a more convincing case about how people respond to the absurd, we would need to show that our participants weren't just responding to some unique peculiarities of any of the individual situations that we put them in. Rather, we would need to find a common kind of reaction among people across a wide variety of different kinds of absurd experiences.

So our challenge was to find ways to reliably lead people into the absurd. Within the confines of the psychology lab, where the participants we studied were often students from the University of British Columbia, who were typically quite suspicious of what might transpire in a psychology study, we needed to find ways to make them feel *meaningless*. Over the course of their time in the lab, we needed to thoroughly discombobulate our participants, find ways to alienate them, provide them with an impactful "WTF experience," or have them go through what Martin Heidegger called "a breakdown in the machinery." And, of course, we always needed to do this in an ethical manner that carefully protected our participants' well-being. Importantly, in all of the studies that I describe throughout this book, we sought guidance and approval from the ethics review board of our university. Also, at the end of each study we explained in detail to our participants what all had just happened to them, so that they were able to understand precisely why they had just had this experience in the absurd.[8]

Coming up with ways to make our lab a gateway to the absurd was a challenging task as there was no standard lab manual that we could turn to. And so, we ended up spending many of our lab meetings talking about the various ways that we could create experiences that would cause our participants to tumble into the absurd. These were some of the most interesting lab meetings we've ever had as people came up with a variety of really creative ideas for alienating people, although most of these ideas were just too impractical to actually conduct. But over the course of these meetings, we were able to come up with several different successful experimental designs, and these were easily the most unusual studies that I've ever been a part of.

Our very first attempt to deliver a WTF experience in the lab came out of these lab discussions. We decided to have our participants unwittingly be part of a magical trick. At the time, we had been eagerly following a fascinating line of research on something called *inattentional blindness*. This research shows that people will often not notice something—even something very striking—when their attention is directed elsewhere. It's the key psychological foundation of many magical tricks. You may have already encountered an example of a famous study on inattentional blindness by the cognitive psychologists Daniel Simons and Christopher Chabris where people watch a video of a group of students, and they are asked to count how many times the students tossed a basketball back and forth between them. I'm about to deliver a big spoiler that will forever change the way you experience this study, so if you have not seen a video of this study before, I encourage you to visit the URL in the notes to watch it before reading any further.[9]

The big spoiler for this famous study is that while participants were busy counting the basketball passes, a person in a gorilla suit casually walked into the center of the scene, turned to face the camera, pounded their chest, and then walked slowly off to the side. When you expect the gorilla to be there you really can't miss it—it literally is the gorilla in the room—and when it crosses the screen, it becomes the center of your attention. But the participants in the study had no reason to expect any such gorilla to appear. Moreover, their attention was diverted by trying to track a moving basketball in a chaotic scene. In the most distracting scenes, quite remarkably, most people in the study simply did not see the gorilla. After, when people were asked whether they had seen a gorilla, they often had no idea what the experimenter was talking about, and they needed to see the footage a second time before they could be convinced that they had stared at a scene for thirty seconds without even noticing the gorilla.

But did those participants really never see the gorilla? One of my colleagues at the University of British Columbia, Ronald Rensink, had been demonstrating in his research that even when people say they couldn't see a change in an inattentional blindness task akin to the gorilla study, they still often reported having the feeling that something had happened. They had the uncanny sense that something was not right, but they didn't know what was making them feel that way. Their experience is reminiscent of Jerome Bruner's participants who, when shown a red six of spades, would fake a sense of meaning and say they saw it as a six of hearts, but would then become distressed. Those participants also had the acutely uncomfortable sense that something wasn't right, despite not consciously identifying any problem. This led us to the idea of designing a magical trick in our lab: in front of our participants, we would magically transform one experimenter into a completely different person. More specifically, in the study the participants would interact with an experimenter, who would briefly step out of view to retrieve a questionnaire, and without missing a beat, another experimenter would reappear, wearing the exact same outfit.[10]

Although the two experimenters were dressed the same, they really didn't look anything alike. They had different colored hair, one was a few inches taller than the other, one wore braces and the other didn't, and one spoke with a bit of a Farsi accent. You would never mistake them for the same person. But, quite remarkably, at the end of the project, across three separate studies, we had found that fewer than 10 percent of our participants had consciously noticed that the second experimenter was a different person. The rest had no idea that the experimenter was different, despite interacting with both experimenters before and after the switch. We even had one participant show up who unexpectedly was a friend of the second experimenter. After the experimenters had switched, and the participant was for the first time looking at her friend, she was definitely in an absurd situation. But she immediately responded to this senseless situation by creating a story that could potentially make sense of things. She said: "Oh my God! I can't believe how out of it I am today! I didn't even recognize you when I first came in!" Just like someone seeing the red six of spades, the participant tried to force this absurd anomaly into her usually reliable meaning framework that people remain the same person while you're interacting with them.[11]

We had switched the experimenters on our participants to see how they would respond to this blatant violation of expectations. Would they reground themselves in the face of this absurd experience? We compared those who interacted with this transmogrifying experimenter with those who were in a control condition, where the experimenter stayed the same throughout the study. We found that people regrounded themselves by exaggerating their other meaning frameworks, and they did this in each of the three separate changing experimenter studies that we conducted. Specifically, in this instance, the participants were provided with a situation where someone broke the law, and they had to determine the punishment. People normally operate with a belief that rules are there to be followed, but after seeing the changing experimenter, they were especially likely to embrace this belief, and they assigned a much larger punishment than those in the control condition. Our participants' reactions to the changing experimenter, even though they couldn't consciously see it, were very similar to the kinds of reactions you see in other studies when people reflect on their mortality or are acting in ways that they can't make sense of. One way that people respond to the absurd then is by becoming more committed to the other meaning frameworks in their lives.[12]

In the years that followed, we conducted several other experiments that explored how people react to the absurd. In these studies, our participants have been shown surreal David Lynch movies, have been subliminally shown word pairs that don't make sense, have been led to write an essay arguing against a position they believe, have reflected on close relationships with people who betrayed them, have read stories by Franz Kafka, or have reflected on the fact that they are going to die. Regardless of the many ways that we have put people in the absurd, they responded by showing similar efforts to reground themselves by increasing their beliefs in other meaning frameworks. These findings suggest that when things don't make sense and feel meaningless to people, they respond by trying to regain the sense that things are meaningful. Their sense-making system reacts by trying to orient them back to a situation where they can feel that all is well again.[13]

As I've argued here, people can respond to meaning threats in a few different ways. Often their first response will be to fake meaning, by pretending that everything is as it's supposed to be. This strategy can often work reasonably well, allowing people to feel that nothing odd has happened, but there are limits to how much people can fake meaning, and people often have the disturbing sense that something is not quite right. A second strategy is that people can respond to any absurd encounters by trying to make meaning and adjusting their meaning frameworks to account for what has transpired. But making meaning is by no means a simple affair, and often people don't have the time and resources to figure everything out and adjust their meaning frameworks. In extreme cases, such as scientists encountering data that is at odds with their preferred theory, they may not be able to make meaning by coming to accept a new and improved theory. They, along with many scientists before them, may stick with their existing but flawed theory until their deaths. And a third strategy is that people may respond to a meaning threat by ignoring it, and instead reground themselves by becoming more committed to their other meaning frameworks. These regrounding efforts don't directly solve the meaning threat, but they help to dispel the bothersome and uncanny feelings that the meaning threat had elicited and can lead people to conclude that all is meaningful again. After their regrounding efforts have helped people to restore the feeling that things make sense, they may return to think about the troublesome meaning threat again in the future, and with enough time and thought directed at it, they may ultimately be able to make new meanings from it.

We are often vulnerable to tumbling into the absurd when our meaning frameworks are violated and we rely on our sense-making system to help get us back on track. We depend on so many meaning frameworks to make sense of ourselves, our world, and our places within the world that the absurd is always lurking just around the corner.

In the remaining chapters, we'll explore other ways that we can become undermined and how we can respond in ways to help us to build a meaningful life. We'll delve into how people strive to pursue meaningful lives through the choices that they make, and how they come to live with those choices, even when they're bad ones. We'll investigate how people can maintain a sense of meaning when they confront their mortality and come to terms with the realization that regardless of how fulfilling a life they may be leading, it will nevertheless soon be coming to an end. We'll consider the many devastating ways that our life experiences can wreak havoc with our meaning frameworks, and how we can rebuild our lives in the aftermath of trauma. And we'll discuss some practical steps that you can take to deepen the sense of meaning that you have in your own life.

Chapter 6

# Learning to Live
# with Our Choices

In the World through which I travel,

I am endlessly creating myself.

Frantz Fanon, *Black Skin, White Masks*

Modern philosophy hadn't given much thought to the topic of anxiety until Søren Kierkegaard came along and shone a spotlight directly on it. Anxiety was, for Kierkegaard, a core feature of the human condition. He felt that anxiety was a relentless driving force behind people's behavior and that there was no aspect of human existence that was shielded from it. As Kierkegaard put it, "No discerning judge knows how to interrogate and examine the accused as does anxiety, which never lets the accused escape, neither through amusement, nor by noise, nor during work, neither by day nor by night."[1]

It really is no surprise that anxiety is the topic Kierkegaard stumbled upon, as the poor man was an anxious wreck throughout his life. It was Kierkegaard's feelings of self-doubt and fear of failure that kept him putting off his university exams again and again and again. It wasn't until he was ready to ask the love of his life, Regine, to be his wife that he finally took his exams, a full ten years after starting his studies. Kierkegaard was madly in love with Regine, but he was tormented by the thought that he wouldn't be able to make her happy. And so, he abruptly decided to cancel his engagement with her, leaving everyone mystified and upset by his actions. This decision ate away at Kierkegaard for the rest of his life—he called it the "thorn in his flesh." He covertly dedicated many of his writings to Regine, and he kept trying to reach out to her to better explain his decision. On his deathbed, he remained so tortured by his decision to break his engagement with Regine that Kierkegaard asked his brother to give her all of his remaining assets, even though she was long married to another man.

A key worry for Kierkegaard was how others received his work. He disguised his identity by writing his many books under bizarre pseudonyms, such as Johannes de Silentio, Hilarius Bookbinder, and Frater Taciturnus, and he would often use multiple pseudonyms in a single book, each arguing with the other. Kierkegaard's worries about his public image were continually fanned as he was the target of much gossip: everyone knew him as the eccentric son of a wealthy merchant, who had inexplicably broken his engagement to Regine and could always be found nervously pacing the streets of Copenhagen at night. His anxieties about his reputation were inflamed even further when he became an early victim of something akin to cyberbullying: the editor of a local newspaper, who had been irritated by Kierkegaard's incessant oversharing of his inner ruminations, started running a regular series of cartoons that mocked him mercilessly—caricaturizing his curved spine and ill-fitting clothes. Kierkegaard fretted a lot about how others always seemed to have the wrong impression of him: "Well, such is my life. Always misunderstanding. At the point where I suffer, I am misunderstood—and I am hated."[2]

Kierkegaard was all too familiar with the experience of anxiety. Curiously, he felt that the root of people's anxieties comes from something that many people often celebrate—the freedoms that we have. Kierkegaard felt that we need to embrace the freedoms in our lives, and to choose to live an authentic existence. He saw that having the freedom to chart the course of our own lives meant that we were ultimately in charge—the lives that we lead are up to us. But Kierkegaard was well aware of the challenges that our freedoms can pose for us. He felt that we approach our futures as though we were standing at the edge of an abyss. The abyss represents the unknown that stretches out in front of us, reflecting all the possibilities of our futures. We don't know where the unknown will take us, but we recognize that we need to act—we need to make the best choices that we can and then live with the consequences.

"Anxiety," Kierkegaard wrote, "is the dizziness of freedom." The abyss contains the many possible paths that we can pursue in our lives, and we are responsible for our choices. Our choices have consequences for our futures, and we don't know how those futures are going to unfold. Kierkegaard felt that as we plan to act in our lives, without being able to know how our choices are going to pan out, we are left with the awareness of "an indeterminate horror of existence that finds no worldly foothold, since it senses an infinite nothingness beneath every step." He recognized that there is no set path that we can count on to follow to safety. We always need to figure out for ourselves the route that we're going to take. And there is no guarantee that we'll make the right choices. Kierkegaard, despite having enough inherited wealth to have more freedom to choose many aspects of his life than most of his compatriots, was well aware of how painful it can be to live with the questionable choices that he made in his own life.[3]

Kierkegaard's realization that people's freedoms lie at the root of their anxieties is of much importance, and it can help to explain a lot of the difficulties that people face in their lives. As we'll see below, people's freedoms are what can make adolescence such a challenging time, as it's the life stage when people need to make so many of their key life choices. While we tend to revel in having the freedom to choose, these freedoms by no means ensure that people will be making good choices, and we'll explore some of the psychological strategies that people rely on to help them to live with their own questionable life choices. We'll consider how life in this new age of anxiety, particularly in the United States, is more replete with choices than perhaps in any other cultural context before, and this creates some obstacles for people in their pursuit of meaningful lives.

## Adolescence at the Abyss

When people stand at the edge of the abyss, they are facing the many potential life paths that extend in front of them. The thought of choosing a path, without knowing where it will go, lies at the root of many people's anxieties. But it is during adolescence, in particular, that people find themselves standing at the edge of the deepest and widest of abysses. People typically make many of the most consequential decisions of their lives during adolescence and the years of emerging adulthood that come right after it. It is then that people's whole lives extend in front of them, and people need to act to choose a path to go forward. Should they continue with their schooling? What career path should they pursue? Should they settle down with their partner? Should they move to a new city? Should they stay with the religious commitments that they may have acquired from their parents? As if making such far-reaching decisions weren't hard enough, young people are making them at a time when most people are still trying to figure themselves out. They may be questioning their identity and trying to work out what it is that they really stand for. Given all that is at stake for adolescents, it's no surprise that this is typically the most anxious period of life.

A common trope in graduation speeches that are directed at adolescents is to remind the graduates that they can become whatever they want. They are at an age when the doors to so many different possible lives remain open to them. Those offering those words of guidance are probably trying to inspire their audience, to help them to dream big. But such encouragement is a stark reminder of just how much is on the line for adolescents as they face these key life decisions. They need to choose the path that their lives are going to follow. The legendary founder of Taoism, Lao Tzu, stated that "a journey of a thousand miles begins with a single step." While standing at the edge of the abyss, it can be rather overwhelming to decide which direction one will set off in. With all of these choices in front of them, it is not surprising that it is during adolescence that many people face their first existential crisis. They need to figure out who they are going to be as a person and what kind of life they are going to lead. They must summon the courage to take those first steps into the abyss.[4]

I had my first existential crisis at the age of nineteen. I was in my second year of university, and I was studying business at the time. My dream then was to have a career with an international marketing firm—I envisioned a life that was full of travel, excitement, and wealth. These were all things that I had only imagined from afar, as I had grown up in a working-class family and had never been anywhere farther than where you could get to at the end of a long day's drive. I had joined an international business student club at university, known by the acronym AIESEC, and was thrilled that the club had been able to arrange for me a summer internship at a marketing division of a large company in Helsinki, Finland. It was my first time to be away from home, my first time to be abroad, and the first job that I had that had any career prospects. I couldn't believe my good fortune at having this opportunity to pursue my dream career. I loved living in Helsinki and getting to travel around Europe, and I was having a lot of fun hanging out with all of the other international interns who were there on the same exchange program. It really was the time of my life.

Except for one thing. Rather than feeling happy that I was working at my dream job, I instead felt a profound sense of alienation. The job was not at all what I had imagined. I felt like I just wasn't interested in anything that the job was about, and I really couldn't imagine myself having a career like that. And it was then that I started to realize that perhaps it was meaningful that I had always found it boring to read the business section of the newspaper each day—it had always felt like such an unpleasant chore. I've always loved reading, and at the time the reading that I was doing for my own interest usually took me to pop psychology books and books on Eastern mysticism. I realized then that must be where my interests really were. And so, it was at the moment when I thought I had been so lucky to get the job of my dreams that I realized I was on the wrong path, and I decided I would switch from studying business to studying psychology. I told my friends in Helsinki about my decision, pretty much all of whom were business students themselves, and almost everyone thought I had gone crazy.

They kept asking me why I was willing to throw away this amazing opportunity. I didn't have any good answers for them either, other than to say that I had realized this wasn't what I wanted to pursue for a career. It felt quite scary to be changing paths, not having any idea where I would be headed, but at the same time I felt quite certain that this new direction was a better fit.

As adolescent crises go, mine was rather tame. Though it was a rather confusing and unsettling time for me, I didn't go out and rebel against the world or start breaking any laws or anything. But adolescence is commonly one of the most turbulent and chaotic periods of life. Psychologists describe it as a time of "storm and stress." When people are in their adolescent years, it is common for them to resist and rebel against any adult authority. In their efforts to become more independent and to prepare themselves for adult roles, adolescents will often push back at any adult efforts to guide their behaviors. This rebellion often comes paired with some problematic behaviors. This is the period of life when people are most likely to engage in antisocial or criminal behavior. It is an especially violent time, and the relation between adolescence and violence is so clear-cut that sociologists can predict crime rates by tracking the percentage of the population that is between fourteen and twenty-one years old. It is also during adolescence that substance use peaks, as well as other risky behaviors that lead to higher levels of accidents and of sexually transmitted diseases. And adolescence is the stage of life when people are more likely to suffer from mood disruptions and anxiety. The storm and stress of adolescence can take quite a toll on families and society, let alone the adolescents themselves.[5]

But we can understand the problematic aspects of adolescence better by comparing people's lives across societies. What does adolescence look like in other cultures? Remarkably, research finds that it's not storm and stress everywhere. One analysis of more than one hundred traditional small-scale societies from around the world found that in most of those societies people did not expect adolescents to act in more antisocial ways or to act more aggressively. While in all of these societies people thought of adolescence as a distinct stage between childhood and adulthood, in most smaller societies it was not commonly thought of as being a particularly tumultuous period. However difficult adolescence may be in some societies, it isn't an especially challenging stage of life in many parts of the world.[6]

So where is it that adolescents are most likely to struggle with all of the storm and stress? Research finds that it's in WEIRD (Western, Educated, Industrialized, Rich, and Democratic) societies that adolescents have the most tumultuous lives. Adolescents in these societies have more possible roles to choose from: they have a lot of options for the kind of lives they will lead. Adolescents there need to find for themselves the path that they are going to follow in life. WEIRD adolescents are facing an enormous number of potential roles that they have to choose from. In contrast, in most small-scale societies becoming an adult means accepting the adult roles that are offered to you; few key decisions need to be made. For example, if you're from a society where everyone farms, then you don't need to figure out what you're going to do with your life—you're going to be a farmer. But in WEIRD societies, with so many different possible lives that one can pursue, the abyss in front of people extends so much further. It contains so many different possible paths, resulting in a far more difficult and anxious time in choosing the life that one is going to lead. Not surprisingly, adolescents in WEIRD societies are among the most anxious people in the world.[7]

These findings that the difficulties in adolescence vary so much around the world challenge some earlier theories, which viewed the struggles of youth to be the natural outgrowth of hormonal changes in puberty. These theories assumed that a tumultuous period of life emerged as reliably as the development of breasts or a deepening of the voice. Hormonal changes in puberty certainly can make the challenges of adolescence more difficult, but I think that the reason adolescence is so difficult in WEIRD cultures is because these biological changes are interacting with the challenges of living in a culture where people need to figure out what kind of life they are going to lead.[8]

People's experiences in adolescence, just as in other aspects of their lives, are shaped by the surrounding culture, and as cultures have continued to change over time, so has adolescence. Let's compare the experience of American adolescents during the original age of anxiety with that of the twenty-first century. One thing that stands out is that people in the twenty-first century are taking far longer to embrace adult roles. One milestone for becoming an adult is to get married. In 1953, an article in the *New York Times* warned that a "girl who hasn't a man in sight by the time she is 20 is not altogether wrong in fearing that she may never get married." This advice sounds grossly off the mark by the standards of the twenty-first century: in 2022 the median age of first marriage in the United States was 28.2 years for women and 30.1 years for men. But in the 1950s, the median age of first marriage was only 20.3 years for women and 22.8 years for men. One reason marriages are delayed is that people are often reluctant to get married before they have finished their education, and people are spending far longer in school now. In 1950, the median number of years of education in the United States was only 9.3 years, and fewer than 7 percent of people had a bachelor's degree or higher. But by 2019, 39 percent of Americans had at least a bachelor's degree, and students have been taking longer and longer to finish their studies. More than half of US undergrad students are over 25 years old, and nearly 40 percent of students plan to pursue postgraduate studies, keeping them in school even longer. This extended period of education has delayed the onset of other adult roles, such as moving out of their parents' houses, starting careers, becoming financially independent, and having children. Americans are taking much longer to begin "adulting" than they used to.[9]

This dramatic extension of the period before people take on adult roles has led to the identification of a new stage of life termed *emerging adulthood*. During this period, people continue to explore their identities, which they have been doing since their early teens. They continue in their efforts to figure out precisely who they are. This is a particularly unstable time in life, as people have often not settled down with a romantic partner, haven't found a place of their own to live yet, and have yet to begin whatever career they're aspiring for. This tends to be a very self-focused period, as emerging adults tend to have very few obligations to anyone other than to themselves—their time is largely dedicated to doing what they wish to do. And this tends to be a particularly anxious time: more people are struggling with anxiety disorders than in other stages of life. It is also during this period that emerging adults continue to spend much time reflecting on the kinds of possible futures that await them. Young people now are left living an uncertain life, and their various explorations of who they are going to be will continue to persist for many more years than they used to. This period of emerging adulthood is seen to extend to the time when people come to take on adult roles and fully enter adulthood, which commonly doesn't occur now in the United States until around the age of thirty.[10]

This extended period that people go through now before they fully enter adulthood has consequences for people's well-being. Relative to older adults, the personalities of adolescents have some rather undesirable characteristics that can be a problem for their mental health. On average, adolescents are less conscientious and responsible than older adults, they tend to be more disagreeable and inconsiderate, and they are often more anxious and neurotic. Part of the struggle being an adolescent is that their personalities make their lives more difficult for them. But people's personalities have been found to change once they take on adult roles. The good news is that once people start adulting, their personalities mature in a number of specific ways. In particular, when people take on adult roles, such as getting married, having children, or getting a career, their personalities become more self-disciplined and dependable. The dark moods that so often characterize people's adolescent years begin to fade, and they become more pleasant to be around. And they become more emotionally stable and less likely to worry about all that is going on in their life. I suspect that these changes in people's personalities may be partly due to them having fewer looming key life choices to make after they have become an adult. And because people come to take on adult roles at different ages around the world, we can see evidence that this pattern of personality maturation starts at different times in different cultures. In cultures where people take on adult roles earlier, their personalities begin to mature at an earlier age. With Americans now taking so much longer to take on adult roles, it is also taking them longer to grow out of their rather problematic adolescent personalities. For a longer period of time, they continue to be relatively irresponsible, moody, and anxious.[11]

## Confronting Our Choices

Jean-Paul Sartre became known as "the philosopher of freedom," and he earned this moniker both from his provocative ideas and from his unorthodox lifestyle. As noted in Chapter 1, Sartre's life was a celebration of freedom, which he paraded to the world, and the freedoms that he extolled were a key reason why existentialism was so popular in his time. Sartre always abhorred following rules and norms, which he viewed as unnecessarily restricting his autonomy. He failed his university exams the first time that he took them because he chose to ignore the exam's questions. He instead used the exam as an occasion to write about his own philosophical ideas. Sartre wouldn't allow anyone to dictate how he should act. He despised everything that was nice, bourgeois, or conventional, as he felt that one needed to be free of any societal expectations or pressures, and scoffed at any traditions or obligations that he felt might limit his freedoms. He didn't want to be bound by any contracts or debts, so he never owned a house or car. He even once gave away all of his possessions except for his pipe and his pen. Sartre didn't like to feel beholden to any societies that might influence his writings, so he turned down all awards and honors, including the Nobel Prize in Literature and the Legion of Honor for his activities in the French Resistance.[12]

Sartre remained so adamant about fighting anything that might constrain his freedoms because he felt that people could only be authentic if they were the authors of their own actions. He believed that people were prone to let their actions be dictated by their situation or their roles, which prevented them from following their own choices. Sartre felt that when people allowed their roles to take over they would be in a state of "bad faith" and would be acting on the basis of external pressures, rather than from the wellspring of their own voluntary will. Sartre felt that people could only live authentically when they acted in accordance with their own preferences and choices. He urged people to embrace their freedoms and to let them guide their lives.

As Sartre put it, "Man is condemned to be free; condemned, because he did not create himself, yet nonetheless free, because once cast into the world, he is responsible for everything he does." He felt that we become who we are from our choices and not because we were born a certain way or lived in a certain situation. Sartre maintained that we didn't arrive in the world prepackaged, facing a set life course, but rather, we create ourselves through the lives we choose to lead, making ourselves up as we go along. And he emphasized that we *always* have choices to make. Even in situations that deprive us of all but a few options, Sartre argued we still have a choice. He maintained that even if someone is standing on the gallows about to be hung, they still have a choice about how they confront this moment. Do they approach their death cowering in defeat, or do they confront it standing tall? We may not always be able to choose what will happen to us, but we can always choose what we make of our situations.[13]

Sartre's focus on individual freedom was largely shared by the other existentialists, who agreed with the idea that we live our lives through our choices. It can be exhilarating to consider the freedom we have to create any kind of life we wish. This perspective offers the individual a tremendous amount of power: people are free to choose to pursue any kind of life they like. But at the same time, this view that people's lives are up to them to figure out makes their choices far more consequential. Choices are not just about what to have for dinner or what movie to watch—they provide the foundation of what our lives are built upon. Take a moment to think about how your own choices have shaped your own life. What would your life be like right now if you had made different choices along the way?

In my own case, I often look back to the decision I made during my own adolescent existential crisis. I had been enthusiastically pursuing a career in business when I rather abruptly decided to drop it all to study psychology. It was a key decision in my life, and I often reflect on what would have happened if I had never made it. What would my life be like today if I had instead just decided to stay in business school? I imagine I would have ended up with some kind of career in business, and my days would have been filled with business kinds of tasks as opposed to the kinds of activities that make up my life as a psychology professor. I probably would have a very different social network—more friends who were also in business and fewer friends who were professors. It's quite likely that a business career path would have resulted in me living in a different city or maybe even in a different country. I probably never would have met my first wife, and I wouldn't have the particular kids that I have. Had my adolescent self, facing my first existential crisis, not made that key life decision to change my course of study, my life would have been vastly different from the one that I have been leading.

Our lives are filled with opportunities for choices, and the choices we make determine the direction that our life path takes us. If we had made some different choices, we may have ended up on different life paths. But the life paths that we follow only run in one direction. As tempting as it may be to reflect on how different our lives would have been had we made different choices, we can never really know for sure where those alternative life paths would have taken us. And we don't know where our current path will take us either. As Kierkegaard said, "Life can only be understood backwards, but it must be lived forwards." We can never know what lives await us as we make our choices. We also usually don't learn whether the choices we've made have worked out better than the alternative choices that we didn't make.[14]

While the trajectory of people's life stories is importantly shaped by the choices that they make along the way, most people are presented with a challenge in building their life stories around the premise *I am good.* When people look back on their lives, they are generally motivated to conclude that the life choices they have made have been good ones. They chose the right major at college, the right career, the right spouse, and the right number of kids to have. After all, how could a person convince themselves that they are good if they felt that they kept making poor life decisions? As such, most people are prone to tell their life stories around the premise *I have made good choices.*

## Rationalizing Our Choices

John Bolton had a long and storied career overseeing the international relations of the United States and served in various top governmental posts under four different Republican presidents, including US ambassador to the United Nations under President George W. Bush and national security adviser under President Donald Trump. Bolton has always been a polarizing figure, as throughout his career he has been one of the most committed foreign policy hawks in the US government. International diplomacy is typically a balancing act, where officials try to cajole other governments to act in ways that align with their own interests, either by offering them different kinds of carrots to incentivize their cooperation or by coercing them to go along by threatening them with various kinds of sticks. Bolton was clear where he stood on this issue: "I am not much of a carrot man." He has consistently pushed the United States to take aggressive positions against other countries. He pushed strongly for the United States to invade Iraq in 2003, and he advocated bombing Iran and North Korea. Bolton definitely earned the nickname that was given to him by President Trump, "Mr. Tough Guy." At almost every point when the United States has faced a key decision in its international relations, Bolton has pushed for the country to take a more belligerent position. This preference for an aggressive foreign policy has been common across his life story. But like everyone's, Bolton's life story has hinged on some key decisions that he made along the way.[15]

In 1969, at the age of twenty-one, Bolton was faced with a particularly difficult decision that a lot of young American men were confronted with at the time. For years the United States had been embroiled in a devastating war in Vietnam, which many saw as futile. As Bolton later said about his thinking at the time, "I confess I had no desire to die in a Southeast Asian rice paddy. I considered the war in Vietnam already lost." But it didn't really matter whether Bolton or anyone else wanted to go fight in the Vietnam War; the United States had implemented a mandatory draft that required all of those who were selected to drop everything they were doing to go fight. It is hard to overstate how unpopular the draft was at the time, and desperate young men tried anything possible to avoid getting drafted, such as escaping to Canada, faking mental illnesses, or aspiring to get a coveted medical exemption, such as the diagnosis of heel bone spurs that was obtained by President Trump. But one of the more common strategies to avoid the draft was to enlist in one of the service branches of the US Armed Forces that likely wouldn't be sent to Vietnam, such as the National Guard. The advantage of this strategy was that one would probably remain stationed in the United States, far from all the carnage. However, this choice came with a steep downside. People had to commit to up to four years of their life to serving in the National Guard. When you're only twenty-one, four years of service can seem like an eternity. It was not a decision one could make lightly.[16]

This was the decision that John Bolton faced in 1969. Should he enlist in the National Guard to avoid getting drafted to Vietnam? The stakes of his decision were compounded by the looming draft lottery. On December 1, 1969, a lottery was held for every man who was eligible for the draft that year. A large rotating bin was filled with numbers corresponding to every date of the year, and they were selected in order until all of the dates had been drawn. Everyone who was eligible for the draft received a lottery number corresponding to their birthday. If someone received a low number, they were almost certain to be drafted and could be sent to the front lines. On the other hand, if someone received a high number, they were almost certain to avoid being drafted and would be able to continue on with their lives in the United States without having to worry about ever being sent to the war. However, John Bolton and many of the other potential draftees had to make this key life decision about whether to enlist in the National Guard *before* the draft lottery was held. It was a huge gamble with enormous consequences.

In Bolton's case, he opted to enlist in the Maryland National Guard, which meant that he committed himself to four years of service regardless of the results of the draft lottery. This decision to enlist in the National Guard gave the results of the draft lottery an entirely new meaning. If Bolton's birthday was selected early in the draft lottery, then his decision to enlist in the National Guard would seem very prescient, as it would mean that his life may have been saved by avoiding having to fight in Vietnam. On the other hand, if Bolton's birthday was selected late in the lottery, his decision to enlist in the National Guard would seem to have been a bad bet. It would mean that he never would have been at risk of getting drafted in the first place, and his choice to enlist in the National Guard to avoid the draft would have all been for naught.

When the lottery was held, John Bolton received number 185. Everyone with a number lower than 195 was drafted, so Bolton's decision to enlist in the National Guard to avoid fighting in the war would seem very prescient and may have saved his life. But imagine that the lottery had turned out differently. What if Bolton had instead drawn number 285, which would have meant that his decision to enlist in the National Guard would have been entirely unnecessary? How do you think Bolton's experiences in the National Guard would have been different if he had learned that he never would have been drafted in the first place? Of course, as with most of our life decisions, we never get to know for sure how our lives would have unfolded if circumstances had been different. But in this case, a real-life natural experiment sheds some light on this question and reveals how people come to live with their choices.

The social psychologist Barry Staw was able to survey 550 American men who had enrolled in the US Army Reserve Officers' Training Corps (ROTC), prior to the draft lottery being conducted in 1969. At the time of the Vietnam War, enrolling in the ROTC served a similar function as enlisting in the National Guard. The enrollees would avoid being sent to fight in Vietnam, but it required that they commit the next few years of their lives to the ROTC.

Staw had asked these men why they had enrolled in the ROTC, and the men had reported, with no uncertainty, that their primary reason for enrolling was to avoid being drafted into the war. None of the other reasons that they offered for enrolling in the ROTC were even close. Each of these men had decided to take a big gamble to commit themselves to a few years to the ROTC in case their birthday would get drawn early in the draft lottery. Just as in Bolton's case, the ROTC enrollees had to make their decision to join the ROTC *before* the results of the draft lottery were announced. Staw wanted to investigate how the results of the draft lottery affected these men's experiences in the ROTC.[17]

After the draft lottery was conducted, the men were able to find out whether their gamble had paid off. Setting aside the group of men who received lottery numbers in the midrange (and for whom it wasn't immediately clear whether they would have ever been drafted), Staw focused on the men who received lottery numbers with clear implications for the draft. Approximately half of these men received a low lottery number and found out that they definitely would have been drafted had they not enrolled in the ROTC. These men had learned that their enrollment had prevented them from having to fight in the war. The other half received a high lottery number and learned that they never would have been drafted. They were faced with the realization that their enrollment in the ROTC had all been for naught. Several months after the results of the lottery were announced, Staw surveyed these same men again to learn about their experiences in the ROTC.

Knowing how their gamble to enroll in the ROTC had since paid off, which group of men do you think enjoyed being in the ROTC more? Well, it would seem that it should be the group that would have been drafted to the war, right? Enrolling in the ROTC may have saved their lives, whereas the other group should be regretting that they took this gamble and ended up having to unnecessarily spend a few years of their youth in the ROTC. But this prediction fails to consider the deep lengths that people will go to defend the premise *I have made good choices.*

In actuality, the results of the survey showed the precise *opposite* pattern. Those men who had received a high lottery number and had found out that they would have never been drafted reported being *much more satisfied* with their time in the ROTC compared with those who had received a low lottery number and had learned that enrolling in the ROTC had saved them from being sent to the war. This result certainly seems surprising. Those who had received a high lottery number were faced with what must have looked like a bad decision to them. They would seem to have been much better off had they never decided to enroll in the ROTC, as they would be free to live their lives as they wished. These men faced an absurd situation: they largely saw themselves as good and sensible people who had made a key life decision that had turned out badly for them, and they responded to this absurdity in a way that is probably all too familiar: they rationalized their decisions.

Our ability to rationalize our decisions is a key weapon in our arsenal to defend our life stories. When people rationalize their decisions, they take what would seem to be evidence of a *bad* decision and instead convince themselves that they have actually made a *good* decision. In the case of the ROTC enrollees with the high lottery numbers, if they could convince themselves that they actually enjoyed their time in the ROTC, then the gamble they took would no longer seem like a bad decision; their enrollment would seem to have been a good decision. Of course, participating in the ROTC does provide an individual with many positive experiences, and these men who were motivated to rationalize their decisions were able to appreciate them. They were able to recognize all the benefits that they had received from their time with the ROTC. They had learned a number of useful new skills, enjoyed the camaraderie of a new group of friends, and served their country proudly. They had the opportunity to develop themselves more and to mature. These are all positive outcomes and are consistent with the ROTC enrollees having made a sound life choice.

But those enrollees who had received a low lottery number saw things quite differently. They had enrolled in the ROTC to avoid getting sent to fight in Vietnam, and it had worked. Their gamble paid off—it would seem to have turned out to have been a very good decision for them. They didn't need to try to find ways to rationalize their decision or to see their ROTC experiences as rewarding. As a consequence, they ended up not really liking their time there.

We might expect that John Bolton's own reactions might be similar to those of the ROTC enrollees with the low lottery numbers. Bolton learned that his gamble to enlist in the National Guard had paid off—it saved him from having to fight in the Vietnam War. Given that his decision had worked out in the way he had hoped, he had no need to rationalize it. He didn't need to convince himself that serving in the National Guard was especially rewarding. Bolton had a long career serving his country and influencing its decisions for national security. You might expect that he would have seen his first experience of serving his country through the National Guard as inspiring. Yet, it is striking that in Bolton's various memoirs where he details so many of his life experiences, he never once mentions his time in the National Guard. The only comment in his memoirs about his decision to enlist in the National Guard is to say, "Looking back, I am not terribly proud of this calculation." Perhaps if Bolton had instead received a higher lottery number he would have become more committed to having had a rewarding time in the National Guard. He may have worked harder in his service, and this may have ultimately shaped his subsequent career and, potentially, US foreign policy.[18]

The rationalizations that we make play a key role in the ways we lead our lives. This point was highlighted by a character played by Jeff Goldblum in the 1983 film *The Big Chill*, in an exchange he had with a character played by Tom Berenger.

> **Goldblum:** *Don't knock rationalization. Where would we be without it? I don't know anyone who could get through the day without one or two juicy rationalizations. They are more important than sex.*
> **Berenger:** *C'mon, nothing is more important than sex.*
> **Goldblum:** *Oh yeah? Have you ever gone a week without a rationalization?*

I think Goldblum's character is right—we are deeply indebted to our rationalizations as they play a key role in our efforts to tell our life stories. We have an urge to keep our life stories straight; we need them to make sense and to be consistent with all of the key premises that we embrace. Our rationalizations ensure that the events in our lives can always fit into the stories we tell about ourselves. If, say, someone took a gamble to try to avoid the draft by enrolling in the ROTC, only to find out that they were never going to be drafted in the first place, they have an urge to convince themselves that spending a few years in the ROTC was precisely what they had wanted to do. People's rationalizations come to shape the life stories that they tell.

"We are our choices," Sartre exhorted. Our lives unfold on the basis of the choices that we make. It can be thrilling to consider the freedom that we have to create any kind of life that we wish. But if our lives really are the choices we have made, then we are often facing some looming existential anxieties if we consider the possibility that we might sometimes be making the wrong decisions. A life of bad choices is hardly something to celebrate. We may wish to be the captains of our own lives, but we are imagining we'll be a competent captain and not one that is failing. We don't want to feel that the difficulties that we've experienced in our lives are the result of our own bad choices.

And this brings us to the flip side of the exhilaration that comes with embracing the freedoms in one's life. Being able to choose one's life path also brings with it a lot of unwanted responsibilities, and these lie at the root of people's existential anxieties. At the same time that Sartre celebrated our freedoms, he felt that the responsibilities that come with our choices stand to threaten our peace of mind. "It is anguish pure and simple," Sartre said, "of the kind experienced by all who have borne responsibilities." If what we don't like about our lives are the result of own choices, then this can bring a crippling amount of responsibility. How can we feel that we have made good choices? We depend upon our rationalizations. Our rationalizations enable us to live with the choices we have made. They ensure that we are able to feel that our lives are not absurd and that everything appears to make sense.[19]

We probably don't ever go a week without a rationalization. People are constantly making choices in their lives, and they are motivated to ensure that they have been making good ones. Many psychological studies conducted with American participants have investigated people's reactions to their choices. Typically, these studies find that, when given a choice to make between two alternatives, most people respond by rationalizing their choice and convincing themselves that they have clearly made the right decision by selecting the better option. People will show these kinds of rationalizations even for minor decisions such as choosing a new kitchen appliance or even a pen, let alone their more important life decisions, such as the choice of their spouses or their careers. These studies most often find that whenever people are making choices, they are also making rationalizations.[20]

People's efforts to rationalize decisions are the product of the most studied defense mechanism in psychology, known as *cognitive dissonance*. Cognitive dissonance is the unsettling feeling that people get when they realize their lives aren't making sense. People feel dissonance when they recognize a glitch in their life stories and realize they are acting in a way that runs afoul of their deepest values. They might have noticed that they've made an argument they don't agree with. They may have chosen something they don't really want. When people catch themselves acting in these nonsensical ways, they get a disturbing, uncanny feeling that something is not quite right—their life feels absurd. They need to escape the absurd, and this feeling motivates them to engage in some rationalizations. These rationalizations help people feel *I have made good choices*.

Thousands of psychological studies have explored situations that elicit dissonance and the many kinds of psychological acrobatics that people engage in to reduce their dissonant feelings. Commonly, people react to dissonance by rationalizing so that their lives don't seem so absurd. They make new kinds of meaning, such as the previous example of the ROTC enrollees. When they learned they were never going to get drafted, the enrollees came to see their time in the ROTC as a life-enhancing experience, whereas before the draft lottery was conducted, they had seen it primarily as a means to avoid going to war.

One key function of our rationalizations is to make ourselves feel better about the decisions we have made. Rationalization calms our anxieties about having acted absurdly. But dissonance is not just about changing our feelings. People's efforts to get rid of the absurd feelings of dissonance can also direct them to lead their lives differently. In the ROTC study, the enrollees who had received the high lottery numbers were not *just saying* that they liked the ROTC more. They had very different experiences there too. They worked harder and received better grades in their ROTC coursework than did those who had received low lottery numbers. Faced with a decision that seemed to have turned out badly, they had a stronger urge to commit themselves to the ROTC.

This is an important point about our rationalizations: they can change the ways that we lead our lives. People can be so committed to convincing themselves that they are not absurd that they will actively engage in behaviors, such as studying more for their courses, so that their decisions can better fit with the life stories they wish to tell. Sometimes people seem to be living their lives in service of their rationalizations. They make decisions about what to do with their lives so that their life story fits better with their rationalizations.

The full extent that people will go to protect their rationalizations was evident in what has to be the most striking study of dissonance. The founder of dissonance theory, Leon Festinger, understood that people will go to great lengths to rationalize their beliefs. But what happens to people when they learn that their most important beliefs are utterly disconfirmed? How will people respond when they confront unambiguous evidence that their most strongly committed beliefs are proven wrong? This question seemed impossible to study in the laboratory. But

Festinger saw an opportunity when he came across a Chicago newspaper article describing a local mystic, Dorothy Martin, who had shared a message with her devoted followers, called the Seekers. Martin had said that the message had been sent to her by superior beings from the distant planet Clarion. They had informed her that a great flood would come to devastate the earth on December 21, 1955. However, a series of flying saucers would be sent from Clarion to help evacuate the Seekers.[21]

Upon reading this article, Festinger felt he finally had the rare opportunity to explore what happens when a committed belief system is disconfirmed. What was going to happen to the Seekers after December 21 had passed and neither the great flood nor the UFOs had arrived? Festinger and a team of others decided that they would infiltrate the cult, participate in their rituals, and observe what happened to people's rationalizations in real time as they came to terms with their looming failed prophecy.

Festinger and the other observers began to regularly attend the meetings of the Seekers in the few weeks prior to December 21. They learned that the other Seekers were extremely committed to the prophecy that God was going to destroy the world with a great flood. Some of them had given away their life savings. Others had cut off their relationships with their families and friends. The Seekers had made an enormous gamble with their lives. In poker, this kind of bet is called "going all in." The Seekers had a lot of commitment to a belief system that was about to be proven wrong.

The night leading up to midnight of December 21 was extremely tense. The Seekers all gathered around to hear any new guidance from Martin. They waited and waited, silently. And then the clock in the living room chimed twelve poignant times as midnight arrived. The Seekers sat still, with their faces frozen and expressionless. But nothing happened. The clock kept ticking on past midnight, but there was no great flood or flying saucers. The big bet the Seekers had placed seemed to go bust.

A few hours after midnight, things were getting extremely tense among the Seekers. The group was in desperate need of a sign that they hadn't been duped. And then, at 4:45 a.m. that night, one arrived. Dorothy Martin received another message stating that God had been so inspired by their devotion that he had decided against destroying the earth. The Seekers had not been duped by a crazy prophecy. Rather, it was their steadfast devotion that had saved the world! They were offered an enormous rationalization for why they should stay committed to their meaning framework.

And then the Seekers' behavior changed. During the previous few weeks, they had tried to avoid attention as much as they could. When potential new believers arrived, they often tried to steer them away. When the press called, they refused to talk to them. They hadn't been trying to spread the word about the upcoming flood. They were a small group of people, and they were much more concerned about ensuring that they got a seat on the flying saucers than they were in letting others know about the encroaching Armageddon. But in the days following the failed prophecy, this all changed dramatically.

Dorothy Martin immediately started contacting the press. On the day of the failed prophecy, her house was crowded with reporters. The Seekers sought out anyone who would listen and explained what had just happened. For the first time, they shared tape recordings of Martin receiving messages and pictures of the Seekers. They reached out to people to convince them that they had just missed being destroyed. Their sudden change from being a publicity-shy group to one that had become deeply committed to proselytizing shows the beginning of a new kind of rationalizing. By recruiting other new members, they could ensure that they had more evidence around them—all of these devoted followers who shared their views—to convince themselves that everything about their lives made sense again. They needed to create the social reality that others saw things as they did too.

Festinger's study of the Seekers' reactions to their failed prophecy exposed the sheer power of people's rationalizations. What more proof could the Seekers have received than to be convinced that the crazy prophecy was wrong? The absence of a flying saucer and a destroyed planet was not enough to make them concede they had been mistaken. Upon learning that the prophecy had failed, the rational thing would have been for the followers to have condemned Dorothy Martin, as she had been so obviously proven wrong. And indeed, a few of the followers did abandon the group at this moment and never came back. They could no longer justify their commitment. But the more common response was for cult members to double down and become even *more* committed to the group, convincing themselves that their purity of heart had saved the world from the flood.

The reactions of the Seekers are a lot like Max Planck's observations about how scientists often die before they are able to accept new evidence and give up on their theories. People are so dependent upon the meaning frameworks that guide their lives that they will embrace almost anything that allows them to conclude that their views of the world are sensible after all. They are usually quite resistant to changing them. Now most people's worldviews aren't built on such a tenuous relation to reality as were the Seekers'. On the other hand, most people *do* share something in common with the Seekers in that they will usually remain strongly committed to defending their worldviews.

## Love and Rationalizations

Romantic relationships are particularly rife with rationalizations. It wouldn't be easy to fall head over heels for our partner and want to stay committed to them for the rest of our lives without a good dose of rationalization to keep us going through the rough patches. Before someone has decided to love a particular person, they may have had a long list of characteristics that they're looking for in their partner. On dating apps they may swipe right and left with confidence, knowing what it is that they're looking for. And often, after a single date, people are quite adept at ruling out people for not being a good fit. When people are single, they seem to be pretty good at knowing what it is they want. But once they commit themselves to a long-term choice, their rationalizations will typically kick in and help to ensure that they continue to want to stay with their partner.

Benjamin Franklin recognized the benefits of rationalizations in marriage when he advised, "Keep your eyes wide open before marriage, and half shut afterward." The reason why rationalizations are so important in marriage is because it's such a big commitment. It is one of the most important choices in your life. You become emotionally committed to this person. You have pooled your financial resources. The world recognizes you as a couple. You may have raised a family together. Married couples are not that different from the Seekers who gave up their life savings. They have gone all in with their chosen partner. And once an individual is this committed to a choice, it's important to justify their commitment.

There are many other kinds of choices that we make in life without a whole lot of commitment. For example, we don't have much at stake about what foods we like to eat or the music we like to listen to, and as a result, we can more easily let our feelings ebb and flow about these preferences. But if people let their feelings about their partners fluctuate the way they do about, say, fettuccine Alfredo or Taylor Swift's new album, they'd be in big trouble. While it is natural for people's feelings toward their partners to shift because the events in their lives change, if they acknowledged that they didn't feel much love toward their partners anymore, they'd be left with a big inconsistency: I promised to spend the rest of my life with this person, but I don't feel that I love them much anymore. These kinds of conflicting thoughts can create much dissonance and leave one stuck in the absurd.

Over the course of a relationship, people encounter both the best and the worst of their partners. And when they see the worst, their rationalizations can become especially necessary. If people looked at their partners with the same kind of objective detachment they do with other things in their lives, love would be more difficult to sustain. If people saw their partner "warts and all," it would be hard to integrate the feeling *I love my partner* with the many shortcomings that they see. Research finds that the more people rationalize their partners, the more successful their relationships are. By looking at their partner through rose-colored lenses, people can help to keep away those feelings of dissonance. One can rationalize their partner's less desirable traits such that they seem more tolerable. So, say, if one looks at the mess their partner has left around the house, they might instead conclude that their partner is "carefree," rather than a slob. If one's partner has a vicious temper tantrum, they could conclude that their partner is "in touch with their emotions," as opposed to being hostile. Friedrich Nietzsche perceptively observed that "love is a state in which a man sees things most decidedly as they are not." When we're in love, our rationalizations distort how we see our partners.[22]

I've described rationalizations in people's relationships in fairly positive terms as they can be so important to keeping a marriage together. But, as with everything, people can go too far in their rationalizing, and sometimes these rationalizations can cause more harm than good. In extreme situations, people's rationalizing can keep them in a bad relationship. They can sometimes be so potent that people have a hard time leaving an abusive partner. Abused women are in a terrible situation, which often does not offer an easy way out. They may be better off if they could leave, but they might not have the financial means. They may be worried about how their children would fare. They may feel the social pressure of their extended family and friends who view them as a loving couple. It can feel easier to not do anything rather than make an abrupt life change, and they may be terrified of what their husbands might do to them if they left. Faced with a horrible situation that they can't easily leave, they may experience an urge to rationalize their abusive husband's behavior so that it doesn't seem so bad to them. Staying with an abusive husband that one doesn't love seems rather absurd, but if a woman can convince herself that she really *does* love her husband, she can reduce some of that dissonance. This reaction is called *psychological entrapment*. The entrapped individual may keep escalating their rationalizations because they feel they have too much invested in the relationship. Research finds that women who are in relationships with abusive husbands often report loving their husbands and viewing them in more positive terms than do women who have left their abusive husbands. Sometimes it can seem easier to change one's feelings— "I love my husband so much that it's worth staying with him, despite his abuse"—than to leave one's marriage. Often, our attitudes are more amenable to change than our behaviors.[23]

## Rationalizing Across Cultures

Rationalizations play a key role in people's life stories. They help to ensure that people can live with the choices they make. This is especially true in cultures where people's lives are guided so much by the choices that they have. It's no coincidence that the existentialists were all from Western cultures, emerging from individualistic societies that emphasized the power of individuals to choose how to direct their own lives. But choices are not celebrated to the same degree everywhere.

Arguably, the high temple of choice is Starbucks. Before there were Starbucks coffee shops, people used to just order a coffee. But Starbucks made the decision to prioritize its customers' choices so it could create a bespoke coffee experience. Starbucks's slogan became "Make it your drink," and the company allowed customers to specify in granular detail precisely how they would like their cup of coffee made for them. The customer can ask for a very specific kind of drink, say a grande half-caffeinated latte with oat milk, warmed up two extra degrees, with chocolate sprinkles on top, and the barista will obey their every command. Starbucks claims that there are more than 87,000 permutations for customers to have their coffees. Ordering a coffee at Starbucks can be a celebration of choice. But it's a very different experience getting coffee in Japan.

I know an American instructor who teaches at a university in Japan. His favorite way to get his coffee is to have three shots of espresso over a cup of ice, and then filled up to the top with milk. But his local coffee shop in Japan wouldn't sell him this drink. He begged the barista to make it for him. He offered to pay them however much they would ask for such a drink. The barista would just look back at him with a puzzled look on her face—she couldn't sell him his coffee that way because it wasn't on the menu. Embittered by this lack of choice, the instructor brought up this experience in one of the classes that he was teaching. But the manager of the coffee shop later learned about this class discussion. The manager didn't like that her business was being used as a case study for the lack of freedom in Japan, and she wanted the instructor to stop ranting against her coffee shop. She proposed a compromise to the instructor: from then on, whenever the instructor was in that coffee shop, they would give him a cup with three shots of espresso over ice, topped off with milk. They came up with a reasonable price, and it was programmed into the cash register, and the staff received training about how to make it, although it was not advertised to anyone else. The manager even let the instructor come up with his own name for this concoction, which he called "The Captain." It was set up just for the instructor so that he could order it whenever he went into that store. But to the instructor, the manager was completely missing his point. It was never really about the coffee. It was about having the freedom to choose. The instructor wants to live in a culture where people have the freedom to get whatever they want, and not just because they could cajole a manager into creating a private exception just for them. But Japan doesn't celebrate choice in the ways that Americans do.

Westerners who live in Japan commonly complain about the lack of choices that they have there. But one of the key life lessons that I learned from living in Japan has been to come to appreciate the value of surrendering one's choices. I learned to embrace *omakase* and would always recommend that people try it at a Japanese restaurant. *Omakase* literally means "I leave it up to you"— meaning the chef, in the case of a restaurant. The chef then makes a meal they know they can make exceptionally well. These skillful, highly trained experts know which flavors pair well together. They use ingredients that are fresh and in season, and the meal often costs more than a regular entrée. I have found that an *omakase* meal is always a good meal.

I know that many Westerners may balk at the idea of ordering *omakase*. They are reluctant to give up their freedom to choose, and they are concerned that the chef doesn't know about their particular idiosyncratic preferences. How can they enjoy their meal knowing that their particular desires are being ignored? This is the trade-off with going *omakase*. But focusing on always trying to have one's idiosyncratic tastes met results in a failure to adequately consider all that is psychologically on the line when one makes a choice.

Making choices requires a lot of psychological work. Research finds that people can become somewhat mentally exhausted after making a series of choices. Making choices also comes burdened with the responsibility of ensuring that it is a good choice, which may require some additional rationalizations later on. *Omakase* spares one from all these costs. I think it serves as a good recommendation for approaching life more generally. Sometimes there can be real benefits to surrendering your choices to an expert and recognizing that making choices lies at the root of your anxieties. When the choice is made by an expert, it'll probably result in a positive outcome, and importantly, you are spared the effort, anxiety, and responsibility of having to make the choice. You do not need to rationalize a choice made by someone else. There is much to be gained by not trying to force the world to fit into your own particular fixed choices.[24]

Cultures vary tremendously in the amount of choices they offer in life. The United States, hands down, is the world champion of providing choices. Americans have so many more choices to make in their lives than people from other cultures because they desire more choices than do people elsewhere. Take the case of India. Comparisons between Indians and Americans find many differences in how they make choices. Research finds that Indians are considerably slower than Americans when making choices, as Indians just aren't as practiced at it. In addition, there are many domains of life where Indians indicate that they do not desire choices. In contrast, Americans are more likely to say that across almost all situations they would rather have the freedom to choose, and the more important the choice is, the more likely Americans are to insist to make it on their own. But for Indians, the pattern is the opposite. The more important the choice, the more Indians want trusted *others* to make their choices for them. This is particularly evident in what is arguably the most important choice that people have to make in their lives—their spouse. The most common form of marriage in India is an arranged marriage, where typically the parents play a key role in choosing partners for their children. I find in my teaching that this is the one cultural difference that students really struggle to wrap their heads around. They just can't imagine having a spouse that they didn't choose. They are convinced that arranged marriages must be inferior, but curiously, studies that have compared love versus arranged marriages within countries usually find that arranged marriages are at least as successful as love marriages and lead to more love over the long term, although it's important to note that the popularity of arranged marriages has been decreasing over time. Arranged marriages usually lead to largely positive outcomes, and they do so without the individuals having much choice.[25]

People living in Asia have fewer choices to make in life compared with Americans, and when there are fewer choices to make, there is less need for rationalizations. And, indeed, there is far less evidence for cognitive dissonance in Asia. I conducted a cross-cultural experiment along with Darrin Lehman where we had Japanese and Canadian students make a choice between two music CDs. To compensate them for their participation in the study, the students had to choose between two CDs that they had earlier rated as being equal in desirability. After making their choice, the students were asked to rate the two CDs again, and the Canadians then rationalized their choice by rating the CD they chose as more desirable, and the CD that they didn't choose as less desirable, compared with how they had originally rated them. It was no longer a close call: they had convinced themselves that they had made a good decision. The Japanese, in contrast, showed no evidence of rationalizing their decision. Their ratings of the CDs didn't change. It just doesn't seem to be as important to the Japanese to feel that they had made a good decision. In cultures that celebrate the importance of choice and encourage people to make choices throughout their lives, people depend more on rationalizations.[26]

## Making Choices in the Twenty-First Century

People living in different cultures have very different opportunities for making choices. But cultures also vary across historical time. Let's reflect on what Western cultural life was like in the Middle Ages for most Europeans. In contrast to life in the twenty-first century, far fewer key life choices were available to most people. For example, it was common for people to inherit their occupations from their parents—surnames such as Miller, Smith, and Cooper described the jobs that people were born into. It was relatively rare for people to break into a new line of work. People then also had far less say in who they married. Arranged marriages were not uncommon, where families strived to form alliances with other families or to ensure the smooth transfer of property. People didn't usually have much say in the religions that they practiced either. Often, people were only exposed to one religion during their lives. Society at the time was also very hierarchical. People knew their place within the hierarchy, and there were few opportunities available to change one's status. As St. Augustine said, "A person should not aspire to change position in society any more than a finger should wish to become an eye." People commonly lived in the same community into which they were born and didn't have much say in where they lived. The life paths that people followed were largely laid out in front of them, with few points along the way where people could consider an alternative path.

But today, particularly in the United States, it is hard to find key aspects of people's lives that are not subject to their own choices. People today live in a time of what the sociologist Zygmunt Bauman calls "liquid modernity." The traits that used to be assigned to them by their communities must now be chosen by the individuals themselves. Unlike in the past, people today need to figure out how they are going to sculpt their own selves. They have to figure out their identities, which they often showcase on social media, where they are often left worrying whether they will be approved by others.[27]

People today need to decide for themselves what careers to pursue, but this has become far more challenging because of how much career opportunities are in flux. One hallmark of the twenty-first-century labor market is the gig economy. For many young people, there is no set career path that they are following; they have to figure out for themselves how to combine various temporary lines of income to earn a living. This do-it-yourself approach to career planning is also becoming more common in university curricula. Typically, when students select a major, they are provided with a set series of required courses, with only a little flexibility around which optional courses they can choose. But there has been a growing trend for universities to offer custom-designed majors, in which students select for themselves the different collection of courses they will take. Students are able to customize their education and their future careers to fit with their own idiosyncratic preferences.

People also confront more choices now in their search for a mate. The most common way of finding a romantic partner now is through dating apps, which are at odds with previous generations, when people usually met their partners through their social networks. The process of finding a partner has become not that unlike flipping through a catalog with thousands of options. People search through all of these potential partners, and, somehow, they're supposed to find the one that is best for them.

Having the freedom to choose has also come to characterize many people's spiritual experiences. Rather than staying with the religion they are born with, approximately 42 percent of American adults have a different religious affiliation than they did in childhood, and an increasing number of people are turning away from organized religions. One of the fastest growing religious categories is "spiritual but not religious." People are rejecting the structure of organized religions in favor of figuring out for themselves what set of transcendental beliefs they will subscribe to. Their new belief system may involve a sampling from a number of different faiths or mystical traditions. An individual may create their own bespoke set of spiritual beliefs and practices that might involve, say, some pagan rituals, Zen meditation techniques, yoga poses, astrological tables, and crystals, along with some ideas from a New Age book. People have been increasingly choosing for themselves how to figure out the right path to the hereafter. Their personal responsibility has taken on cosmic dimensions.[28]

In contrast with the past, there are scant few aspects of life that people can count on as fixed and predetermined. Young people today are even choosing their own genders. The many freedoms that Americans, especially young people, are enjoying today are unusual in the context of human history. It's individualistic societies that provide more choices in life, and America is the most individualistic country in the world today. It celebrates these freedoms to a degree not matched elsewhere. Moreover, much of the world, the United States included, has been becoming progressively more and more individualistic over time, and people are encountering new choices that their ancestors never had to make. In many ways, Americans are living at the vanguard now: there has probably never been a previous culture that had as many freedoms as twenty-first-century Americans do now. Americans are serving as the guinea pigs that are testing how well humans can live their lives with so many freedoms, and it is particularly their youth that are bearing the consequences of their many life choices. We need to consider how people can best embrace all of their freedoms without succumbing to the anxieties that come with them.[29]

With so much of our lives resting on the choices we have made, we are more dependent upon our rationalizations than ever before. Our lifestyles are unique, capturing our own propensities and partialities, and our freedom to choose keeps extending to more and more domains of life. We bear a lot of responsibility for each of the choices that we make, and this brings with it more need for rationalizing. The new age of anxiety is replete with individual freedom and all of the rationalizations that come bundled with it. It is a time, perhaps more than ever before, that people feel the urgency to conclude *I have made good choices.*

# Chapter 7

# Reckoning with the Hereafter

Therefore never send to know
For whom the bell tolls,
It tolls for thee.

John Donne, "For Whom the Bell Tolls"

On the frigid morning of December 22, 1849, Fyodor Dosto-evsky was woken early in his prison cell. A guard handed him the clothes that he had been wearing at the time of his arrest and, without explanation, ordered him to get dressed. Dostoevsky was then escorted in a carriage to Semenovsky Square in St. Peters-burg, where he stepped out and struggled to gain his bearings—it was the first time that he had seen the sun in months. Together with a group of fourteen other prisoners, all emaciated with long untrimmed hair and beards, he was ordered to walk across the square through a foot of freshly fallen snow to a platform that had been erected. The prisoners lined up on the platform, shivering in the cold, and waited to be met there by a civil service official. The official, documents in hand, walked up to Dostoevsky and read to him the decision for his crimes: he had been convicted of being part of a secret revolutionary society that was plotting against the government. As the official continued reading, he then announced, unexpectedly to the prisoners, that they had all been condemned to death by firing squad. As the prisoners struggled to process this horrendous news, a priest walked up to them, presenting them each with a cross to kiss, and they were then given long white peasant blouses and night caps to put on. The first group of men were then tied to stakes and their caps were pulled over their heads. A drum-roll began and the firing squad took aim. The drumroll continued for the most excruciatingly long minute that Dostoevsky had ever experienced. Suddenly, the drum roll changed, signaling a retreat, and the rifles were lowered. The official then announced that, by order of the merciful czar, the men had been granted a reprieve. Their execution had been halted, and Dostoevsky was instead sentenced to four years in a Siberian prison, followed by six years of military service in a remote outpost.

As one might surmise, this experience in Semenovsky Square left quite the impact on Dostoevsky. In his novel *The Idiot*, which he wrote twenty years later, Dostoevsky recounted the horror that he had experienced in this mock execution: "His uncertainty and revulsion against this new thing which was bound to happen at any moment were terrible," he described. But "nothing was more awful than the incessant thought, 'What if I was not to die! . . . I would turn each minute into a century. I would miss nothing. I would reckon each passing minute and waste nothing!'" Upon facing his imminent death, Dostoevsky had been struck by just how precious life is. This harrowing experience did not break his will but instead inspired him to strive to live his life to the fullest. Upon returning to his prison cell that day, Dostoevsky wrote a letter to his brother, Mikhail, announcing that "never before have I felt welling up in me such abundant and healthy reserves of spiritual life as I do now. . . . Now deprivations mean nothing to me and this is why I am not afraid that any kind of material hardship will destroy me. . . . Life is a gift, life is happiness, every minute can be an eternity of happiness!" Moreover, from that moment on, Dostoevsky replaced the primarily secular perspective that had previously guided his contemplations of human life with a deeply religious faith. Dostoevsky came to believe that life was a gift from God and always needed to be embraced. He recognized that life was so precious because we never know when it will be taken away from us.[1]

As we'll see in this chapter, Dostoevsky's commitment to live life to the fullest is but one of many kinds of responses that people often have to thoughts about their impending deaths, and we'll be considering below the variety of ways that people come to terms with their own mortality. Dostoevsky's inspired reactions to his near-death experience may seem rather curious because, oftentimes, intense negative experiences can be seriously debilitating to people. Indeed, one of Dostoevsky's fellow prisoners, Nikolay Grigoreyev, appeared to be psychologically broken from his mock execution and was rendered a helpless mental invalid for the rest of his life. More generally, it is not uncommon for people who experience traumatic life events, such as losing a loved one, having an accident, or being laid off from a job, to spiral into a depression. Experiences with trauma often hurt people's well-being, for the obvious reason that trauma usually makes people's lives worse off than before. In stark contrast to this general trend, though, is how common it is for people who have near-death experiences to respond like Dostoevsky and have a more inspired outlook on life.

## Inspirations from Encounters with Death

People often seem to respond to encounters with death in ways that align with Albert Camus's declaration: "Come to terms with death. Thereafter anything is possible." Frequently, people who have gone through such experiences gain a new appreciation for life like Dostoevsky. For example, the former chief of staff of President Jimmy Carter, Hamilton Jordan, described the experiences from his own battle with cancer. "After my first cancer, even the smallest joys in life took on a special meaning—watching a beautiful sunset, a hug from my child, a laugh with Dorothy. That feeling has not diminished with time." Sally Walker, a professor of geology, survived an airline crash that killed eighty-three people. As she described her experiences, "When I got home, the sky was brighter, I paid attention to the texture of sidewalks. It was like being in a movie. . . . [Now] everything is a gift." These kinds of positive reactions to near-death experiences are strikingly widespread. One study interviewed a couple hundred Americans who had survived life-threatening dangers. Approximately one-quarter of people showed evidence of positive psychological changes after their life crises, a response called *posttraumatic growth*. They responded that their experiences had made them appreciate the preciousness of life and had led them to reevaluate their priorities and commit to a less cautious approach to life. Many became more religious. It is encouraging that posttraumatic growth is a common response to tragedy; however, as the example of Dostoevsky's fellow prisoner, Grigoreyev, reminds us, not everyone gets to enjoy these benefits.[2]

People do not necessarily have to directly confront death themselves to experience posttraumatic growth; they can show similar kinds of positive benefits after having just witnessed tragedies among others. For example, one study provided people with an online survey that assessed people's character strengths—positive traits that enable people to work toward achieving the better things in life. In the survey, people were asked to rate statements such as "I know that I will succeed with the goals I set for myself," or "I never quit a task before it is done." The survey was accessible from January 2001 to June 2002, and several months after the survey had been made available, the United States was hit by the terrorist attacks of 9/11. Suddenly, all Americans faced the fact that their country and way of life were under attack. They watched television footage showing over and over again the airplanes crashing into the World Trade Center, killing thousands. The researchers recognized that the time frame in which they had collected their data provided an opportunity to assess the psychological changes brought about by those terrorist attacks. The researchers identified that many of these character strengths were endorsed more by Americans in the months that followed 9/11 compared to the responses collected before. After the terrorist attacks had occurred, Americans reported that they had more of the character strengths such as gratitude, hope, perseverance, kindness, leadership, love, teamwork, and spirituality. The experiences of the terrorist attacks seem to have prompted Americans to strive to cultivate these character strengths. Like Dostoevsky, they responded to these reminders of their mortality with an enhanced commitment to live their lives more fully than before.[3]

One reason that near-death experiences can so often lead to an enhanced appreciation of life may be because death reminds people of the scarcity of life. It highlights how we have only a limited number of chances to pursue our goals in life. Viktor Frankl noted that "if we were immortal, we could legitimately postpone every action forever. It would be of no consequence whether or not we did a thing now. . . . But in the face of death . . . we are under the imperative of utilizing our lifetimes to the utmost, not letting the singular opportunities . . . pass by unused." In general, when we perceive any commodity as scarce, it leads people to view it as more valuable, which helps explain the great value accorded to scarce objects such as jewelry, trading cards, or original works of art. Appreciating the scarcity of life similarly seems to enhance its value.[4]

The inevitable fact that we're going to die has broad psychological effects on us. One consequence of a recognition of our impending mortality is that it casts the passage of time in a whole new perspective. Tick, tick, tick . . . each second that passes brings us closer to our own deaths. We can see the effects that people's looming deaths have on them by comparing the ways of thinking between young and old people. Of course, there are many differences between young and old people. Older people have a lot more chapters in their life stories as their lives contain more episodes. They've also matured, taken on responsibilities, and had a broader range of experiences. But much research finds that, curiously, many of the psychological differences between young and old people are not so much the product of the different sets of experiences that people have had but rather are due to *how much time people think they have left*. As our impending death gets closer and closer, our remaining lives feel scarcer and scarcer. And people change how they live when they realize they are facing an ending.

When people are young, they feel rather immortal. With time stretching out so long in front of them, they rarely consider that their life stories will have an ending. They are often thinking about the future and all the potential possibilities that lie within it. Young people are typically interested in gaining new experiences, meeting new people, and improving themselves by learning new things and acquiring new skills. They have an aspirational mind-set and want to achieve the most out of life. But as people get older, the future shrinks in front of their own eyes, and they become aware that time is running out. Older people come to realize that their remaining time is scarce and precious. Studies find that rather than trying to pursue new experiences in life and meeting new people, older people become more focused on spending quality time with their closest relationships. As people age, they tend to shift their priorities to savor the most that they can from their existing relationships. Their social networks become smaller, as they spend time with those whom they know the best.[5]

As people age and get closer to the end of their lives, they also go through other changes. People come to embrace the positive aspects of their lives more and come to feel a greater proportion of positive over negative emotions. One of the most encouraging findings to emerge from all of the social sciences is that most people start to feel happier in their lives after they progress through middle age and begin to approach old age. This upward-sloping happiness curve of middle age documents a trend of improving general satisfaction with life after people have reached their late forties. On average, upon emerging from their forties, people come to feel better and better about themselves, and each year they become increasingly positive about their lives. This trend continues upward until around the age of seventy-five or so when negative emotions become more common again after the infirmities of old age have set in. Quite remarkably, this upward-sloping happiness curve has been identified in every country where it's been explored—it appears to be a universal feature of our species. The scarcity of their remaining days leads people to shift their priorities and to focus more on those aspects of their lives that bring them joy and satisfaction. While it is not uncommon for people to struggle in their forties and to reevaluate their lives in the throes of a midlife crisis, it is reassuring that the typical pattern is that people's lives subsequently get much better through most of the later years in life. It is quite likely that your fifties and sixties will be associated with more happiness than were your thirties and forties.[6]

## Death and Empowerment

Leo Tolstoy, Dostoevsky's fierce rival, suffered through a brutal midlife existential crisis. He became obsessed about death and found his own encroaching ending made his lifework rather pointless. He asked, "Is there any meaning in my life that will not be annihilated by the inevitability of death which awaits me?" Tolstoy's experience reminds us that not everyone responds to death like Dostoevsky, who found meaning and a greater appreciation for life. When I had my own near-death experience, I, too, unfortunately, did not gain a greater appreciation for life. However, my experience taught me something else that is important about death.[7]

My closest brush with death occurred while I was teaching English in Japan. I was living in a small hot springs resort town in Nagasaki prefecture that was named, of all things, Obama. The town consisted of just a few streets that were pinned along the shore of Tachibana Bay on the west slope of Mount Unzen. People always spoke about the mountain in hushed tones, and I often stared up at it in awe. It was the site of one of the deadliest natural disasters in Japan's long history when in 1792 the mountain violently erupted, causing a massive earthquake and tsunami, which ultimately killed over fourteen thousand people. Two centuries later when

I was living there in May of 1991, the mountain started spewing steam and ash, and we started experiencing regular earthquakes several times a day. It was clear that the eruptions were likely going to get worse, and given the mountain's past history, everyone was very concerned. We had long meetings at school discussing what safety measures we could take, but it turns out that there's really not all that much that you can do when you live on the side of an active volcano. I don't know if I've ever felt more helpless when the meetings concluded with the only solution that we came up with being that all of the students and teachers were to be given a plastic helmet to wear. I watched the news every day to learn of the latest developments and had felt somewhat reassured when some of the world's leading volcanologists, who had raced to the mountain to study it, described how we weren't in any immediate danger.

But that all changed on June 3, when the mountain erupted violently, and a pyroclastic flow of scalding hot ashes and rocks swept down the east side of the mountain, killing forty-three people along the way. I had the dumb luck to be living on the opposite side of the mountain, and aside from the fact that everything was covered in a thick coat of volcanic ash, it looked as though our town had survived the initial eruption OK. From then on, I was glued to the television news in a state of panic, my plastic helmet cinched on tight. Things were looking very bleak that week, and I seriously thought that I might be facing my own death. The television news used to consist of daily updates from the volcanologists Maurice Krafft, Katia Krafft, and Harry Glicken, but they had all been tragically killed in the eruption. It was terrifying to realize that no one really knew what would happen next. The news showed a graphic depicting how the entire mountain was surging, as though a balloon were being pumped up with air, and the news anchors discussed that in a worst-case scenario the entire mountain would be obliterated in a massive explosion. I didn't get much sleep that week, constantly jumping out of bed at the slightest noise or rumble, and it was a real struggle to put on a brave face in front of the students, especially during the many earthquakes that would shake the school. I developed the reputation for being the fastest one in class to dive under a desk during each earthquake, which I rationalized as me trying to "lead by example," but truthfully, I was just really scared. In the end, the town of Obama was very fortunate, and everything remained fine on the west slope of Mount Unzen. By the time I left two months later to start my graduate studies, the earthquakes had stopped, and there were no more major eruptions or deaths.

I didn't respond to my confrontation with possible death in quite the same way as Dostoevsky had to his mock execution. While the incident at Mount Unzen was awfully frightening, I don't think I came out of it with a new focus on the preciousness of life. It unfortunately didn't prompt me to strive to live every moment to the fullest. Also, unlike Dostoevsky and many other survivors of natural disasters, the event certainly didn't make me more religious either. But since that stressful experience, I have noticed one big change in me: I am no longer afraid of volcanoes or earthquakes. Now I live in Vancouver, and every now and then various news stories remind us that Vancouver is long overdue for a massive earthquake, which my friends and family discuss with much anxiety. When my colleagues and I were informed that the psychology department was in one of the most seismically unstable buildings at our university, many of my colleagues looked highly distressed. I nodded along as other people told me how worried they were about the next "big one," but frankly, it no longer concerns me in the least. Rather, I feel strangely *empowered* whenever the topic comes up. I feel that I've been there before: I had faced regular earthquakes that I had thought might kill me, and I had come out just fine. I recognize that my feelings of invincibility toward volcanoes and earthquakes are very irrational, and even foolish, and I at least have made sure to take basic precautions, such as fastening our heavy furniture to the wall. But, at the same time, I feel fortunate to not have to share the nagging anxiety that plagues so many others who live in earthquake zones.

While I was surprised to discover how invulnerable I came to feel after my experience on Mount Unzen, my reactions are not unusual. Some other studies have found that people who emerge relatively unscathed from disaster situations often come to feel more invincible. The psychiatrist John MacCurdy, writing during the Second World War, described how the bombing blitz on London only served to embolden people who had survived the attacks without damage. He described one Londoner's reactions: "When the first siren sounded I took my children to our dug-out in the garden and I was quite certain we were all going to be killed. Then the all-clear went without anything having happened. Ever since we came out of the dug-out I have felt sure nothing would ever hurt us." Other research has found that those who remain unharmed by disasters such as hurricanes or tornadoes often come out of the experience feeling empowered; however, those who actually suffer damage from such events commonly become even more anxious and risk averse afterward. Likewise, an investigation of Americans who had survived life-threatening dangers found that about 40 percent of these people reported that their own fear of death had been reduced by this experience. These people had experienced tremendous fear that their lives might be ending, but in the end realized that those fears had been proven wrong. Often, when people have a near-death experience, they became less afraid and less defensive about thoughts concerning death. They can start to feel invincible.[8]

But, of course, such feelings of invulnerability are only an illusion. As the English novelist Neil Gaiman put it: "Everybody is going to be dead one day, just give them time." And this recognition of our inevitable mortality can wreak havoc with our meaning frameworks.

## Striving for Immortality

The Dutch philosopher Baruch Spinoza stated that "everything endeavors to persist in its own being." All organisms are instinctively driven toward a goal of self-preservation. When they are hungry they seek out the food that they need to live; when they encounter threats they quickly respond to get out of danger. But the human predicament is that we all know that someday, regardless of what we do, we are ultimately going to fail at this quest to preserve ourselves. This realization of our inevitable mortality weighs heavily on us. Every day we live our lives with the awareness that at some point we will reach the last page of our life stories.

Of course, all other species of animals will also reach the moment when they take their final breath. But herein lies a key difference between humans and other species: humans have the ability to engage in symbolic thought, made possible by us having a language. This aptitude enables us to consider scenarios that go far beyond the immediate present. We can imagine ourselves in other times and contexts. For example, I can imagine what it might be like to sail around the world, to have gone to a Beatles concert, or to have stormed the beaches at Normandy. I can reflect on what it was like on my first day of elementary school, and I am able to imagine what it will be like to retire someday. Ultimately, this ability to mentally time travel means that I can also envision myself lying in a coffin, hopefully far in the future. This ability that we all share, to be able to imagine what it will be like to die someday, is at the root of some of our deepest existential anxieties.

Young children are largely spared this anxiety. They do not develop these anxieties about their mortality until they are at least nine, when they start to face the realization that they and all of their loved ones will someday be dead and that there is nothing they can do about this. From what we can tell, other species, including our closest animal relative, chimpanzees, are also unable to recognize the inevitability of death. Chimpanzees appear to have an understanding of death that shares much in common with that of young children. They recognize when others die, and they often mourn the loss of those close to them, but chimpanzees don't seem to have made the key conceptual leap to be aware that their own lives are similarly mortal. The primatologist Tetsuro Matsuzawa describes an account of an adult chimpanzee who had become paralyzed from the neck down following a spinal infection. He was in a dire situation, having lost all control over his body, and he would die soon after. Imagine how terrified you would be in such a situation. But the chimpanzee's caretakers were all struck by how he showed no signs of anxiety or depression about his new state—it was as though nothing had happened to him. He remained in a positive mood and continued to play with his caretakers as he had done before, by spitting water at them. He didn't seem at all concerned that his life was forever changed and was in deep jeopardy. Chimpanzees likely don't have a fear of death because they just can't imagine future scenarios well. Without an awareness of their own impending mortality, chimpanzees would seem to be spared much of the existential angst that comes bundled with that awareness.[9]

But because we humans depend so much on our meaning making, the knowledge of our inevitable mortality can be a real problem for us. We can wonder how an individual can build a life that feels rich in meaning on a foundation that they recognize will collapse as soon as they die. Martin Heidegger realized how the knowledge of our impending deaths stands at odds with people's efforts to live a meaningful life. He recognized that death ultimately severs all the relations that make up the meanings that people care so much about. Indeed, in his writings, Heidegger would replace the word *death* with the clumsy neologism "our ownmost nonrelational potentiality-for-being." Thoughts about our impending death stand to annihilate all of the things that we relate to in our lives that make them meaningful. After death, every one of our interpersonal relationships will be dissolved, our aspirations and plans will all be thwarted, we will no longer be connected to all of the things that we care so much about, and the ongoing stories from our stream of consciousness will reach an abrupt and permanent end. We can no longer look to our futures as sources of possibility or hope. As Søren Kierkegaard put it, "In every human being there is a spontaneous, immediate hope; it can be more robust in one than in another, but in death every such hope dies and changes into hopelessness."[10]

How can we maintain the sense that our lives are meaningful when we realize that all of the connections that give our lives meaning will soon be gone? In *Macbeth*, William Shakespeare offers that the inevitability of our own demise renders our lives to be nothing more than "a tale, told by an idiot, full of sound and fury, signifying nothing." Most distressingly, we come to realize that this is all beyond our control—it doesn't really matter how hard we work, how much we sacrifice for others, or how healthy a lifestyle we lead. Nor would it matter if you could realize all of your wildest dreams. You could become the president of the United States, you could win a Nobel Prize, win the Powerball, perform the top song on the Billboard charts. None of these things can change the fact that our future selves will all ultimately become dust in the earth.

Perhaps more than any other individual, the anthropologist Ernest Becker was fascinated by the predicament that arises from people's recognition of their own mortality. He viewed that our awareness that the entire show of what is happening around us will someday end abruptly elicits a paralyzing existential terror within us. "What does it mean to be a self-conscious animal," he wrote. "The idea is ludicrous, if it is not monstrous. It means to know that one is food for worms. This is the terror: to have emerged from nothing, to have a name, consciousness of self, deep inner feelings, and excruciating inner yearning for life and self-expression—and with all this yet to die. It seems like a hoax."[11]

Becker pondered how it was that humans were able to cope with the enormous existential anxiety that the awareness of their mortality posed for them. People have to accept that their existences will really come to an end, no matter what they may try to do to stop it. People come to realize that after they die, the world will just continue on without them and at some point everyone that knows them will also die, leaving the world with no interpersonal trace that they ever existed. Thoughts of their death remind people that the universe doesn't acknowledge the specialness that they feel about themselves, and these realizations can make people's lives feel much less significant. Becker saw that all of this existential anxiety could be overwhelming for people to cope with, and he proposed that humans have come up with a novel solution to this problem: they have created a symbolic cultural worldview that imbues their existence with a sense of order, meaning, and permanence. He believed that this cultural worldview gives people the sense that they matter and that their existence extends far beyond their brief time walking on the earth. They are participating in a drama that connects them with all of the other people from their culture, including those who were alive long before them and those who will live long after they have passed away. This cultural worldview renders their actions as significant, meaningful in the grand scheme of things, and provides their lives with a sense of value. Their lives transcend their animalistic natures, connecting them to something that transcends the natural world.

Becker's ideas have been highly influential in spawning a key theory called *terror management theory*, which was first proposed by the social psychologists Jeff Greenberg, Tom Pyszczynski, and Sheldon Solomon. The terror management team was interested in how people manage the anxiety that derives from the awareness that their own lives are finite. The theory proposes that people can disarm this particular existential threat by aspiring for a sense of what is termed *symbolic immortality*. These aspirations arise because people are aware that their cultures have existed long before them and will continue to exist long after they die. They see the monuments, art, traditions, folklore, and scriptures that date back to many centuries earlier, reminding them of just how enduring their culture is. In many ways, people's cultures can feel somewhat immortal given how they keep persisting despite the ravages of time. This perceived immortality of one's culture can come to influence people's feelings about their own lives. The theory proposes that people can strive to feel symbolically immortal by defending their cultural worldview. They are motivated to view the meaning framework that their culture provides as something that is stable, meaningful, true, orderly, and better than the worldviews of other cultural groups. Moreover, people wish to believe that they are living up to the standards and ideals that are inherent in their worldviews. They wish their lives to be exemplars of their cultural values, and this makes their own lives feel valuable. These feelings of symbolic immortality provide the sense that people will be part of something eternal—even after they are buried in the ground, people can feel somewhat reassured that some aspect of their identity will continue to persist.

Various ideas from terror management theory have been tested in several hundreds of experiments thus far. These studies typically explore what happens to people after they think about the fact that they are going to die someday. For example, studies have shown that people who have reflected on their own mortality temporarily become more patriotic—they come to think of their culture as the best. People also become more insistent that others follow the norms and laws of their culture. Those who break these norms are viewed to deserve more punishment when mortality is on one's mind. People also become more likely to want to possess high-status goods—goods that broadcast they are meeting the standards of success in their culture. They also become more interested in having children, so that they will be able to see their own traits, such as their singing voice or their brown eyes, passed down through the family line and into the future. All of these findings provide evidence that thoughts about death lead people to strive for a sense of symbolic immortality. They are motivated to view themselves as a key player in a meaningful cultural drama, and when they do so they can feel that their own existences are part of the same immortal forces that characterize their cultures. These feelings of symbolic immortality give meaning to people's lives and serve to stave off the harrowing existential anxieties that thoughts of their own death elicit in them.[12]

To give you a better idea of what a typical terror management theory study looks like, consider the following example: American college students were brought into the lab and randomly assigned to two different groups. One group was the "mortality salience condition," and these students were led to consciously reflect upon their own mortality. Specifically, they were asked to respond to two prompts: "Please briefly describe the emotions that the thought of your own death arouses in you," and "Jot down, as specifically as you can, what you think will happen to you as you physically die and once you are physically dead." Another group of participants was randomly assigned to the control condition, and they were asked to write about two questions that had nothing to do with their death; in this instance, they were asked to write about their experiences watching television. Following this, the participants were told that they would be taking part in an unusual task that would assess their creativity. They were shown a cup of sand and then watched as an experimenter poured some black dye into the sand, staining it. They were told that their job was to separate the sand from the black dye using any of a series of objects that were arrayed in front of them. The objects included some cotton balls, a thin rope, a nail, a paper clip, and some netting; however, the only way that one could effectively remove the dye from the sand was to strain the sand using a large cloth. Half of the participants in both groups were provided with a piece of white cloth along with the other items. The other half were given an American flag.

The participants with the white cloth solved the problem fairly quickly, and they rated the task as quite easy, regardless of whether they had been thinking about their own death or the neutral topic. But those participants given a flag were faced with a more difficult problem: if they strained the dye out of the sand with the flag, the dye would then discolor the flag. They would be besmirching a key icon of people's worldview. The study found that those participants who had been thinking neutral thoughts solved the task with the flag quite quickly, and they rated the task as fairly easy—comparable to those who had been given the white cloth. On the other hand, the participants who had been thinking about death really struggled and took 70 percent longer to solve the problem than did those who had been asked the neutral questions. Apparently, when people are thinking about death, they are especially motivated to protect any icons that remind them of their cultural worldview. In the face of their own mortality, people are motivated to protect anything that reflects upon their cultures, and this includes not befouling the American flag in the course of a psychology study.[13]

Terror management theory may sound a little bit wacky, and in the early days of its research program, it had a rather limited following. But that changed rather abruptly after September 11, 2001. The United States had just witnessed widespread death and destruction from terrorist attacks, and it appeared that its culture was under direct assault. The whole nation was forced to confront its own mortality. The overall reaction of people living in the United States aligned rather neatly with what would be expected of a national effort to achieve symbolic immortality. Patriotism skyrocketed, people became more likely to trust the government to take care of them, many condemned the worldviews of people from other countries, particularly those living in Muslim nations, the military showed a large jump in enrollments, and religiosity temporarily spiked upward. While Americans as a whole had leaned right politically beforehand, the political center of gravity shifted decidedly further to the right, and the Republicans made large gains during the next midterm elections. The world witnessed a real-life confirmation of many of terror management theory's predictions, and the theory attracted a much broader following.

The theory remains somewhat controversial and still has its share of detractors, with some researchers questioning how reliable some of these findings are. With this in mind, Lihan Chen, Rachele Benjamin, Yingchi Guo, Addison Lai, and I applied a set of rigorous statistical meta-analyses of the entire underlying database of the terror management literature to assess whether the findings were valid. Overall, we found that in general there was good evidence for the theory's validity.[14]

## Dying to Matter

A key reason why thoughts of our own mortality are so bothersome is that they are at odds with our motivation to believe that our lives are significant. How much can our lives really matter if we're just an animal spending a brief time on earth, destined to become dust? Much research has found that people have powerful desires to feel that their life matters in the grand scheme of things. People who feel that their life is significant tend to have much better psychological well-being and health. The feeling that one's life matters has been found to be one of the strongest predictors of living a meaningful life. We desire to feel that our lives are significant and special; we wish our lives to transcend our mundane physical realities. The fact that we are just another kind of animal, with animalistic urges, foibles, and an inherently weak physical body, runs counter to this desire to feel that our lives can transcend our earthly limitations. Sometimes it can feel bothersome when we reflect on our animal natures. Or, as one of the founders of terror management theory, Sheldon Solomon, put it in his inimitable words: "The explicit awareness that you are a breathing piece of defecating meat destined to die, and are ultimately no more significant than, let's say a lizard or a potato, is not especially uplifting." Our desires to reach for the stars and to feel that our existences are special are undermined by the gross reality that our existence is just like that of other biological creatures.[15]

People strive to feel that their lives matter by trying to distance themselves from other animals. The Bible noted that the first thing that Adam and Eve did upon eating from the Tree of Knowledge was to try to cover up their nakedness in shame—their newly recognized resemblance to animals caused them to recoil in disgust. Such revulsion at our animal natures is not just something that people learned from Judeo-Christian teachings but is found around the world. For example, a review of all of the small-scale societies in the world that have been studied by anthropologists found that there are norms for people in every culture to make efforts to hide themselves from others when they are defecating or when they are having sex. People do not want to be seen when they are driven by these biological urges, which they have in common with other animals. Other species are rather shameless in comparison—dogs certainly don't share these same modesties. The desire that people have to hide from their creaturely natures gets even more pronounced when they consider their mortality. Research finds that when people have reflected on their mortality, they are more likely to prefer an essay that describes how humans are starkly different from other animals as opposed to one that emphasizes that humans are just another kind of animal. In our efforts to aspire for symbolic immortality, we want to make sure to fortify any walls that distinguish our species from other animals.[16]

But our efforts to highlight our uniqueness are undermined because our creaturely nature is never too far away. It doesn't matter how accomplished one might be, or how refined an image one tries to cultivate. Someone might be dressed to the nines at an evening at the opera, praising the hints of cloves and stone fruits that they detect in their glass of Bordeaux, and going on about their concerns about the latest humanitarian crisis. But that same person, upon returning to their bedroom that evening with their partner, may find themselves on all fours, rutting, panting, grunting, moaning, body sweaty and face contorted into a strange grimace, as they exchange bodily fluids. The beastly aspects of sex can be quite bothersome, despite how much pleasure people derive from them, and many people can feel quite ashamed of their sexual urges. Much of this shame surely comes from the ways religions speak about sex. A common feature of many religions in the world is to condemn the pleasures associated with sex and to encourage people to repress their animalistic urges. For example, Jewish law forbids masturbation, and Catholicism maintains that sex should be limited to procreation: better yet, people should aspire to celibacy and become spiritually pure like the nuns and priests. Some fundamentalist Islamic states threaten the death penalty for premarital sex, and though Hinduism has an ancient manual, the *Kama Sutra*, that offers guidelines for achieving sexual pleasure, the religion strongly condemns any sex outside marriage.

The fact that sex is so often cast in such strongly moralistic terms and is subject to so many religious restrictions highlights the challenges that people face in their efforts to transcend their animalistic urges. The inherent conflicts between the powerful sexual urges that people have and their desires to transcend their creaturely nature results in sex being the basis of so many people's anxieties. Sigmund Freud felt that a key role of civilization was to curb people's libidinous urges, but given how potent people's animal instincts were, this often leads people to develop persistent neuroses. Indeed, Freud viewed people's primal animalistic urges to be the underlying cause of almost all of people's psychopathologies.

While most psychologists question many of Freud's views about sex, they would agree that sex is a common feature in many people's anxieties.

Sex creates a predicament for people. People have strong creaturely desires, but these can commonly provoke anxieties and neuroses. In the face of these anxieties, people will often talk about sex in ways that disguise its more unseemly aspects. People instead focus on the sublime romantic aspects of sex, which are celebrated in poetry, song, and romantic comedies. They use euphemisms to describe sexual acts, such as "making love," "sleeping with," or, in the case of the Bible, "to know" another. People strive to control their neurotic anxieties by downplaying the animalistic aspects of sex and focusing instead on the emotional connections with their partner. One study explored how thoughts about mortality affected how people felt about sex. After answering some questions about their mortality or a neutral topic, the participants were shown a list of statements that characterized sex. Some of these statements captured the animalistic side of sex, for example, "Feeling my partner's sweat on my body," "Feeling my genitals respond sexually," and "Tasting bodily fluids." Other statements emphasized the more transcendent romantic aspects of sex, such as "Opening up emotionally with my partner," "Being loved by my partner," and "Connecting spiritually." The participants were asked to select those items that were the most appealing to them about sex. The study found that people who were more neurotic found the animalistic aspects of sex, but not the romantic aspects, to be less appealing when they reflected upon their mortality in comparison to those who were thinking neutral thoughts. When people are aspiring for a sense of symbolic immortality, they have a stronger desire to couch sex in ways that transcends its animalistic urges.[17]

## Turning to God

As the hundreds of experiments from terror management theory have demonstrated, people often respond to thoughts about their mortality by aspiring for symbolic immortality—they hope that some aspect of their identity can continue on after their death. People can do various things to cultivate these feelings, such as by having children and recognizing parts of themselves continuing to exist in their child. Some may donate a small fortune to an institution or organization and thereby ensure they'll be remembered, by, for example, having their name emblazoned somewhere on a plaque or on a building. Or, in my own case, by writing a book, where my words and ideas could continue to exist even after I've departed. But there are limits to how well our anxieties can be assuaged by these efforts for symbolic immortality. As Woody Allen put it, "I don't want to achieve immortality through my work. I want to achieve it through not dying." This remark points to the second way that people often respond to thoughts about their own death: they come to desire *literal* immortality. We want the stories that we are telling about our lives to continue indefinitely.

Throughout recorded history, people from around the world have shared one particular fantasy. They imagined that there are ways to gain immortality, such as by visiting a mystical fountain of youth or by ingesting various magical substances. In Greek mythology, people were believed to achieve immortality by consuming ambrosia; the ancient Hindu text the Rig Veda similarly describes the immortal properties of drinking *amrita*. Likewise, many medieval alchemists in Europe succumbed to mercury poisoning in their efforts to concoct a potion that would enable them to live forever. You can identify similar beliefs in Japanese folklore, where people seek out the magical springs of a mystical Mount Horai to gain immortality, or in Alexander the Great's quest for the Fountain of Youth.

More recently, people have been trying to pursue immortality in other ways. People discuss the possibility of uploading their consciousness into the cloud to achieve a kind of digital immortality. Futurists, such as Ray Kurzweil, promise that a kind of near immortality may be obtained when science is able to insert nanobots into our bloodstream that would continue to patch up any cellular wear and tear from the inside, thereby keeping our bodies in a perpetual state of youth. Several people, including baseball great Ted Williams, have spent small fortunes to have their bodies or heads cryogenically frozen after their death, with the hope that they would be brought back to life in the future once medical science has solved the problem of mortality.

Our physical bodies place some cruel limits on our fantasies to live forever, and at least for the time being, it doesn't seem realistic to expect that anyone's life will be immortal on earth. But it's an entirely different matter for our souls. People the world over are deeply committed to the belief that some core internal aspect of their identity will continue on even after their bodies have long decayed. These beliefs in an immortal soul are common across religions, even though the details differ so much. Christianity and Islam ensure that one's soul will spend an eternity in either heaven or hell, Hinduism promises that one's soul will be reincarnated into a different life-form, and many tribal religions envision that one will continue to live on as a ghost or a spirit. Religions are found in all cultural groups on the planet, and virtually all of them promise some kind of immortality of one's soul or, at the very least, are somewhat ambiguous about what happens to people's minds after they die.[18]

But the problem is, no one can be certain what awaits them after they die. As Hamlet stated, "Death, the undiscovered country from whose bourn no traveler returns." Living with the awareness that the unknown awaits us is a rather terrifying prospect, and people often seek God to receive some solace. As former talk show host Larry King argued, "I think the only reason for religion is death. If you didn't die, there would be no religion." A key reason that religions are so appealing is that they promise that there is more to our existence than the lives we've been leading. They render the life story that we are telling to be but a single chapter confined to earth, with the assurance that the story will continue in some form in another cosmic realm. What could be a more effective counter to people's existential anxieties than the promise that one's soul will never die?

People's religious leanings are tightly interwoven with their fears of dying. We can see how the two are inseparable in some terror management studies that have found that when people are reminded of their mortality they respond by reporting greater beliefs in God. In general, there is more evidence for religion whenever there is more presence of death. Religious beliefs spike when people encounter life-threatening situations, and studies have found that encounters with natural disasters or war are associated with increased religiosity. When people confront the possibility that they may die, they are more likely to turn to God. There is much truth to the expression, "there are no atheists in foxholes."[19]

Religions play a key role in helping to quell people's anxieties. When people are worried, or struggling, they are more likely to turn to God to help them to cope with the difficulties in life. Indeed, researchers have identified these calming effects among religious participants in their patterns of brain activation. For example, the psychologists Michael Inzlicht, Ian McGregor, Jacob

Hirsh, and Kyle Nash measured the brain activity of Canadian university students when they made simple errors while completing a task. Whenever the students made an error, the researchers identified a burst of neural activation that was centered around the anterior cingulate cortex (ACC). This brain region, as we discussed in Chapter 4, is a key hub in the salience network, and it signals to people whenever they have experienced something that needs their immediate attention—this cortical alarm system would go off when the students realized that they had made an error. The researchers had also asked the students to indicate the degree that they believed in God. When analyzing the results, the researchers identified a striking pattern: the more that participants said they believed in God, the less pronounced was their neural activation in the ACC when they made errors. Religion seemed to be exerting palliative effects on people's minds: they were less bothered by the errors that they made. In many ways, Karl Marx seemed to have it right when he declared religion as the opium of the people. It can dull the anxieties that people have about their lives.[20]

These palliative effects of religion are only recently being appreciated by scientists. Religions don't just help calm people's feelings about all of the stress in their lives; it also has direct benefits on their physical and mental health as well. Participating in a religion, especially if one is regularly attending services at a house of worship, is associated with lower rates of mortality across a variety of health conditions and, in particular, protects people from so-called deaths of despair, such as suicide, alcoholic liver disease, and drug overdoses. Research finds that among people who develop cancer or those who have cardiovascular disease, those who are more religious suffer from fewer physical symptoms and report better well-being. Religions seem to provide these kinds of health benefits because it helps people feel more optimistic about their situation. They feel they can turn to God to help them out, and they also benefit from the social support they receive from their religious communities.[21]

Another benefit of religions is that they offer people a worldview to explain what is happening around them. For example, religions provide an origin account of how people came to be: every society has an origin story as part of their religious beliefs. And religions provide ultimate explanations for why events in the world are occurring. These explanations provide a sense of order to the chaos of the world. But religions do not have a monopoly on providing worldviews that can explain what is happening. Science also offers a competing perspective on why things are as they are, and since the Enlightenment, people have increasingly turned to scientific accounts to make sense of what is happening around them. Like religions, scientific worldviews can provide people with a sense of order. People can feel at ease knowing that events do not happen randomly but are governed by natural laws. Science can also help people feel optimistic in the face of their challenges, as they can count on science to provide solutions to many of the pressing problems of the world, such as helping to create an effective COVID vaccine in a relatively short period of time. These aspects of scientific worldviews can also be helpful in providing people with some optimism about how they can face the challenges ahead.

Nonetheless, despite the many practical benefits that scientific worldviews provide people, they suffer from one big drawback— they don't seem to provide people with the sense that their lives are meaningful. Dunigan Folk, Bastiaan Rutjens, Michiel van Elk, and I investigated American adults' feelings about meaning in life together with their views on science and religion. We found that belief in God was reliably associated with stronger feelings of meaning in life, while faith in science was associated with less meaning in life, even among a sample of scientists, who are obviously very committed to a scientific worldview. Despite all of the many ways that science has improved our lives by enhancing our abilities to control the world we live in—the striking boost in people's lifespans around the world is just one obvious example—the scientific worldview doesn't do a good job of soothing our existential anxieties. For example, Darwinism describes a world where life-forms emerged through the cold calculus of natural selection, an endless series of random genetic mutations that increased a species' survival advantage. A worldview that is based on the survival of the fittest hardly offers much guidance when one is questioning the purpose of one's life, nor does it provide any solace when, say, one's child has just been diagnosed with a life-threatening disease. In contrast, religions provide people with many existential benefits. Religious believers can feel encouraged by praying and petitioning for some supernatural aid and comforted that they are connected with hidden mystical forces that may be able to help them out. In contrast, the scientific worldview comes up short as it doesn't offer any existential reassurance.[22]

By connecting people with the apparent supernatural forces that surround them, religion provides one of its most important benefits. It helps people to feel that, in the grand scheme of things, their lives have some cosmic significance, are meaningful, and transcend their mundane physical nature. Religion makes people feel that they are participating in something immense and important. This sense that one is connected to something much larger than oneself was emphasized by the Zen philosopher Alan Watts, who said, "You are something the whole universe is doing in the same way that a wave is something that the whole ocean is doing." People who are religious can feel that their lives are connected to powerful forces that envelop them.[23]

## Losing Religion

As we've seen, religions provide people with various psychological benefits, and these benefits help to explain why religions are found in every society around the world. But the many psychological benefits that people receive from religion raise an important question: What happens to people when they leave their religion? When people walk away from their religion, will they also leave all of these psychological benefits behind?

This is not a hypothetical question, as in recent decades large swaths of the population from many countries have been leaving organized religion. Even in the United States, which has long been recognized as the most fundamentalist Christian country, there has been a sea change in the number of people walking away from religion. At the turn of the millennium, approximately 70 percent of Americans belonged to a church, mosque, or synagogue. By 2020, this number had dropped below half of the United States population to 47 percent—the first time in recorded history that a majority of Americans did not belong to a house of worship. People are not just becoming less likely to attend religious services, but they are also increasingly saying that they do not identify as a believer. When posed the question, "What religion do you follow?," in 1972 only 5 percent of Americans said "none," yet by 2020 this number had reached 30 percent. If these trends continue, the United States is expected to become a country that consists of a majority of nonbelievers by 2070.[24]

We might wonder what a world of nonbelievers would be like. When people walk away from their religions and come to base their worldview exclusively on an atheistic scientific understanding, they face some existential penalties. Compared with believers, atheists report having less meaning in their lives. Studies find that atheists have a more difficult time embracing a sense of purpose than do believers. Most notably, atheists are considerably less likely to feel that their life matters in the grand scheme of things. Moreover, atheists suffer more than believers in a wide range of measures of well-being and health. Atheists appear to pay a significant existential cost for leaving their religions, and with so many regions of the planet secularizing at a rapid pace, this suggests that much of the world may be facing an ominous existential crisis.[25]

But there is one consideration that should dampen any worries about a looming global existential crisis. Most people who turn their back on the church will likely not face a sharp uptick in their existential concerns, and this is because people tend not to change all that much after they part ways with their religion. Most people who turn away from their religion still preserve a lot of the attitudes, moral values, social networks, and practices that they had previously held when they were religious. Although people who have left their religion may have stepped away from the formal religious doctrine that they used to worship, most people still hold on to a lot of the same psychological habits that they had before. In many countries, a majority of people who leave their religion continue to hold on to their spiritual intuitions. They may no longer believe in the dogma of their former religion, but they still have the strong sense that there is far more to their existence than that of their mortal lives on earth.[26]

In 2017, a survey found that 27 percent of Americans identified as being "spiritual but not religious," representing the rise of a relatively new denomination. In the same survey, only 18 percent of Americans identified as atheists, reflecting that it was more common for people who had left their religion to maintain some sort of spiritual beliefs as opposed to giving them up altogether. People who identify as spiritual but not religious maintain various kinds of mystical and spiritual beliefs, but they aren't following any particular religion's doctrine. Rather, they are choosing their beliefs à la carte from a host of various options. Spiritual but not religious people may choose an eclectic mix of spiritual practices from different faiths such as yoga or meditation, supernatural beliefs such as tarot cards, and various paranormal phenomena such as aliens or ghosts, and they may embrace alternative healing strategies such as psychedelic drugs or shamanism. In stark contrast to the religiously devout, who typically are not presented with a choice of what scriptures to believe, the spiritual but not religious celebrate their ability to choose their path to the afterlife. As Elizabeth Gilbert, the author of the bestseller *Eat Pray Love*, puts it: "You have every right to cherry-pick when it comes to moving your spirit and finding peace in God. . . . You take whatever works from wherever you can find it and you keep moving toward the light." Those who are spiritual but not religious have abandoned formal religious dogma in favor of a do-it-yourself approach to the supernatural.[27]

The choice to abandon the security of a centuries-old faith in favor of a custom-made spirituality may seem rather stark, and we might wonder how well people are managing who have taken this enormous supernatural gamble. How are the spiritual but not religious people faring overall? Will Jettinghoff, Dunigan Folk, Paniz Radjaee, Ara Norenzayan, Aiyana Willard, and I conducted a study to see how the lives of spiritual but not religious people compare with those of atheists and religious believers. Are the spiritual but not religious people more similar to atheists, with whom they share a lack of commitment to any particular religion? Or are they more similar to religious believers, in that they both believe in a spiritual realm that transcends their mundane worlds? First, we considered the kinds of mystical beliefs that people maintained. Quite strikingly, we found that religious people and spiritual but not religious people were overall very similar to each other in terms of their mystical and supernatural beliefs. While the content of these beliefs varied somewhat between the two groups—with religious people expressing greater belief in God and an afterlife and spiritual people reporting slightly more belief in karma, the law of attraction, and superstitions—both reported having many more mystical beliefs than our sample of atheists. There isn't a great deal of distance between spiritual but not religious people and conventionally religious people in terms of their commitment to the supernatural realm.[28]

How are the spiritual but not religious people doing in terms of their existential anxieties? We found that, overall, conventionally religious people tend to be the most likely to say that they have a meaningful life, whereas atheists are far less likely to feel this way. Spiritual but not religious people fall smack in the middle, feeling that their lives are more meaningful than those of atheists but not quite as meaningful as those of religious people. We explored what might be the most likely reason behind the greater sense of meaning among the conventionally religious and the spiritual but not religious. Curiously, we found that it was people's supernatural beliefs that predicted whether they felt they had meaning in their lives. It didn't seem to matter what people believed in: whether it was belief in God, the law of attraction, or karma, any kind of supernatural belief was associated with greater meaning in life. It seems that beliefs that connect people to something much bigger than their own lives, that transcend the physical world, are associated with feeling that one's life is meaningful. Our research confirms that atheists seem to struggle more with living in an existential vacuum, but that those who maintain some sort of supernatural belief after leaving their religion can satisfy their existential needs.

We seem to depend on the supernatural realm to cope with our mortality. By feeling connected to something that transcends us, we can feel that, unlike our bodies, our souls continue to exist in the hereafter. These connections to the supernatural play a key role in numbing our existential anxieties. They serve to help us cope with difficult times, and they can make our lives feel more significant and meaningful.

As much as death can be a problem for our meaning frameworks, there are many things that happen to us in our lives that can also assault our sense of meaning. In particular, suffering is something that is inherent in the human condition, and our sufferings can shatter our most important meaning frameworks. But as we'll see in the next chapter, our experiences with suffering can both bolster and devastate our pursuit of a meaningful life.

Chapter 8

# When Life Breaks
# Our Stories

God whispers to us in our pleasures . . .
but shouts in our pains: it is His megaphone to rouse
a deaf world. . . . It removes the veil; it plants the flag
of truth within the fortress of the rebel soul.

C. S. Lewis, *The Problem of Pain*

In the decades following the Second World War, the East Germans faced a problem. They wished to show off to the world their recently established new communist society, to demonstrate the supposed superiority of their ways. But the new government's efforts were being starkly undermined by a stubbornly growing problem: the regime was enormously unpopular with its own citizens. In the years following the war, more than three million East Germans had escaped to West Germany. The East Germans created the Ministry for State Security, commonly known as the Stasi—the secret police—in an effort to combat the problem of dissidents. But

219

the Stasi would take a slightly different tack than other totalitarian societies. Unlike the Soviet Union, where physical torture and killings were commonly used to control dissidents, the East Germans preferred tactics that didn't leave any visible scars. The Stasi came to employ psychological torture on a vast scale toward any who were suspected of being unfaithful to the state. They achieved this by relentlessly striving to break down the meaning frameworks of suspected dissidents.

The Stasi established the Department of Operative Psychology, and the policies they enacted are considered to be some of the worst abuses ever inflicted on the public by psychologists. A key goal of the department was to create within the state's enemies a condition of *zersetzung*—a word that translates as decomposition. The goal was to decompose and break down the target's meaning frameworks. The Stasi launched a comprehensive assault on the dissidents' ways of living to the point that they could no longer make sense of what was happening around them. The Stasi aspired to leave targets in a disoriented and demoralized state where they felt terrified and utterly alone and questioned their own sanity. The Stasi relied on a number of elaborate sinister methods in its efforts to create a state of *zersetzung* in their targets.[1]

As a first step toward achieving *zersetzung*, the Stasi strove to tear apart an individual's sense of belongingness. Often the Stasi would aim to destroy the family itself. Sometimes secret agents would try to seduce a target's spouse, with the goal of undermining their relationship. They would seek to turn mothers against their children by informing them that their children were involved in illegal activities. They would foster distrust within the target's network of friends, by spreading false rumors that the target was an informant of the Stasi itself, causing their friends to cut off all contact, which further isolated them. Targets could quickly find themselves all alone, with no one to turn to. The Stasi also spread false rumors to besmirch the target's public reputation, such as suggesting that the target had a drinking problem or was involved in immoral activities. The Stasi achieved this through a variety of unusual schemes, such as placing classified ads in the target's name offering various kinds of illicit sexual services. The cumulative result of these assaults on the target's reputation could be severe and sometimes resulted in the person losing their job.

The Stasi maintained a massive surveillance state, which enabled it to keep a constant eye on its targets. The Stasi would regularly intercept people's mail and tap their phones, and spies would follow a target's every move. When a target left their home, the Stasi would sometimes break into their apartment and set up hidden microphones and cameras to record the target's private life. With the knowledge that the Stasi was able to gain about its targets' lives, it could stage elaborate and apparently coincidental chains of events, which would leave its victims completely dumbstruck and mystified, no longer able to tell what was real and what was staged.

The Stasi also endeavored to disrupt all that was familiar in the targets' lives. The targets would return to their homes to find that the contents of their tea and coffee jars had been reversed, their alarms had been set to 5:00 a.m. instead of 7:00 a.m., or objects had been rearranged on shelves. Nothing seemed to make sense anymore. The targets would be woken by phone calls in the middle of the night with no one on the other end. Sometimes their electricity or water would suddenly be shut off. The targets could no longer feel safe or in control even in their own homes, and it was commonplace for the targets to begin to question their own sanity.

These cruel *zersetzung* practices inflicted enormous damage throughout the country, and thousands of those targeted would go on to develop serious mental health problems. The Stasi could be merciless in its efforts and especially targeted those who seemed to be psychologically unstable and thereby more vulnerable to the ministry's *zersetzung* tactics. Sometimes, the *zersetzung* was so overwhelmingly disruptive that the targets were driven to take their own lives.[2]

The ruthless efforts of the Stasi ultimately served to break people's stories about themselves. In the aftermath of the ministry's *zersetzung*, the targets no longer knew who they could trust, nor sometimes who they even were. But while the Stasi may have been somewhat unique in how it intentionally tried to dismantle the meaning frameworks of its targets in such a brutal manner, the effects of *zersetzung* are disturbingly common. There are many experiences in people's lives that can also wreak havoc with their meaning frameworks, leaving them in a disoriented and broken state. In this chapter we will explore other ways that events in our lives can damage our meaning frameworks.

## Boredom and *Zersetzung*

Sadly, there is no shortage of ways that our life experiences can shatter our meaning frameworks, and we'll consider here a broad range of ways that people's sense of meaning can get undermined. Some kinds of experiences, such as traumatic life events, can cause enormous upheaval in people's life stories. But the ways that people's meaning frameworks can be disrupted is not always so cataclysmic, and some experiences can attack people's meaning frameworks in a more persistent and gnawing fashion.

Let's start by considering what might seem to be a rather trivial meaning threat that people frequently experience. One of the most corrosive forces that undermines people's sense of meaning in their lives is boredom. We all get bored on occasion, and the unpleasant feeling motivates people to escape it. Our feelings of boredom signal that we have an absence of meaning in our current activities—we realize that what we are doing feels meaningless. We may recognize that our current activities do not have any sufficient purpose, nor relate to anything that we value. In many respects, our feelings of boredom are very much the opposite of the feelings we get when our lives feel meaningful.[3]

People can get bored from a wide variety of different activities. Attempting something that is too easy can lead to boredom because the activity is insufficiently challenging. Imagine how boring it would be to work on a slow-moving assembly line where your job was to separate the white widgets from the black ones. But the flip side is also true, and things that are too difficult can also elicit boredom because they lie outside an individual's ability to feel that they are making any progress toward them. A math novice sitting through a lecture on advanced calculus would likely soon become terribly bored. Some events are pretty much universally boring, such as being stuck in traffic, waiting in line, or being put on hold, as virtually no one is able to derive much meaning from them. However, much of what bores people is entirely subjective, reflecting just how different people's meaning frameworks are from one another. For example, two friends might watch a sporting event together, with one, an avid fan, being so engrossed that they don't notice anything else that is happening around them. In contrast, the other, who knows nothing about the sport, would be bored to tears as they watched players chase a ball for no apparent rhyme or reason. When people are unable to find any meaning in an activity, they will likely experience profound feelings of boredom. We feel engaged when we are doing something that integrates with our meaning frameworks, and we can feel bored when it's an activity that we are unable to relate to anything that we care about. Because people have different bases of meanings in their lives, we can get bored by different things.

Our feelings of boredom can be excruciating when we're unable to escape them. "If I were to imagine Hell," the existential psychologist Erich Fromm offered, "it would be the place where you were continually bored." Our judicial systems are well aware of how unbearable boredom can be, as it's a key part of the penal system. Criminals are commonly placed in prisons, where they are tormented by the boredom that comes with having too little to do, sometimes for years at a time. And those who break the rules of prison life may find themselves with the even more inhumane punishment of solitary confinement, where the tortures of boredom are further amplified. Some have argued that relying on boredom to punish people is unnecessarily cruel. In his book *In Defense of Flogging*, the criminal justice professor Peter Moskos goes so far as to argue that it would be more humane for societies to whip their prisoners than to submit them to years of boredom in prison.[4]

We find boredom to be so unbearable because it alienates us from all that we care about. Boredom, which Jean-Paul Sartre calls "the leprosy of the soul," obstructs our pursuit of a meaningful life. It leaves us without a sense of purpose, stuck doing things that we feel just don't matter. People hate being bored, and some organizations make elaborate efforts to reduce people's boredom. For example, people tend to get bored and frustrated when they are at the baggage area of the airport waiting for their luggage to arrive. Some airports have come up with the solution of moving the baggage areas farther away from the gates. This solution does nothing to speed up the amount of time that it takes for people to pick up their bags, but because people are forced to walk through a long and convoluted path to get to the baggage area, they are given something that provides them with a sense of purpose, and as a result they don't get as bored.

Boredom is not a trivial inconvenience; it can actually cause people much harm. Because people find their bored feelings so torturous, they sometimes engage in destructive behavior just to escape them. Many of people's riskiest and worst behaviors are done to avoid boredom. One account from an online prisoner message board put it this way: "At the end of the day it's the fucking boredom. I'm surprised prisons aren't worse than what they are. You ever see what happens when you give nothing to do to high schoolers or middle schoolers? It won't last long, they'll come up with something to do which will likely hurt someone or break something." People would lead far less risky lifestyles if it wasn't for their harmful efforts to escape their boredom. A primary reason people abuse substances is because they find their sober lives to be tedious. The altered states of consciousness that alcohol, cannabis, and illicit substances elicit can relieve people from the boredom of their everyday existence. Bored people are more likely to become promiscuous, pursuing short-lived sexual opportunities in an effort to make their lives seem more interesting. Boredom also leads people to gamble, where the risk of striking it big or losing it all provides a cheap thrill to escape the monotony. Even more problematic, boredom can lead people to engage in sadistic behaviors. One study found that high school students who reported more boredom were more likely to agree with items such as "I enjoy physically hurting people," or "I enjoy tormenting people." Søren Kierkegaard was not mistaken in his declaration that boredom was "the root of all evil."[5]

To get an appreciation of just how far people will go to escape boredom, consider this curious psychology experiment. American students were directed to an empty room where they were to spend some time alone. They weren't allowed to bring in any phones, books, or anything to distract themselves with. They were asked to sit by themselves with nothing but their thoughts. However, in the room was an electric shock generator, which the participants were wired up to. At the beginning of the study the participants had all received a single electric shock to learn just how unpleasant it was— the shock really stung. The participants were informed that they were to sit in the room alone with their thoughts for fifteen minutes, but if they wanted, they could press the button on the shock generator to deliver more of these unpleasant shocks to themselves. This seemed like a crazy suggestion: Why would anyone want to shock themselves? But it turns out that many of the participants felt that delivering an electric shock to themselves was a more desirable activity than just sitting by themselves. One-quarter of women and a full two-thirds of men opted to shock themselves rather than to just sit bored with their thoughts. One man shocked himself 190 times during those fifteen minutes! This gives an idea of just how much people hate the feelings of boredom—they'd rather hurt themselves instead. Indeed, boredom can sometimes lead people to engage in self-harm and even suicide. As the psychologist Roy Baumeister put it, "Suicidal people resemble acutely bored people: the present seems endless and vaguely unpleasant, and whenever one checks the clock, one is surprised at how little time has actually passed."[6]

We all collectively experienced new thresholds of boredom during the COVID pandemic. During the lockdown people were unable to get together with friends, many lost their jobs and had nothing to occupy their days, and people had few places to go to. People came to realize just how long a day could feel like if they were unable to pursue their usual distractions. Many people turned to television to pass the time, but there are limits to how long people can stay engaged with their programs, and some claimed that their viewing felt pointless, and the repetitious news coverage became monotonous. People started to do things that they had never had sufficient time or interest to try before, such as baking bread, gardening, or learning a musical instrument, but many of these efforts faded away as the pandemic stretched out longer and longer. As much as parents may love their children, they came to realize how much harder parenting was when their children were constantly in need of attention. One stay-at-home mom likened her pandemic isolation with her three-year-old to the movie *Castaway*: "We speak an entirely different language that no one else understands. We are literally on an island alone, together—he is my Wilson and I am his Tom Hanks." The endless feelings of tedium contributed to the sharp spike in depression and anxiety that occurred over the pandemic.[7]

Boredom presents a real threat to our meaning frameworks and can often bring out the worst in people. However, just as with other kinds of meaning threats, people will sometimes respond constructively to their boredom by trying to boost their sense of meaning in other ways. Our feelings convey information to us that we rely on for guiding our behaviors. Our feelings of hunger indicate that our stomachs are empty and lead us into the kitchen, whereas our lonely feelings alert us that our belongingness needs aren't being met and we may reach out to a friend. Our feelings of boredom also serve as a valuable signal: they signal that our current activities are insufficiently meaningful, and these can sometimes lead people to seek out new activities that are more meaningful to them. Sometimes people respond to their boredom by becoming more curious about the world or more creative. Bored people are more likely to engage in nostalgic reflections, as they attempt to regain a sense of meaning by considering the past events in their life story. Feelings of boredom also lead people to identify more with their groups and their nationality, as they can derive some meaning from feeling connected to the important groups that they belong to. The meanings that people get from religion are also protective against boredom. In general, religious people report being less bored compared with the nonreligious, even when they're in a psychology experiment engaging in an activity that is designed explicitly to elicit boredom, such as writing down references from the literature about lawn mowing. Our feelings of boredom signal that our current actions are lacking purpose and meaning, and they can function to guide people toward making the efforts needed to lead a more meaningful life.[8]

## *Zersetzung* by Traumatic Life Events

Boredom is one of many ways that people can undergo a *zersetzung* experience, whereby their meaning frameworks begin to erode. But perhaps people endure the most shocking collapse of meaning when they suffer from traumatic life events. Sadly, there is no shortage to the many horrible ways that people can experience trauma—someone may get diagnosed with cancer, a natural disaster may destroy their home, a loved one might die, an accident may leave them paralyzed, or they may be the victim of a criminal assault. It is of course a truism that trauma can be devastating to us. But traumatic events can shatter and overwhelm not just because they cause direct losses—such as loss of certain capabilities or loss of a close relationship—but also because they can cause a massive *zersetzung* experience. Following a traumatic life event, people may be forced to realize that some of their core meaning frameworks no longer hold, and they may no longer be able to make any kind of sense of their lives.

People embrace broad meaning frameworks about themselves, the world, and their place within the world. We rely on these meaning frameworks to predict what will happen and to guide how we should best act, and these meaning frameworks shape the narratives that we tell about ourselves. Broadly speaking, most people narrate their life stories around the ideas that they are good and the world is a benevolent, orderly, and meaningful place, and these narratives enable people to figure out how to live their lives. But after a traumatic event, people may no longer feel that they are inherently good, and the world can feel like a cruel and senseless place. The psychologist Ronnie Janoff-Bulman argues that victims of traumatic life events endure "a double dose of anxiety." In addition to suffering from the direct victimization they have experienced, they now have to contend with the feeling that they no longer understand the world or how to function within it. In studies that compare people who have experienced traumatic life events with those who have thus far avoided any major tragedies, the victims are less likely to agree with statements such as "People are basically kind and helpful," "I am very satisfied with the kind of person I am," or "Through our actions we can prevent bad things from happening to us." Even after many years have passed following their ordeals, the survivors of traumatic life events are less likely to narrate their life stories around the premise *I am good* or that they live in a benevolent, orderly, and meaningful world. The stories about who we are and what our worlds are like are so fundamental to people's lives that when they are devastated by trauma it can feel as though a hole has been blown clear through the center of their being.[9]

In the face of their broken meaning frameworks, people often respond to tragedies by trying to find meaning in them. They are driven to make sense of why the event happened to them and what impact it has had on their lives. This search for meaning is not in vain, as those who are able to find meaning in their tragedies tend to fare far better in their overall well-being and physical health and are better able to get on with their lives and to stop ruminating about the past. In contrast, survivors of trauma who have yet to find sufficient meaning in their tragedies often remain stuck trying to make sense of what happened. They typically have more intrusive thoughts about their trauma, which can continue to cause much distress, even decades later.

For example, one study interviewed Canadian women who were survivors of incest.[10] Although these events had, on average, occurred more than two decades earlier, the women still showed many signs of lingering distress from their traumatic experiences. However, those women who reported that they had been able to find some meaning from their trauma were faring much better and had less distress, higher self-esteem, and better social adjustment compared with those who were still searching for meaning. Similar findings have been observed in people suffering from a wide variety of tragedies, including survivors of the 9/11 terrorist attacks and those suffering from a cancer diagnosis. Religious people often find meaning in their suffering by understanding their trials as part of God's plan for them, which leads them to stop obsessing so much about what has happened, whereas atheists are more likely to try to understand their trauma in terms of causal events in the world.

The ways that traumatic experiences threaten people's meaning frameworks can have lasting effects. We conducted a study to investigate how traumatic life events may impact people's efforts to maintain meaning in their lives. Daniel Randles, Michael Poulin, Roxane Cohen Silver, and I examined the questionnaire responses of a sample of more than 1,600 American adults. The participants were asked whether they had ever experienced any of a long list of traumatic life events, such as enduring a divorce, physical assault, or natural disaster. In addition, the participants were asked some questions about their political attitudes. We were interested to assess whether participants who had past traumatic experiences were more likely to reground themselves by becoming more committed to their political attitudes. This is precisely what we found: the more traumatic experiences that a person had endured, the more likely they were to show regrounding tendencies by having more polarized political views. Trauma appears to cause conservative people to become even more conservative, and liberal people to become more liberal. Interestingly, these victims of traumatic life events showed the same kinds of responses that we have observed in various other studies, where we tried to nudge people into the absurd. Our findings suggest that years after these traumatic events, people are still feeling the lingering aftereffects that challenge their ability to find meaning in their lives, and one way that people respond is by becoming more politically polarized. But traumatic events can upend the meaning in our lives far more deeply than this.[11]

## Broken Life Stories and Suicide

Cedar and Sage (the names are pseudonyms) were two brothers raised in a First Nations reserve in Alberta. Cedar, a very active child, loved to go snowboarding and skateboarding and enjoyed many of the traditional aspects of his culture, such as fishing and hunting. His younger brother, Sage, was a rather shy child who had a deep passion for music. He could often be found practicing some of his tribe's traditional dances, and he had a dream that in the future he would become a famous Aboriginal violinist or perhaps a rapper. Their hobbies offered them some respite from the troubles that were brewing at home. Cedar and Sage were often left on their own, with no adult supervision, as their mother struggled with her addictions. Their problems at home escalated after they saw their mother being abused by a number of men that she was seeing. Their troubles ultimately caught the attention of child welfare services, and the boys were taken away from their mother and spent a few years moving among foster homes. These were especially difficult times for the boys, and they stopped going to school. Sage fought with his anxieties and started drinking heavily. Sometimes he would have bouts of uncontrollable rage in which he would punch holes in the walls. His mental health got progressively worse, until, at the age of fifteen, he tragically took his own life. Sage's suicide was devastating for Cedar. He felt that he had failed his younger brother and that there must have been something that he could have done to have prevented this tragedy. Four months later, overcome by guilt, Cedar too died by suicide.[12]

Cedar and Sage's story is heartbreaking. Suicide is always devastating, especially when a young person who has so much ahead of them takes their life. But what makes the tragedies of Cedar and Sage even more difficult to bear is to know just how common they are. Their suicides were described in a provincial governmental report in 2016, along with five other suicides of Indigenous teenagers that had recently occurred in the province. In the same month that this report came out, about a dozen teenagers in a First Nations community in Northern Ontario attempted suicide. The province declared a state of emergency as it struggled to find a way to contain this horrific epidemic.[13]

One of Canada's deepest shames is the astonishingly high rate of suicide among its Indigenous youth. On average, their suicide rate is about seven times higher than the national average. Clearly, the country has been failing its Indigenous communities. If we are to try to address these tragedies, we need to ask why the suicide rate of Indigenous youth is so high. At first glance, the answer may seem obvious: the horrors of colonialization and the accompanying brutal treatment and neglect of First Nations communities in Canada are well known and are a likely cause. Suicide rates also tend to peak among adolescents in many cultures as they struggle with the anxieties associated with adolescence. But answering the question of why so many Indigenous youth take their own lives becomes more challenging when we take a closer look at the suicide rates of the different communities. One extensive analysis found that while the suicide rates for some Indigenous communities were far lower than the national average, some other communities had suicide rates that were hundreds of times higher than that of the national average and are among the highest suicide rates on the planet. Any compelling explanation for the high rate of suicide among Indigenous youth needs to consider why the rates vary so much among the different communities.[14]

We can begin to provide an answer to this question by considering one key risk for suicide. Generally, the life stories of most people are integrated and provide a sense of continuity across their lifespan. A healthy life narrative provides a story of how one's identity has a constant thread running through it, despite the changes that people go through as they age and have different experiences. These life narratives connect the episodes of one's past to the present, and further provide a glimpse of the path going forward, resulting in the sense that one's life story is coherent and meaningful. But people who are at risk for suicide often lack this sense of continuity. They don't feel that the different episodes of their lives are tied together. The events of their past feel as though they happened to a different person, and their imagined future doesn't really seem to feel like part of their self. It's hard to care much about one's future self when it feels so disconnected from the present, like a stranger one has never met. And if people don't care enough about their future self, they are at greater risk for suicide.

One study investigated a group of Canadian youth who were receiving treatment for mental illness. About half of this sample was judged to be at high risk for suicide, whereas the other half was not deemed to be at risk. Researchers asked them questions about their lives and identified how much of a sense of continuity they felt in their selves over time. This task was quite straightforward for the group that was at low risk for suicide. A full 94 percent of them were able to identify how their selves felt continuous across their lives. They could describe how they had always been the same person, proceeding through events in the various chapters of their life stories. In stark contrast, this question was extremely challenging for the highly suicidal group—only 12 percent were able to identify a continuous identity that connected the different episodes of their lives. Similar findings have been observed in other groups that are at a high risk for suicide, such as veterans, who are often struggling to reintegrate into society. In response to this, new clinical interventions have been developed to try to enhance a sense of continuity in people's life stories, with promising results for reducing suicidal ideation.[15]

Having a sense of continuity in one's life story is an important protective factor against suicide, and it is also key to understanding the high suicide rates of some Indigenous communities. But to understand people's life stories more fully, we need to consider them in the context of the cultures that have shaped them. People's own feelings of continuity of their selves are shaped a great deal by their sense of continuity of their cultures. But the stories of many Indigenous communities do not have a clear sense of continuity across time because of the massive disruptions of colonialism. Historically, the Canadian government has viewed Indigenous culture as backward, and for more than a century, the government sought to stamp it out by forcing Indigenous people to assimilate into the mainstream culture. Indigenous children were taken from their homes, often never to return, and raised in underfunded and barbaric residential schools where they were punished for speaking their own languages. The ways of their ancestors were often no longer available to them; they were no longer able to live off their former lands. For many Indigenous youth in Canada, it is not at all obvious how their current ways of living are connected with the lifestyles of their ancestors.

Although colonialism was deeply disruptive and traumatic for all Indigenous groups, the different communities vary in terms of how much their present culture has been severed from its past. The psychologists Michael Chandler and Christopher Lalonde studied the almost two hundred Indigenous bands that live within the province of British Columbia. They documented how much these individual bands had the presence of various markers of cultural continuity. For example, some of the bands had taken steps to secure Aboriginal title to their traditional lands; some had obtained certain rights for self-government; and some had been able to establish officially recognized cultural facilities to preserve their past traditions, whereas other bands had not. In total, the researchers identified six different markers of cultural continuity that varied across the bands, and they compared how the presence of each of these markers related to the youth suicide rates of the individual bands, controlling for other relevant variables, such as socioeconomic status, population density, and geographical location. The researchers found that some of the bands had all six of these markers of cultural continuity, and for these bands their suicide rates were approximately the same, or even lower, than that of the national average. On the other extreme, some of the bands had none of these markers of cultural continuity, and their suicide rates were many times that of the national average. In the bands that had an intermediate number of these cultural continuity markers, the suicide rate was in lockstep with the number of protective features their communities had. These findings underscore the importance of having a life story that is connected to the past. Any features of one's past culture that continue to exist, and can be incorporated into one's life story, help provide a foundation to one's sense of identity, and this is protective against suicide.[16]

Though the suicide rates of some Indigenous communities are depressingly high, the risk of suicide is a problem that all people around the world must confront. Whenever people's life stories get broken, they are at greater risk for mental health problems, anxiety, and suicidal ideation. A lack of cultural continuity is one way that people's life stories can get disrupted, but many other factors can shatter one's life story. One of the highest risk factors for suicide is when people's lives unfold in a manner that falls far short of their expectations. People's expectations for their lives are core features of their meaning frameworks. As people go about their lives, they have a set of expectations that allows them to feel a sense of control over their world, as they are able to predict what kinds of things will happen to them. But sometimes people confront events in their lives that are grossly at odds with what they expect. People often have positive expectations for how their lives will unfold, and when these expectations are violated, they can experience a tremendous amount of psychological pain. In particular, when people experience a fall from grace—when they lose a sense of status they had previously enjoyed—they can suffer a devastating disruption in their life stories.

The particular psychological pain that comes with a failure to live up to one's past expectations helps to explain one of the more ironic facts of suicide. When one surveys the different lifestyles of people in the world to consider who might be most at risk for suicide, it may seem that the people with the most disadvantages in their lives should be the ones who are most at risk. After all, the destitute, those born with physical disadvantages, and those that are the targets of discrimination would seem to have some of the least optimistic prospects ahead of them. Yet, strikingly, such people are relatively unlikely to consider suicide. In stark contrast, the people who are most at risk for suicide are those who have largely lived lives full of privilege and advantage. For example, suicide rates are higher in wealthier countries than they are in poor countries. Curiously, it is in the very countries where people generally have their basic needs met that people are more likely to kill themselves. This fact led the nineteenth-century sociologist Emile Durkheim to call suicide "the ransom-money of civilization." He saw a heightened suicide rate as the price that comes with growing modernization.[17]

Looking within the United States, we can see a parallel trend as suicide rates are higher in wealthier states than in poorer states. Likewise, suicide rates are more than twice as high among white

Americans than they are among Black Americans, and suicide is more common among college students, particularly those who have enjoyed higher grades, than they are for students with lower grades or among similarly aged working-class peers. The key reason for this ironic trend is that privileged groups have loftier expectations, which makes them more at risk of falling short of those expectations. In accordance with this logic, the people who are particularly at risk for suicide are those who have recently experienced a sharp downturn in the quality of their lives. When people lose their jobs, they are especially vulnerable to suicide, and national suicide rates spike during recessions. Likewise, people who divorce show a sharp spike in their suicide rates. When college students who are used to receiving good grades start to fail in their courses or are forced to drop out, their suicide rates tick upward. And it is in the first month of imprisonment, as well as in the first month after people have been admitted to a psychiatric hospital, before people have been able to adjust to their new situation, that suicide rates are the highest. With positive expectations, privileged people have further to fall and are more vulnerable.[18]

As noted in Chapter 3, sometimes people's life stories include a *contamination theme*. Some people narrate the arc of their life story as one that began with a favorable early period, when everything was going well, followed by a period when things started to fall apart. They may have broken up with their partner, gone bankrupt, had a child who died, or developed harmful addictions. The contamination theme provides a way for people to interpret a destructive episode in their lives. But when people build their life story around this theme, they tend to take a fatalistic approach to life where they come to expect only failure and hard times ahead. They feel broken by their sudden change in fortune, and their positive life story has been irrevocably destroyed.

Fortunately, people are not bound by a particular life narrative. When people experience a sudden turn of negative events, the decision to narrate their lives around a contamination theme is not inevitable. They have some say in how they construct their life narratives and can rewrite their stories. They can choose which events they view to be most significant and have some say in how they respond to those events. For example, one study found that college students who had adopted a contamination theme became less likely to describe their life narratives in this way after they had graduated: they came to write their life stories in more optimistic ways. But when people's life stories are written around a contamination theme they are frequently in a vulnerable place. These themes have been found to be associated with depression, lower feelings of coherence in one's life, lower self-esteem, lower life satisfaction, and poorer physical health—all of which can be precursors of suicide.[19]

There are other ways that people's meaning frameworks can be broken and contribute to an increased suicide risk. Virtually all major theories of suicide highlight how feelings of disconnection can increase one's risk of suicide. Recall that meaning is ultimately about connections—with other people, a sense of purpose, work, and the transcendent. These kinds of connections help to provide people with a sense that their life is meaningful and are protective against suicide. However, when people lose these kinds of connections, their risk of suicide can increase.[20]

Arguably, the most reliable predictor of suicide risk is feelings of social isolation. As an ultrasocial species we depend on being connected with others, and it can be agonizing when people feel detached from those around them. As T. S. Eliot noted, "There are moments, perhaps not known to everyone, when a man may be nearly crushed by the terrible awareness of his isolation from every other human being."[21] Accordingly, suicide rates closely track various markers of social disconnection: rates are higher in smaller families than larger ones, among divorced or widowed people than married individuals, and among people with fewer rather than larger groups of friends.

The connections that people feel toward their work can also be important for providing a sense of meaning in life. Work can give people a sense of identity, purpose, and mastery, as well as a set of important social relationships. Of course, work can also be tedious and unpleasant and can get in the way of more desirable activities, so it's not uncommon for people to dream about the freedom that they'll enjoy once they retire. But as attractive as retirement and the so-called golden years may seem, for some people the transition from work to retirement can be fraught. Some individuals derive so much of their meaning in life from their work that the experience of leaving their career behind them can be associated with depression, feelings of worthlessness, and suicidal ideation. For these individuals, their transition to retirement can be facilitated by efforts to find other ways of building meaning in their lives.[22]

Religion is also a key source of meaning in many people's lives, as it connects them to mystical forces that transcend the here and now and provides people with the sense that they are part of something much larger than themselves. Religious people are less likely than the nonreligious to report any kind of suicidal ideation. The kinds of meanings that people derive from religion seem protective against suicide, particularly for those who regularly attend a house of worship and feel part of an active religious community.

The classic sociological study of suicide by Durkheim identified the emergence of societal disintegration to be the key cause underlying people's risk for suicide. He felt that the social bonds that used to link individuals to each other were being weakened. The loss of social cohesion that Durkheim witnessed in the nineteenth century threatened the social order, and he considered it to be a by-product of modernization. Durkheim saw that families had become more likely to break apart, people were at a greater risk of being disconnected in their work, communities were becoming less integrated, and religion was losing its grip on people's lives. Durkheim was concerned that as the constraints and traditions of a society weakened, people would find themselves lacking a sense of purpose to guide them, and their mental health would be at risk.

Durkheim was ahead of his time, as the signs of social disintegration that he identified in Western Europe in the nineteenth century have only gotten worse in the existential vacuum that pervades the twenty-first century. In many countries, some of the key connections that provide meaning in people's lives have gotten much weaker since that time. As we discussed in Chapter 1, Americans have steadily interacted less with their neighbors, are less likely to have dinner with their family members, are less engaged in various forms of community activities, and are less likely to identify with a religion in comparison with earlier decades. Given how much people's connections have been unraveling and the foundations of their sense of meaning has eroded, it is perhaps not surprising that the suicide rate has also reached unprecedented heights. From 2000 to 2018, the suicide rate in the United States increased by 36 percent—a brutally sharp uptick. In a time of such a mental health crisis, and the disintegration of many of the vital sources of connection in people's lives, we need to find new ways to rebuild people's sense of meaning.[23]

An increasing amount of research has risen to the challenge and has explored how people can be helped to improve their mental well-being and reduce their risk for suicide by rebuilding a sense of meaning in their lives. A number of clinical interventions have been developed that strive to make people feel a greater sense of connection in their lives. For example, one intervention targeted men who were struggling with their transition to retirement and sought to help them identify the sources in their lives that provide them with meaning. The intervention significantly reduced suicide ideation and also improved mental health and well-being. Other kinds of interventions have also sought to build people's connections in their lives with promising results for reducing suicidal tendencies. When people are given tools to help them to build a sense of connection and meaning in their lives, evidence indicates that their well-being increases and their risk for suicide reduces. In the following chapter, we'll consider more ways in which people can make efforts to rebuild a sense of meaning in their lives.[24]

## Suffering and Posttraumatic Growth

People function at their best when their lives are sustained by viable meaning frameworks and a coherent life story. But as research on mental health and suicide has revealed, people can be at greater risk when they experience the breakdown of their meaning frameworks. As we discussed earlier, traumatic life events can wreak havoc on people's meaning frameworks and make it much harder for them to cope with life's travails. But, importantly, not everyone is equally likely to be broken by traumatic life events. And the different ways that people respond to trauma can offer some guidance for how people can approach the most difficult times in their lives.

Friedrich Nietzsche proclaimed, "That which does not kill me, makes me stronger." He recognized that the struggle and suffering people endure when they experience adversity can potentially have a beneficial impact on their lives. Nietzsche felt that the hardships people confront can sometimes provide them with a sense of resilience, courage, and self-mastery. In some circumstances, past trauma can lead to personal growth and better equip people to face future challenges.[25]

Nietzsche identified something that is important about the role of suffering, and research provides much support for his observation. Our sufferings have the potential to make us stronger and more resilient. People don't necessarily get broken by the difficult times they face but can often emerge from them even tougher than they were before. For example, we can see evidence that aligns with Nietzsche's aphorism in one study that tracked more than two thousand American adults over a three-year period. The participants had been asked about their past history of experiences with trauma, and the researchers were able to assess the reactions that participants had to any new adversities they experienced over the three-year duration of the study. When the researchers examined how these people were faring, they identified something important. Individuals with no past experience with trauma found these difficult events to be especially challenging to cope with. On the other extreme, those individuals who had reported that they had endured a large number of past experiences with trauma were also struggling with their more recent ordeals. Their past difficulties seemed to accumulate over time, making it even more difficult for them to face new adversities. But the researchers found that those individuals who had experienced some past traumas but not so many that they had been overwhelmed by them fared the best when facing new adversities. These people had become more resilient; they had learned to cope with adversity and that enabled them to better confront their new hardships. This research (which is also supported by other findings) identified that some degree of trauma helps people to build resiliency and grow from their misfortunes and better prepares them to face the future hardships of life.[26]

Our suffering doesn't only help to bolster a sense of resiliency in us. The difficult times that we endure also play a key role in helping us to lead more meaningful lives. As Sartre put it, "Human life begins on the far side of despair." That is, many of the ways people feel their lives are meaningful are grounded in the sufferings they have experienced. One research project investigated the differences between people who found their lives to be happy and those who found them to be meaningful. While, on average, happy lives and meaningful lives overlap a great deal, the researchers focused on those aspects of a meaningful life that were distinct from happiness. And, remarkably, they found that people who had more meaningful lives reported that they had more experience suffering through past negative events. They also reported worrying more and enduring more things that caused them stress. On the other hand, these past experiences with suffering tended to reduce people's overall levels of happiness. Our sufferings, then, seem to help to provide people with the sense that their lives are more meaningful, even if these events are associated with lower feelings of happiness.[27]

We can also see evidence of the relation between suffering and a meaningful life in another intriguing research finding. If you look around the world to identify where people are more likely to be leading meaningful lives, you don't tend to find many of them in places where people's basic needs are easily satisfied; rather, people who are leading meaningful lives are more common in places where life is *harder*. On average, the poorer a country is, the more likely its citizens will report that their lives are meaningful. For example, in one large multinational survey, the places where people were most likely to report leading meaningful lives were poor countries, such as Senegal and Ecuador, whereas meaning was near its lowest in wealthy countries, such as Japan and France. This finding is all the more striking because, on average, people living in poorer countries tend to report feeling less happy and less satisfied with their lives in comparison with those living in wealthier regions. Money can make life easier, after all. But the comfort and ease that people living in wealthier countries are able to enjoy appears to come at an existential cost. A comfortable and easy life doesn't seem to provide the sufficient struggles that people rely on for building a sense of resilience and meaning.[28]

The portmanteau *affluenza* was coined to describe the state of many modern postindustrial societies. These societies are affluent, but their citizens seem to be struggling in a state of malaise as though they were suffering from a bout of influenza. Without any real objective threats to their well-being, many people in these societies are caught up chasing shallow concerns of wealth, fame, and materialism. Affluenza refers to a situation in which people are unable to be satisfied with their comfortable lifestyles. They may pursue a lifestyle of the rich and famous, but no amount of consumption seems able to satisfy their itch. Regardless of how much they acquire, people are still left with a collective sense that their lives are somehow empty and unfulfilled. People in affluent societies can have trouble building a meaningful life as they're often living in an existential vacuum, in a context where they don't have the traditional foundations of meaning, such as sufficient connections to others or to things that really matter. Instead, their primary concerns are shaped by advertisements, television shows, and social media that make them feel that their comfortable lives are somehow inadequate and they need to chase after a more luxurious lifestyle.

But it's not at all the case that a meaningful life is only a concern to people who are living in a state of comfort and plenty. Rather, it was precisely in a context of unimaginable suffering that Viktor Frankl, the founder of existential psychiatry, witnessed humanity's fundamental need for meaning. In the Second World War, Frankl was a prisoner at four different concentration camps, over a period of three excruciating years. He lost absolutely everything during that time: his brother, both of his parents, and his newlywed wife all lost their lives in the camps. He tried in vain to keep hidden a copy of a manuscript of the first book he was working on, *The Doctor and the Soul*, which was an introduction to the field of existential psychiatry, but he lost this too when it was taken from him in the disinfection chamber at Auschwitz. Under this relentless assault on everything he valued and loved, we might expect that Frankl would collapse and lose the will to live. He noted that this happened to many of his fellow prisoners. But, somehow, Frankl persevered.

How was Frankl ultimately able to bear the unbearable suffering in the camps? Ironically, perhaps, he says that what kept him going through his darkest periods was his desire to rewrite the book manuscript that had been taken from him. It had been heartbreaking for him to lose his manuscript, yet this loss ultimately provided him with a new sense of purpose. He had a resolve to rewrite this lost manuscript, and this is what kept him moving forward throughout the agonizing conditions he suffered through. It was while facing the most painful and hopeless of situations that Frankl found a reason to live. Frankl liked to quote one of Nietzsche's aphorisms, which stated that "he who has a *why* to live for can bear with almost any *how*." Frankl and Nietzsche both recognized that people are able to face the suffering in their lives precisely because they are able to construct a sense of meaning and purpose from them. They recognized that we need a purpose to help us to lead a meaningful life.

When Frankl looked at his fellow prisoners, he recognized what the survivors of the camps seemed to have in common. It wasn't that they were facing different circumstances: all of the prisoners experienced unimaginable horrors. Under the soul-crushing weight of this relentless torture, some of the prisoners seemed to experience a kind of spiritual death: they would suddenly appear to be broken, numb to the horrors, and shut out from everything. They would no longer respond to any of the beatings they received, and they seemed to surrender to their death. But others were able to surmount their suffering and survive. Frankl thought the survivors were able to identify the reasons they had to live. They had found a why, and with that, they somehow were able to bear the most unbearable of hows. Frankl recognized that even in such an indescribably bleak situation, people always have a choice of how to react to their circumstances. They have a spiritual freedom to seek and find a sense of meaning in what they are doing.

In this context of unrelenting suffering, Frankl recognized that striving to find meaning in one's life was a key motivational force for people. He called this striving the "will to meaning"—a deep-seated drive to find meaning wherever we can. We struggle to make sense of our lives and to find meaning in our actions, and especially in our suffering.[29]

But Frankl recognized that our sufferings can come even in situations that are far less severe. As Frankl saw it, all of our sufferings are ultimately relative—even the most comfortable life will have many moments of anxiety. He saw that our basic need for meaning was operating in the same way during times of peace and abundance. Frankl likened the suffering we face to that of gas in a vessel. Regardless of the size of the vessel, the gas will expand to fill it completely and evenly throughout. If your day-to-day life is largely safe and comfortable, even relatively small kinds of suffering can be deeply bothersome, and our concerns with those problems can envelop our entire consciousness. In the context of a comfortable life, a single rather trivial worry, such as wondering if one offended one's boss with a joke that didn't land well, might hang heavily over someone's head for days. Given the way that our sufferings always find a way to dominate our consciousness, there really is no life we can lead that would be free from suffering. He found that having a sense of purpose would help people to thrive. How people approach their trauma and respond to their suffering determines how well they cope with their travails. Even people living comfortable lives in an affluent society still need a sense of purpose to guide their lives.

Frankl's descriptions of concentration camp survivors show how remarkably resilient people can be even when enduring extreme suffering. Frankl's work inspires people because, in the face of the dire futures that may be awaiting them, they are encouraged to see that people typically rise to the challenge of their suffering. As George Bonanno, an expert on posttraumatic stress disorder, put it: "Most people exposed to potentially traumatic events are able to continue on with their normal lives relatively quickly and without suffering *any* long-term difficulties. . . . When we look across the full range of research that has been conducted—studies on all kinds of highly aversive or potentially traumatic events—resilience is almost always the most common outcome." We can't avoid suffering in our lives, but it is reassuring to know that when the time comes, we will likely be able to endure the most difficult of times.[30]

People don't just survive their sufferings; they also often emerge showing a great deal of growth and can find themselves on a path toward a more meaningful life. As Frankl put it, "Even the helpless victim of a hopeless situation . . . may turn a personal tragedy into a triumph." Research reveals that people's experiences with adversity can spark a new set of meaning-making efforts, as they come to terms with the threat from the suffering. They are often forced to try to make sense of things differently. They can come to recognize that their past view of themselves and their world was not adequate, and they come to understand their lives quite differently than before. It is their struggles with the new reality in the aftermath of their tragedy that ultimately serves to make their lives more meaningful. A great deal of research has found that people's sufferings can pave the way to posttraumatic growth, where their lives can ultimately become better in many ways because of the very difficulties they have endured.[31]

While not everyone goes through posttraumatic growth, it is reassuring that most people experience growth when confronting adversity. The meaning-making opportunities that come with trauma provide people with a few kinds of common beneficial reactions. First and foremost, people often come to develop closer and more meaningful relationships with others. Traumatic experiences often force people to become more dependent upon others, and in doing so, they come to appreciate their relationships more. For example, one study that explored the reactions of parents who had lost a child found that their relationships became more intimate and meaningful to them. As one parent said, "When he died people just came out of the woodwork. . . . I realize that relationships with people are really important now . . . and I cherish my husband a lot more." These kinds of difficult experiences provide occasions for learning who one's real friends are. People's relationships often deepen following tragedies as they become grateful for the social support they are receiving.[32]

Traumatic experiences can also lead people to develop new purposes in their lives. In the face of such dramatic change, people often come to reevaluate what they are doing with their lives. Commonly, trauma survivors become more altruistic toward others who have suffered tragedies. They often get involved in charitable work. And by trying to give something back to their communities, they often experience greater well-being in their lives.

Through trauma, people also discover inner strengths they didn't realize they possessed. In a happy and comfortable life, people's strengths are not tested that much, and they can largely lie dormant. But when one faces adversities in life, these hidden strengths come to the fore, as people rise to the occasion. People are typically resilient, and often in ways that they hadn't foreseen beforehand. They may realize that if they can handle this new challenge, then they can handle just about anything. It is as though they have discovered some new superhero powers that they hadn't been aware of.

People's lives also often become more meaningful because their spiritual lives tend to deepen after their trauma. When people are confronted with the most difficult times in their lives, they often turn to God. People become more religious in times of trauma because they are seeking a transcendent explanation for their suffering. They want to understand why they have had to face such a terrible event, and they can feel more reassured by seeing the event as a spiritual opportunity, or as a test from God. People frequently come to feel more connected to God and secure in their belief that God will continue to look after them. The kinds of spiritual connections that people develop in the face of tragedies can also help to make people's lives feel more significant and meaningful than before.[33]

A final way that people show posttraumatic growth is that their tragedy can often provide them with a renewed appreciation for life. They become aware of just how vulnerable they are and recognize that their lives could end at any time. Just as Fyodor Dostoevsky discovered the preciousness of life following his mock execution, many survivors of traumatic life events emerge with a newfound commitment to savor all that life has to offer. They no longer take their lives for granted and come to appreciate all of the good things in their lives.

I don't want to paint an overly rosy picture of life after tragedy, and a key point that needs to be emphasized is that not everyone benefits from posttraumatic growth. Sadly, many people's lives become much harder after they experience tragedy. For many people, life no longer makes much sense, and their losses can sometimes lead to much unwanted ruminations and depression. But research has helped to identify the kinds of situations in which people will be more likely to become resilient in the face of adversity. In particular, people tend to fare better after trauma when they can interpret their adversity as a challenge, rather than as a threat. This enables them to feel that they have the capability to cope with their new situation and can lead them to feel more optimistic about their futures. When people recognize that they have the wherewithal to keep going forward in the aftermath of their trauma, they are in a far better position to grow from their experiences.[34]

## Writing Your Way to Recovery

People who have experienced trauma can become overwhelmed with distress, and this can pose some significant challenges to their mental and physical well-being. But there are some ways that people can be guided onto a path of recovery. When the psychologist James Pennebaker was working with people who were struggling with traumatic life events, he noticed that those who were suffering the most from their past history with trauma had indicated that they had tried to keep their experiences a secret from others. Pennebaker wondered why these people might be struggling so much more than those who had discussed their past traumatic experiences. He felt that the people who had hidden their trauma were suffering more because they had not taken the time to understand and make sense of their traumatic experiences.

Pennebaker developed a very simple exercise that has provided extensive benefits for people coping with past traumatic experiences. He asked people to sit in a room that had a box of tissues and some blank sheets of paper for about fifteen minutes at a time. They were given the following instructions: "For the next 3 days, I would like for you to write about your very deepest thoughts and feelings about an extremely important emotional issue that has affected you and your life. In your writing, I'd like you to really let go and explore your very deepest emotions and thoughts. You might tie your topic to your relationships with others, including parents, lovers, friends, or relatives; to your past, your present, or your future; or to who you have been, who you would like to be, or who you are now. . . . The only rule is that once you begin writing, continue to do so until your time is up."[35]

This simple intervention led to some rather striking results. People reported that this writing activity was a very painful process as they confronted their thoughts regarding their deepest traumas, and many of them broke down in tears while writing. But this temporary pain seemed to pave the way for many other benefits later on. Many of the people showed quite dramatic improvements in their physical health and well-being, which persisted for months. They didn't need to go to the doctor as often in the following year. Their body's immune system improved, and they often showed sharp drops in depression and anxiety. College students showed improvements in their grades, and the unemployed were more likely to find new jobs. This writing exercise helped to take people out of their experience of feeling devastated, overwhelmed, and confused by their trauma, to a state where things started to make sense all over again. By writing about what had happened, they created a narrative of events unfolding in sequence, identifying an apparent sense of cause and effect and linking the various implications of the event, with the result creating a bit of a sense of order out of the chaos of their trauma. They came to feel that things made sense again in their lives.

This writing experience doesn't work as well for people who have already made some progress in coming to terms with their tragedy, but it is especially effective for people who have suffered from posttraumatic stress disorder. By creating a story of what happened to them, one that they may have not yet tried to tell, people can begin to get their lives back in order again. Such is the way that stories help us to construct a meaningful life.[36]

However, the tactics that people can use to construct a meaningful life are not just restricted to those who are struggling with a past history of trauma. The science of existentialism has much to offer for everyone in identifying a set of strategies that can be applied in their efforts to lead a more meaningful life.

## Chapter 9

# Building a Meaningful Life

One must cultivate one's own garden.

Voltaire, *Candide*

Albert Camus was looking for a metaphor to capture people's pursuit of meaningful lives, and he chose, of all things, the Greek myth of Sisyphus. Sisyphus was sentenced to spend eternity in the underworld trying to roll a giant boulder up a steep hill, only to have it roll back down whenever he was about to reach its crest. He had been cursed with an endless and futile task that appeared to be maddeningly meaningless. Camus felt that, like Sisyphus, we too are caught up in an endless struggle. We all have a need to create a meaningful life, and we work relentlessly at this throughout our lives. But Camus believed that our efforts to find meaning in our lives would, in the end, be futile, as he felt that the universe was fundamentally meaningless. Even though we keep pushing ahead, trying to build a meaningful life, every now and then we are forced to recognize that our lives are not as rational and coherent as we would like, and we stumble into the absurd, finding ourselves yet again at the bottom of a steep valley of despair.

By comparing our own lives to Sisyphus's ridiculously pointless predicament, Camus would appear to have a very cynical and bleak take on human existence. But that's not his point at all. Rather, Camus concludes his book by saying, "The struggle itself toward the heights is enough to fill a man's heart. One must imagine Sisyphus happy." That's right. Camus argues that Sisyphus doesn't feel frustrated and depressed at how futile his existence is—he feels *happy* about it. Sisyphus is happy because of the way he approaches his life. As Camus imagines him, Sisyphus is fully present in each moment and embraces whatever situation he is in. Each time he starts to push the boulder up the hill, he does so with renewed vigor and commitment, fully engaged in the task. He doesn't dwell on the pointlessness of his efforts but instead focuses on what he is working toward in the moment. This is what Camus challenges us to do. We need to live our lives to the fullest, continuing in our endeavors to construct a life story that is full of meaning and authenticity. And when we hit a setback, which we invariably will, Camus urges us to not just wallow in our alienation and despair. Rather, we should just dust ourselves off, get right back at it again, and continue to forge ahead, making efforts to lead a rich and meaningful life. And, if we do this well, working hard toward finding a sense of purpose and significance in our lives despite the obstacles that we face, we'll ultimately enjoy all the peace of mind and satisfaction that comes with the pursuit of a meaningful life.[1]

Pursuing meaningful lives is not a straightforward endeavor, and it has become more challenging in the twenty-first century, particularly in the hyperindividualistic culture of the United States. Living a meaningful life has become more difficult because so many of the foundations of a meaningful life have been erod-ing. They've been eroding as cultures around the world have been becoming increasingly individualistic, and people have been focusing more and more on themselves, leading them to be less socially grounded. We depend upon our interpersonal relation-ships, but people are less connected with their families, friends, and communities than before. We also seek a sense of meaning from our work, especially in more industrialized countries, but it has been getting harder for people to find much meaning in their careers. And we gain meaning from our religious beliefs, but so many people are turning away from organized religions. With so many key sources of meaning being undermined, we are currently living through an existential vacuum, where it's more difficult to gain a sense of meaning in our lives. Our existential needs are not being satisfied, and people are struggling, with increasing levels of depression and anxiety and, most disturbingly, a sharp escala-tion in deaths of despair. In this vulnerable state—an existential ape that's living in an existential vacuum—the question of how we can build a more solid foundation for a meaningful life has become especially urgent.

Fortunately, the science of existential psychology can offer us some guidance for how we can lead more meaningful lives. Over the past few decades, researchers from around the world have been studying the basis of an existentially rich life. This research has pointed to the kinds of factors that help people to gain a sense of meaning in their lives. It provides a blueprint for how we can try to build a more purposeful and satisfying life.

What can we learn from this research in existential psychology to apply to our own efforts at leading a meaningful life? Overall, this research points to two broad kinds of strategies that we can pursue to build more meaningful lives. The first kind of strategies can serve to provide a short-term boost to our sense of meaning. These are useful strategies to turn to when you are feeling that life isn't sufficiently meaningful. These strategies can serve to temporarily help you to get out of those states of apathy or anxiety. The second kind of strategies can help us to build and reinforce an underlying foundation of meaning in our lives. These strategies can suggest ways that we can change the course of our lives such that they will become more meaningful. We'll consider each of these two kinds of strategies in turn.

## Existential Exercises to Temporarily Boost Meaning

Leading a meaningful life does not mean that one's life will feel meaningful at all times. Some days, people's lives might feel rather rich in meaning, whereas on other days, they might really be struggling. On the bad days, people may feel a deep sense of boredom with whatever they are doing. They might feel lonely, alienated, and disconnected from others. Or they might feel that what they are doing is without any purpose. People's feelings of meaning in their lives may fluctuate because their perceptions of their lives will change across time and circumstance.

Research has identified a number of exercises that can heighten people's feelings of meaning in life. I think of these exercises as the existential equivalent of a shot of espresso: they can provide a temporary boost to people's feelings of meaning, although their effects likely won't endure for all that long. Nonetheless, a short-term meaning enhancement can help people to avoid some times of crisis and can help them when they would otherwise be at their worst, even if they probably won't dramatically change the course of their lives. Moreover, people may later remember their experiences during these moments, so some of these meaning-enhancing efforts may have some enduring effects. Let's consider some of these exercises below.

## Self-Grounding

People don't possess a constant capacity for confronting the challenges in their lives. Sometimes when encountering a problem, an individual may feel quite devastated by it, while at other times that same problem might appear to be no big deal at all. Why might people have such different reactions to a threat depending on the circumstances that they're in? A key reason behind people's differing reactions to challenges is whether they are feeling existentially grounded at that time or not. When people are grounded, they feel that the key connections in their lives that provide the foundation of a sense of meaning are solidly intact. They know who they are, who their important relationships are, and what they stand for, and they are in a better position to confront any new threats they might encounter.

Research on self-affirmation theory, proposed by Claude Steele, finds that if people can take a moment to existentially ground themselves, they are better positioned to maintain their sense of self-integrity even when they encounter other threats. Their efforts to ground themselves remind them of how competent, stable, and moral they are, which makes the problems they encounter feel less threatening. They feel more empowered and make whatever changes are required in their lives to handle these challenges, rather than just engaging in unconscious psychological defenses.

Research studies have found that one simple self-grounding exercise can be surprisingly effective. Participants in these studies are asked to reflect upon a personal value that is important to them, and then to write a paragraph or two about why that value is important. Some people write about their concern for their family, or their passion for making music, or the centrality of religion in their lives—and so on. This brief writing task provides people with a better sense of what matters to them; it reminds them of who they are, what they stand for, and how they live their lives in accordance with their values. As people think about their values and why they are important, they become more existentially grounded, and their sense of meaning in life is bolstered.[2]

Despite the simplicity of this exercise, dozens of studies have found that people who ground themselves in this way fare much better when they later encounter various challenges. This self-grounding exercise can help to make people less defensive and more proactive for dealing with challenges. For example, after going through this exercise people who learn that they have an elevated risk for cancer are more ready to change their lifestyles to reduce their cancer risk than are people who didn't go through this exercise. Writing about their values led people to be more proactive about taking care of their health in the face of receiving threatening information. In contrast, those who didn't go through the exercise often remained too frightened by this disturbing news to be able to seriously process this information and take steps toward changing their lifestyle. Other studies have found that this simple self-grounding exercise can help disadvantaged students to do better in their schoolwork, as they become more resilient in the face of the challenges that they confront there. Self-grounding has also been found to lessen people's defensive reactions to death and can help them to better accept the choices that they have made in their lives.

Moreover, people can achieve this self-grounding in a number of different ways in addition to focusing on their values. Similar kinds of benefits have been found by people who were instructed to reflect upon their sense of belongingness with others or consider how their own difficulties are commonly shared by others. Dozens of different studies have found that these simple exercises serve to boost people's sense of integrity and competence and to help them to successfully confront the various challenges they face.[3]

## Nostalgic Reflections

Each of our life stories is made up of a series of events that have happened in the past. We are not able to change what has happened to us, but this doesn't mean that our life stories are beholden to what we think has occurred in our pasts. As the author Gabriel García Márquez put it, "What matters in life is not what happens to you but what you remember and how you remember it." Memories provide people with a key resource for building a meaningful life.

When people are enduring a period in which their life feels rather meaningless, there is a rather easy way that they can give themselves an existential boost. They can engage in nostalgic reflections and consider some of their past memories. Nostalgic reflections serve to help to existentially ground an individual. They help people to feel a sense of continuity across their life course. Reflecting on past chapters of one's life story can make the present seem far more sensible and connected. Nostalgia also helps people to feel more socially connected. People's most nostalgic memories tend to be social occasions, and reflecting on their memories of the key people in their lives can help people to feel that they are loved and protected. Nostalgic memories can help people to feel more authentic as well, as they recognize that what they are currently doing in their lives is connected to their pasts. People's nostalgic memories serve to remind them of the past events and important relationships that have made them who they are. When people wax nostalgically, they get a meaning boost, and they become less distressed by other concerns in their lives. People even become less worried about their own deaths. Nostalgic reflections provide people with a key source of existential benefits.[4]

Given that our nostalgic memories can help to boost our feelings of meaning, it is perhaps not surprising that people are most likely to turn to nostalgia when their lives are feeling short on meaning, such as when they are feeling bored or their lives feel purposeless. People are most likely to turn to nostalgic reflections when they are feeling lonely. Lonely feelings prompt them to think back to past chapters of their lives when they were socially connected, and this gives them the feeling that they are supported by others and have been living a life that is richly connected to its past episodes.

So on those occasions when your life is feeling rather empty, you can do yourself a service by reflecting on your past memories and giving yourself a nostalgic boost. Not all of our past memories are equally good at delivering existential benefits. Try to recall social events from your past, as our relationships play such a key role in our feelings of meaning. Try to think back to some of your more momentous life events, especially ones that revolve around cultural rituals, such as your high school graduation, or family traditions, such as a big Thanksgiving dinner, as these kinds of memories are most nostalgic. And try to recall events when you had surmounted some difficulty, as these memories highlight a theme of redemption, which can be especially poignant. You can make your past memories more accessible to you by trying a variety of things that can help bring them to mind. Make an effort to reach out to a friend that you've lost touch with; look through a photo album from your past; play some songs from a past chapter of your life; or look through a box of old keepsakes and try to recall the times that these were important to you. By making your past memories more accessible, you will be better able to connect the path of your current life with the events that occurred along the way. You will be reminded about how the events of your path have shaped who you are today.

## Self-Transcendent Experiences

Much research has revealed that some of the most potent sources of feelings of meaning in life are self-transcendent experiences. Author Ceridwen Dovey calls a transcendent experience "that elusive state in which the distance between the self and the universe shrinks." Time seems to slow down, and people's attention becomes laser focused on the present moment. The emotion that most commonly accompanies self-transcendent experiences is *awe*. People experience awe when they feel connected with something much larger than themselves, such as when they are contemplating the vastness of the universe. People also feel awe when they see someone who they deeply respect act in a way that rises above their typical expectations. Religious experiences and being out in nature can also reliably elicit feelings of awe.

When people are feeling awe, they are more open to supernatural beliefs: they can more easily believe that the world around them is penetrated by hidden, mystical forces. People become less self-centered and selfish, and many of their concerns and anxieties temporarily fade away. Awe-inspiring events can make people feel rather small; they are reminded of just how trivial their concerns are. However, while feeling small doesn't sound particularly uplifting, people typically don't feel the emotion of awe in isolation; rather, it often comes with many other positive feelings, such as feelings of compassion, gratitude, well-being, and authenticity. During these awe experiences, people's lives often feel more significant and meaningful, as they have the sense that they are connected to something much vaster than themselves and that their existence extends beyond the material world. Self-transcendent experiences can be very powerful, and though they may be relatively brief, they are often especially memorable and sometimes have lasting effects on people's lives. These experiences can help people to see the world in a new way and sometimes motivate them to try to transform themselves.[5]

Given all of the existential benefits that come with transcending the here and now and the feelings of awe that this elicits, what can people do to cultivate more self-transcendent experiences in their lives? Below, we'll discuss three strategies to promote self-transcendent experiences: spiritual practices and meditation, psychedelic drugs, and venturing into nature.[6]

*Spiritual Practices and Meditation.* People's religious and spiritual practices provide one of the most common sources of self-transcendent experiences. Religions are very explicit in their teachings that people are part of something much vaster than themselves, and this is a key reason why religious and spiritual people tend to feel that their lives are richer in significance and meaning. Religious rituals and practices are effective in directing one's thoughts away from one's immediate concerns and heightening the sense that one is connected to something self-transcendent. Formal religious ceremonies frequently combine symbolism with emotionally evocative music, chanting, rituals, and communal participation, which can reliably elicit a sense of sacredness and connection among participants. People frequently experience awe at religious and spiritual services, and they can get a temporary reprieve from the anxieties of their day-to-day lives. If you are a religious person, you likely already have an appreciation for the meaning boosts that come with participating in religious ceremonies, rituals, or pilgrimages. You will likely benefit if you can make room for more of these experiences in your life.

But what about people who don't possess any religious or spiritual beliefs? Atheists and those who explain all aspects of their lives in materialistic and scientific terms would seem to have few opportunities to gain the existential rewards that accompany religious experiences. However, secular people who practice mindfulness meditation can also experience transcendent experiences. Meditation originates in Eastern religions, such as Buddhism and yogic practices in Hinduism, where conscious attention and awareness are cultivated through practice, but in recent decades, it has been embraced by Westerners and secular practitioners. Mindfulness is a mental state in which people intentionally attend to the present moment in a nonjudgmental way. The goal is to develop the ability to observe one's thoughts and feelings as temporary and objective events in the mind, rather than experiencing them as subjective aspects of the self that are necessarily true. Meditators develop the ability to enhance their attention and awareness of their present reality, which helps them to distance themselves from ruminating on the events that are causing anxiety and stress in their lives and achieve a state of self-transcendence. A wide variety of benefits have been attributed to regular mindfulness meditation, including coping with chronic pain, stress, and depression and an overall improvement in a sense of meaningfulness and well-being.[7]

Mindfulness seems to enhance feelings of meaning in life because it helps people to feel separate from their thoughts. By not identifying with their thoughts, people are better able to see who they really are and gain clarity about themselves. The exercise also enables people to feel more authentic, where they feel that their actions are in line with their underlying values and needs.

Mindfulness meditation is a powerful tool that can help people to develop greater feelings of meaning in their lives. However, it is important to know that meditation has a learning curve, and many beginners may feel frustrated as they struggle to feel engaged with the process, and they may not initially gain much benefit from the experience. But people typically improve with practice, and much research finds that the well-being benefits of mindfulness meditation are most pronounced among those who regularly practice it. You may gain some of these benefits yourself if you can learn how to master this meaning-boosting exercise.[8]

*Psychedelic Drugs.* Recently, there has been a sharp increase in interest in using psychedelic drugs to deliver potent kinds of transcendent experiences. The world is currently going through what has been called a "psychedelic renaissance," and there is growing interest in the purported benefits from the occasional use of powerful psychedelic substances such as lysergic acid diethylamide (LSD or acid), psilocybin (hallucinogenic mushrooms), 3,4,5-trimethoxyphenethylamine (mescaline), dimethyltryptamine (DMT—a key ingredient in ayahuasca), and 3,4-Methylenedioxymethamphetamine (MDMA or ecstasy), which some consider to be a psychedelic. The psychological effects these drugs elicit are somewhat unique to each substance, but they all share some subjective experiences, including alterations to the sense of time and space, positive feelings such as love and peace, visual hallucinations, and a sense of connectedness that is usually accompanied by feelings of reverence.

These drugs are illegal in most countries, although some countries have recently decriminalized or legalized some of these for use in therapeutic treatment. In the United States they are classified as Schedule 1 drugs, meaning they are seen as having no medicinal use and a high potential for abuse; however, much research is currently being conducted, exploring the potential benefits of these substances, particularly in therapeutic contexts. Many studies have found promising results in the substances' ability to treat a variety of conditions, including posttraumatic stress disorder, anxiety, substance abuse, depression, relationship problems, and suicidality. Moreover, unlike many other Schedule 1 drugs, none of these substances are particularly addictive, and studies find that their harms are lower than originally feared, although it is important to recognize that these are all powerful psychoactive substances that come with some risks.[9]

The word *psychedelic* comes from the Greek *psykhe* (meaning "mind") and *deloun* (meaning "reveal or make visible"), and this is an apt description of the effects that come with these substances— they are mind revealing. Published studies report some quite dramatic results: for example, an influential study of people taking psilocybin found that about two-thirds of the participants rated their experience as one of the top five most meaningful experiences of their lives. Studies find that people who ingest these substances report feeling greater authenticity, social connection, self-insight, meaning in life, and reductions in death anxiety.[10]

Curiously, the benefits that seem to come with ingesting psychedelics appear to largely be mediated through the mystical experiences that these drugs most potently elicit—experiences such as feeling that one is merging with external reality, sensing the unity of all things, experiencing a sense of sacredness, peace, and love. Studies have found that even atheists, who tend to have more materialist views of the universe, often come to adopt more of a nonmaterialist worldview as a result of their psychedelic experiences. The drugs can facilitate one's connection to the transcendent sphere, where people realize they are connected with all that's around them.[11]

The existential benefits that people experience while ingesting psychedelics are most evident while the drugs are active in people's systems—while they are high; however, there is growing evidence that some of these beneficial effects can persist for some time afterward. It's because of these enduring benefits that there is so much excitement around their potential for therapeutic use, and many are expecting that at least some of these substances will receive FDA approval after the results of more clinical trials are completed.

While I think that there are many potential benefits from careful and responsible use of these substances and that the likelihood of becoming addicted to these particular drugs is low, these drugs do carry some risk. First, there are pronounced legal risks as the drugs remain illegal in almost all countries. Moreover, the drugs that people purchase may be contaminated with other, far more dangerous chemicals. In addition, many of the studies of these drugs exclude people with family histories of schizophrenia because of concerns that these drugs may create risks of triggering psychotic episodes. Furthermore, people taking these drugs can experience bad trips, and they may end up doing dangerous things while they are high. The effects of each of these substances has been found to be strongly dependent on set and setting; that is, people may experience worse outcomes if their mind-set is not sufficiently grounded or if they are taking them in a setting where they do not feel safe or relaxed. Researchers who are experimenting with the therapeutic use of these substances strongly recommend that anyone who is using these substances does so under the watchful guidance of a therapist or a guide to increase the likelihood that they will have a safe and beneficial experience. It is important to note that psychedelics do not seem to be effective for everyone; for example, people who score high on the personality trait of neuroticism appear to be less likely to reap their benefits. But, for many, when taken in a safe context, psychedelics stand to provide a substantial boost to feelings of significance and meaning.

*Venturing into Nature.* The physical environment that surrounds us is an important factor in our well-being. In particular, venturing out into nature is one of the more reliable strategies for eliciting feelings of awe. When people experience some of the most beautiful aspects of the natural world, such as observing a dramatic sunset, the crashing surf of the ocean, towering mountains jutting into the sky, or the vastness of a desert, they can sometimes have a transcendent experience.

Just walking in nature can be beneficial for one's well-being and mental health. People have recognized the restorative powers of nature for some time. In 1873, the American pastor William H. H. Murray exhorted: "Go to the seashore, to the mountains, to the wilderness; go anywhere where you can forget your cares and cast aside your burdens. . . . Let the old, old nurse, Nature, . . . take you to her bosom again; and you will return to the city happier and healthier for the embrace." In recent years, a growing amount of experimental research has provided support for the restorative power of nature. Many studies have demonstrated that time spent in a natural environment leads people to experience a boost in their positive emotions, a reduction in stress and anxiety, and overall greater well-being. When people are out in the natural environment, they are likely to have the sense that they are connected to something much larger than themselves, and they may experience a feeling of awe and all its existential benefits. It does not take much time in nature to enjoy these benefits—just a short nature walk can deliver a real well-being boost. These studies point to a simple and straightforward balm: when you're feeling a bit stressed or emotionally down, go take a walk in a natural place.[12]

Encouragingly, the benefits of time spent in nature are not just that they enhance people's emotional well-being and feelings of transcendence; they also provide cognitive benefits, such as enhancing the quality of people's thinking. Friedrich Nietzsche recognized this himself as he spent his most productive years taking daily walks along trails in the mountains of Europe. He advocated that "all truly great thoughts are conceived by walking," and he cautioned to "never trust a thought that occurs to you indoors." Research supports Nietzsche's aphorisms, as studies find that people have improved working memory capacity, better cognitive flexibility, and greater creativity after they have gone for a walk outside, compared with people who have remained indoors. The benefits of being in nature are perhaps not that surprising when you consider that for the vast majority of humanity's time on earth, people have lived outdoors, and nature represents the environment that we evolved to function within. It is only relatively recently that people have come to spend so much time indoors, and the psychic costs of being separate from our natural environment are only beginning to be appreciated. Don't underestimate the benefits that accrue from spending some time in nature.[13]

## Constructing the Foundation of a Meaningful Life

These various existential exercises may help you to get a boost in your sense of meaning whenever you're feeling a little alienated. But, by themselves, these exercises are insufficient for creating a rich and meaningful life. They only provide a temporary lift but largely fail to address any of the key foundations for a meaningful life. We will now consider how the science of existentialism points to efforts that people can take to build a more solid existential foundation in their lives.

Tending to the existential underpinnings of one's life requires us to focus on what the key bases of meaning are. Recall that meaning is ultimately about connections: the meaning in our own lives is determined by how well our lives are connected in ways that provide us with a sense of purpose, coherence, and significance. Below we'll discuss the various domains of connections that are particularly important for leading a meaningful life. I suggest that as you read through these different kinds of life connections that you conduct an existential audit of yourself. How are you doing in each of these key domains of meaning? Do you feel that your life is sufficiently connected in each of these domains? Most likely, you will find that in at least some of these domains you have room for improvement—hardly anyone feels richly connected in all of these domains. You may benefit by working to improve the connections that you have in any domains where you feel you are currently lacking.

One encouraging point to note is that research finds that meaning, like money, is fungible. That is, one does not need to get meaning from each of these different domains to have a meaningful life. The meaning in life that one derives from one domain of connections can help to make up for a shortfall of meaning in another domain—it's as though we can pay for the meaning in our lives from different accounts. This means that people can still have meaningful lives even if some of their foundations of meaning are wanting. Having said that, it is still easier building more meaning in life in a domain where one has much room for improvement than in a domain in which one already has sufficient meaning. I invite you to consider how your own life sizes up for each of the following domains of connections.[14]

## Relationships

One of the most reliable sources of meaning in our lives is the interpersonal connections that we have—in particular, those of our closest relationships. When people have relationships with others, their actions come to matter to those around them, and likewise, the actions of their relationship partners matter to themselves. Much research finds that, on average, people who have more satisfying relationships tend to report having a greater sense of meaning in their lives.

In general, people's lives feel the most meaningful when they are spending time with the people they love. For example, people's closest friendships are a reliable source of meaning in their lives and usually make them feel understood, valued, and supported, all of which contribute to a meaningful life. People often feel free to disclose personal matters with their closest friends and can open up about the difficulties in their lives. These kinds of exchanges tend to make people's lives feel more authentic and meaningful.[15]

People's closest friendships contribute a lot to their sense of meaning, but it is people's relationships with family members that often have the most significant impact. Family is especially important to meaning because it provides people with a sense of identity: family members typically have a shared bloodline and a common upbringing. Families often have traditions, religious beliefs, and sets of values that they share with each other, which are important for helping people to gain a sense of who they really are. People's family relationships also often extend across many decades, or even a lifetime, so these relationships can connect people backward and forward in time. And, for many people, family relationships are the ones that they feel they can always count on, no matter how bad things may get.[16]

One kind of family interaction appears to be particularly important in helping people derive a sense of meaning in life—spending time with and taking care of one's children. Having children is meaningful because of the same factors that make our other close relationships rich in meaning: they provide people with a sense of identity, support, shared traditions and values, and they connect people across time. Moreover, having children provides people with a rich sense of purpose. Parents not only feel that they are living their lives for themselves, but also that they are helping their children carry on the family line into the future. In general, people feel more meaning in their lives whenever they take on a caretaker role and are making efforts to help others with their lives, whether they are taking care of pets, the elderly, or their children.

However, the meaning boost that comes with children often comes with a significant cost: having children can make it more difficult to enjoy a happy life, particularly in more individualistic societies such as the United States. Much research has found that children can be a drain on people's happiness; in particular, married couples that have young children tend to suffer from more relationship dissatisfaction with their partners, and these feelings of relationship strain are especially evident among women, who typically take on the bulk of the child-rearing duties. Children can be problematic for happiness because they demand so much of their parents' attention, especially in the current generation, with overinvolved helicopter parents having become the norm. Moreover, children are expensive and can lead to much financial stress. They also require enormous amounts of labor—preparing their food, cleaning up after them, helping with their homework, arranging activities—and parents generally report that childcare activities aren't likely to deliver happy feelings. But perhaps it's the

very struggles that come with having children that helps them provide such a boost to people's sense of meaning.[17]

People also derive a sense of meaning from another kind
of interpersonal connection in their lives: belonging to a group
or community. When people belong to groups they care deeply
about, they gain a sense of collective identity; their identity now
transcends the limits of their individual self. These connections
to a broader group identity can importantly boost people's sense
of meaning, as belonging to a group can help to provide one with
a sense of purpose—one's efforts are directed toward a common
mission.[18]

In recent decades, people have become less actively involved
with groups or communities, and this is surely contributing to
their feelings of being in an existential vacuum. You might find
that you would benefit if you found a group to join. These groups
could be based on social and fun goals, such as joining a softball
team or a choir, or they might be directed toward a key value that
you share, such as working for a political action group or a group
that seeks to protect the environment. Research finds that the
kinds of activities that are most reliably associated with feelings of
meaningfulness are when people are engaged in prosocial behaviors that help others, as this helps to provide people with a clearer
sense of purpose. In particular, people are especially likely to enjoy
a boost in feelings of meaning when they volunteer for a cause that
they believe in. You might also find that your life will come to feel
more meaningful and purposeful if you become an active member
of such a group.[19]

## Work

In the seventeenth century, the French polymath Blaise Pascal
noted that "man finds nothing so intolerable as to be in a state

of complete rest, without passions, without occupation, without diversion, without effort. . . . And at once there wells up from the depths of his soul, boredom, gloom, depression, chagrin, resentment, despair." This is a bleak perspective of what happens to people when they don't have any work to pursue. But there is much truth to Pascal's dark pronouncement, and it underscores just how important people's work can be to their feelings of meaning in life. One doesn't have to look hard to find just how much people's careers are tied up with their existential needs. The American writer Studs Terkel interviewed hundreds of people about their work and concluded that work is as much about a search "for daily meaning as well as daily bread." People may not always like to admit it, but the work that most people do helps them to feel that they are valued and significant and have a purpose in life.[20]

People's jobs play a central role in providing meaning to life for a few key reasons. First, people's jobs play a central role in their sense of identity. When people think about who they are, a big part of their answer comes from what they do for a living or whatever organization they belong to. People's jobs carry such existential weight because work importantly contributes to a sense of purpose in life. Working provides people with a sense of a mission: they are directing their efforts toward furthering the goals of their organization in whatever kind of job they have, and the money they earn can help them to feel purposeful by being a provider. People's jobs also commonly afford a sense of mastery and self-worth. People tend to get quite skilled in whatever work they have, and this helps to boost their feelings of efficacy and self-worth. And people's jobs also typically provide them with a key set of relationships in their lives. People often work together with the same group of individuals for many hours each week, and although these interactions aren't always necessarily that positive, they still constitute a large portion of many individuals' social networks.

It may seem discouraging to note that work can serve such a critical role in satisfying people's existential needs because many people really struggle to find a sense of meaning in their careers. Some of the challenges that people face in finding meaning from their work have become more pronounced over time because people are changing jobs more frequently than before, making them less likely to view their jobs as central to their identities. Moreover, as organizations have been getting increasingly larger and more complex, many jobs are directed toward some specialized aspect of an organization that can seem far removed from what that organization is known for, and people may struggle to see the fruits of their own efforts at their jobs. Some kinds of work are more conducive to providing a sense of meaning than are others. In particular, jobs in which people are offering some kind of service toward others tend to feel particularly meaningful. For example, one study found that the most meaningful careers were clergy, teachers, and various health-care practitioners—all jobs in which people can readily identify a sense of purpose underlying what they are doing.[21]

How much meaning do you feel you're getting from your own work? If you're one of the fortunate ones who feels they have a meaningful career, then I'd suggest that you regularly try to appreciate how much your work gives you a sense of purpose, identity, and feelings of mastery. But many people won't find their careers to be conducive for addressing their existential needs, and retirees may also struggle because they lack the sense of mission or social network that they used to have with their jobs. People can make up for a perceived lack of fulfillment in their jobs by engaging in activities in their free time that can give them a sense of purpose and meaning, such as volunteering at a food pantry or animal shelter, joining a hiking group, or taking classes in something that interests them. I encourage you to find some activities that will make your life feel more meaningful.

## Spirituality

One of the strongest foundations of meaning in life comes from people's spirituality. When people believe that there are other forces that transcend their physical reality, they feel they are part of something far grander than their own lives. These feelings of connections with a transcendent realm help people to feel that their lives are significant: they can believe that their lives matter in the grand scheme of things. Believing in a transcendental realm has been found to be associated with many other benefits as well, such as greater psychological well-being and less anxiety, and believers tend to have better physical health. There are few aspects of people's lives that have as many well-being benefits as the belief in a supernatural realm.[22]

Most of the research on the benefits of a spiritual orientation has focused on people who belong to an organized religion, and on average, religious people show greater evidence of existential well-being than others. However, research finds that people gain many of these same existential benefits from having other kinds of spiritual beliefs, even if they occur outside a religion. For example, we found in our own research that people who are spiritual but not religious tend to report that their lives are far more meaningful than people who report that they have no spiritual beliefs whatsoever. Spiritual people see themselves as part of something much vaster than themselves. They are more likely to have mystical experiences that can't easily be explained, and they may feel that everything around them is interconnected. These beliefs are associated with experiencing life as more meaningful.[23]

These findings are very encouraging for the existential prospects of religious and spiritual people. Feelings of connection with the transcendent realm are associated with many existential benefits. But what about those of us who are not particularly spiritual or religious? Are people who have a materialist and secular outlook on the world blocked from accessing these kinds of rich existential benefits? What should one do if one is quite atheistic or exclusively committed to a search for scientific explanations? How might someone who is used to explaining the world in materialistic terms engage with the idea that transcendent forces are operating everywhere?

Søren Kierkegaard struggled with similar questions. He was an extraordinarily rigorous and logical thinker, and many of his ideas sometimes clashed with his sincerely held religious beliefs. Kierkegaard found much of Christian doctrine to be troubling and contradictory, such as how Abraham could be willing to kill his beloved son, Isaac, because of God's command, or how a loving God could subject such a devoted believer as Job to so much suffering and injustice. These puzzling stories would seem to suggest that it would be irrational to have faith in such a seemingly cruel and capricious God. Kierkegaard became rather obsessed with these paradoxical aspects of the Bible, and he wondered how one could keep their faith when their rational capacities couldn't make any sense of them. Does one need to choose between intellectual pursuits and their faith?

Kierkegaard viewed people's rational abilities to be limited, and he thought that many of the mysteries of the universe were not possible for people to fully comprehend using logical or empirically based arguments. He felt that he needed his faith, even though he couldn't always justify the reasons for it. Kierkegaard reached the conclusion that people had to leap from their logical ways of understanding the world and commit themselves to a higher truth that transcended the limits of human rationality. His resolution of this predicament has been influential enough that it has become part of our daily lexicon when we say that someone takes a "leap of faith." By leaping to faith, people could engage with their beliefs on an emotional, experiential, and personal level, without needing to fully articulate the rationale underlying their beliefs. Kierkegaard's own leap was to embrace his deep commitment with the Christian faith, even though he found so much of it to be paradoxical and absurd.[24]

I think recent research in existential psychology suggests that Kierkegaard may have been onto something here. Studies consistently find that people who believe in a transcendental realm lead existentially richer lives compared to those who only embrace materialistic explanations for the world. It's important to note that this research is correlational and thus raises the possibility that there may be other reasons why spiritual people report feeling that their lives are more meaningful. Nonetheless, I think this research suggests that one might benefit from trying to keep an open mind and consider the possibility that there may be more to the world than meets the eye.

If you feel attracted to a particular religion, then you may want to experiment with it—it might help you to feel that your life is more meaningful. But you don't need to belong to an organized religion to get many of the benefits of feeling connected to a transcendental realm. You might find that your life comes to feel more meaningful if you remain open to considering spiritual perspectives. I'm not suggesting that you should try to be open to all kinds of spiritual explanations—there are surely some spiritual accounts that won't fit with everyone's outlook. But if you are able to find any mystical traditions, activities, or experiences that largely fit with your own way of viewing the world, you would probably have more awe-eliciting experiences and feelings about the unity of everything and how everything is interconnected. Spiritual practices may well help you to feel that your own life is part of something far vaster than you are. Such an orientation should help you to feel that your life is more meaningful.[25]

## Purpose

Fyodor Dostoevsky wrote that "for the secret of man's being is not only to live, but to have something to live for. Without a stable conception of the object of life, man would not consent to go on living, and would rather destroy himself than remain on earth, though he had bread in abundance." Dostoevsky wisely recognized that we all need to live for something: we need to find a reason behind what we are doing. People feel that their lives are meaningful when they feel they have something to contribute and some underlying objective guiding their actions. To gain a better understanding of who we are, we need to consider the underlying reasons for what we are living for. People who have a stronger sense of purpose have a greater understanding of themselves and have more meaning in their lives.[26]

Having a sense of purpose in one's life plays a key role in providing people with a better understanding of themselves, but it is of even more importance for keeping them going forward, especially when times are hard. Viktor Frankl found that those of his fellow prisoners at Auschwitz who had a reason to live were more likely to survive the unimaginable horrors of the camp. Since Frankl's time, a great deal of research has investigated the role of having a sense of purpose in life and in circumstances far less extreme than what he experienced at Auschwitz. This research has largely supported Frankl's observations and has found that having a mission in life is associated with many benefits to people's health and overall well-being. Correlational studies have repeatedly found that people with a sense of purpose tend to fare better in countless ways: on average, they are more physically active, show less cognitive decline with age, earn more money, and live longer. A sense of purpose appears to be the ultimate silver bullet—there are few factors that have been found to be as advantageous to people's lives as having an understanding of what they are living for. But while having a sense of purpose is of great importance, it's not the case that just any old purpose will do. People have different kinds of purposes guiding their lives, and these various purposes offer contrasting kinds of existential benefits.[27]

Michael Mask, Dunigan Folk, and I conducted a series of studies where we investigated the different kinds of purposes in people's lives. We asked several hundred American adults what purposes guided their lives. People offered a wide variety of different reasons for why they were living their lives as they did, and when we analyzed their responses, we found that each was associated with somewhat different kinds of benefits. Purposes that were directed at helping others, making a positive impact on the world, and serving their spiritual concerns tended to have the most existential benefits. In contrast, purposes that were guided by a desire to acquire more wealth, being self-sufficient, and pursuing happiness were less associated with having meaning in one's life. The kinds of purposes that we choose to guide our life thus have different kinds of existential payoffs.[28]

## Rich Experiences

Another route to a meaningful life can be observed by examining the kinds of experiences that people pursue in their lives. People find many different kinds of experiences to be pleasant, but not all such experiences contribute to feelings of a meaningful life. For example, a person may be quite content to stay at home every day tending their garden, listening to their favorite radio program, and doing jigsaw puzzles. These activities may be quite comfortable, relaxing, and pleasant; however, it's unlikely that they would lead to enhanced feelings of meaning in life. Rather, the kinds of experiences that are more likely to provide a sense of meaning in life are *psychologically rich experiences.* Psychologically rich experiences are ones that captivate one's interest and curiosity, are high in variety, and ultimately come to change an individual's perspective on things. They are challenging experiences that remove people from their daily habits and routines and make them approach the world with a fresh mind-set. These experiences remind people that there is more to life than what they are already familiar with, and they require people to change their outlook on the world in order to fully understand and appreciate it. Psychologically rich experiences are characterized by novelty, variety, creativity, and complexity. They require a certain degree of mental effort to make sense of them, and as a result they tend to cultivate people's wisdom. Some kinds of rich experiences are quite large in scope, such as a student going to study abroad for a year or someone seriously taking up a new artistic pursuit, such as pottery or painting. But even relatively small experiences can provide richness, such as trying out new ethnic cuisines, visiting a local art gallery, or going to an escape room with friends. Psychologically rich experiences present people with complex challenges, and they provide opportunities for learning and discovery, all of which tend to be associated with enhanced feelings of meaning. So try to keep an open and curious mind-set as you go about your life. Consider that your life is like a journey: make efforts to try out new and challenging things along the way and always grab opportunities to pursue your passions.[29]

Moreover, it's not just the experiences people have, but also the *attitudes* they have toward their experiences that can make a difference. When people strive to savor their experiences and appreciate all that they have to offer, they are more likely to view their lives as meaningful. For example, people who say they appreciate the little things in life or take great interest in their daily activities are more likely to feel they are living a meaningful life. So try to cultivate an appreciative mind-set. Slow down and appreciate the good things that are happening in your life. Take some time to enjoy a beautiful view or the feel of a warm bath. Think about how much you enjoy your time with your friends, and how grateful you are for all the experiences you've had with your loved ones. Try to stop and smell the roses as you go along on your life journey. If you're able to foster an appreciative mind-set, you'll be more likely to see your life as meaningful.[30]

## Life Stories

One of the most significant sources of meaning in our lives comes from our life stories. Our life stories tie together all the threads of our lives, and they draw heavily from the foundations of meaning we discussed above. Our life stories integrate our relationships, communities, occupations, sense of purpose, rich experiences, and our spiritual outlook. A life story that is told well can function to organize all the different meanings of one's life and to provide one with a sense of coherence, purpose, and significance. But the kind of life story that people tell can have a great impact on how meaningful their lives feel. Simply put, some stories are better than others, and this holds true both in terms of the kinds of stories that people like to read and the kinds of stories that help to build a meaningful life.

Judging by its popularity, the original *Star Wars* has to be one of the better stories ever told, and its enormous appeal is no accident. The story follows the template of what the mythologist Joseph Campbell calls the hero's journey, which is characteristic of many of the greatest stories of all time. Stories that follow the template of the hero's journey share the following seven features, which are clearly evident in the story of *Star Wars*, and, as we'll see, in many people's meaningful life stories.[31]

1. *Protagonist.* The first feature of the hero's journey is that there is a clear and defined central character of the story who comes to recognize themselves as the hero. In the case of *Star Wars*, the story begins with the hero, Luke Skywalker, living a rather ordinary life together with his uncle and aunt. He spends his time moisture farming and hunting womp rats but always senses that he is destined for more.

2. *Shift.* The second feature of the hero's journey is some sudden change in circumstances that requires the hero to begin a psychological journey to resolve it. Luke Skywalker's simple and peaceful life comes to an abrupt end when the evil empire attacks his family's farm, preventing him from continuing on with his previous life.

3. *Quest.* A key feature is that the hero feels that they have an overarching quest to devote their lives toward. In Luke Skywalker's case, he receives a holographic message from Princess Leia requesting his help, and he accepts the challenge, ready to risk his life in his effort to save her and defeat the empire.

4. *Allies.* The hero usually depends on some key allies to help them to succeed in their journey. Luke Skywalker doesn't pursue

his quest alone, and soon he has teamed up with his mentor, Obi-Wan Kenobi, along with Han Solo, Princess Leia, Chewbacca, and others. Together, they pursue their shared mission to save the galaxy from the empire.

5. *Challenge.* Key to a hero's journey is a seemingly insurmountable obstacle. Luke Skywalker and his allies' quest seems impossible, given the vast strength of the empire and its evil commander, Darth Vader, and they face many overwhelming challenges along the way.

6. *Transformation.* In facing their challenges, the hero typically goes through personal and moral growth and is transformed into a better version of themselves. Luke Skywalker outgrows his youthful inexperienced past and becomes a powerful Jedi knight.

7. *Legacy.* In the end, the hero's actions come to have a positive impact on their communities, and they are revered for their efforts. Luke Skywalker saves the rebels by delivering an enormous win in the battle against the empire.

*Star Wars* is not at all unique among stories in following this template, and these same elements of the hero's journey can be found in many other epic adventures, from Hollywood productions, such as *Harry Potter, Hunger Games, Lord of the Rings,* and *Wizard of Oz,* to popular legends in other parts of the world, such as *Ramayana,* the *Epic of Gilgamesh,* and *Journey to the West.* Stories that fit this template seem to really resonate with people, and they frequently emerge as some of the most popular stories in literature. But the hero's journey is not just an effective template for making good mythology; it can also play a central role in the telling of our own life stories. People are mistaken if they think that there is only one way to tell their life story. As the novelist Henry James put it: "Adventures happen to people who know how to tell it that way." People can come to fare much better in their lives by crafting their own life story such that it follows the template of the hero's journey.

Take the example of Cheryl Strayed, the author of the popular book *Wild*, which was also the subject of a major Hollywood production by the same title. Strayed's life story follows many of the elements of the hero's journey. She is from a humble background, raised by a single mother who worked hard to make ends meet. But Strayed's life goes through a difficult shift as her mother dies and her marriage falls apart. She goes through a phase of pursuing short-term sexual conquests and turns to heroin to escape her pain. Recognizing that her life needed to be turned around, Strayed decides to quit her job and pursue a seemingly impossible adventure. Despite not having any real experience hiking or even owning any camping gear, she decides to set off on a 1,100-mile solo trek along the Pacific Crest Trail. Her goal seems unattainable—the trek seems impossible to her and her life appears to be at risk on numerous occasions. But she meets people along the way who help her out, and, somehow, she is able to keep plodding along on her journey. Her long trek transforms her from being inexperienced, confused, and purposeless to becoming a determined and experienced backpacker with a clearer set of life goals. After finishing her trek, she has kicked her drug habit, begun a career as a writer, found a new husband, started a family, and written an enormously popular book about her journey.

Strayed's story is very encouraging, especially for anyone who is feeling that their own life is off track. Her ability to turn her life around was probably a function of a few of the elements discussed in this book. She wrote about her own traumatic life events, which, as we discussed in the previous chapter, likely provided her with some greater insight. Her long time in nature may have facilitated some awe-inspiring transcendent experiences, which gave her life a much-needed meaning boost. She benefited from the new perspective that she gained by pursuing such a rich and life-changing experience. And her adventure fit well into the template of the hero's journey and helped her conceive of her life story in this transformational way.

Now I'm not suggesting that most people who wish to improve their life's course would benefit by embarking on an epic adventure like Strayed's. However, it's often possible to reap some of the same benefits by just considering how one's own past life fits the template of the hero's journey. Though there probably aren't that many people who would spontaneously consider their lives to have been heroic, the basic elements of the hero's journey are common to most people's lives. Research finds that when people are instructed to think about how each of the seven elements of the hero's journey are characteristic of their own lives, and then to write a story about the metaphorical journey that they have been on, they benefit a great deal from the experience. After completing this exercise, people commonly come to view their lives more in terms of a hero's journey, adopt a flourishing perspective on their lives, and see their lives as more meaningful. You might also enjoy similar benefits by trying to write your own hero's journey.[32]

## Leaping to a Meaningful Life

Meaningful lives are associated with many kinds of protective benefits, and we all would be better off if we could view our own lives as meaningful. So it is important to attend to the key foundations of meaning in our lives and consider the ways we can reinforce them. As this chapter highlights, our lives are made especially meaningful by our relationships, our communities, our work, and our spirituality. The meaning in our lives is bolstered by having a strong sense of purpose and rich experiences that we appreciate. And we depend upon our life stories to tie all of these elements together into a compelling and encouraging narrative. People who are able to do this well tend to have a more meaningful life. Your existential audit of how your own life fares in each of these key foundations of meaning likely identified a number of places where your current life is lacking. It would be rare for someone to have adequately constructed all of these foundations. You may find that you will benefit if you build foundations of meaning in those areas where you feel you've come up short. If you can shore up any of the underpinnings of meaning that you find are lacking, you'll likely start to feel that your life is more meaningful.

But research in existential psychology points to something even more encouraging: meaning can be transferred across foundations, such that the meaning we get in our lives in one domain, such as our relationships, can help to make up for a deficit to the meaning in our lives from another domain, such as our careers. The meaning in the different foundations of our lives is interchangeable such that having a spiritual outlook can help to make up for an unsatisfying family life, or getting involved in a new community can help to offset some of the costs from having an uninspiring life story. Each effort we make to build on the individual foundations of a meaningful life can help to bolster our overall reserve of meaning, and this can help protect us from any other areas of our lives that remain wanting. I encourage you to try to build a sense of meaning in your own life in whatever ways seem the most amenable to you.[33]

Research in existential psychology suggests that it is possible for people to make their lives more meaningful, although this can take some determination and struggle. Camus also recognized that the pursuit of a meaningful life required a lot of effort. He felt that we are all in a similar predicament as Sisyphus, trying to keep going in our efforts to build a meaningful life despite being upended by obstacles along the way. Camus felt that if we kept trying to move forward in our pursuits of a meaningful life, we would be happy in the ways that he imagines Sisyphus to be.

Camus felt that so much work was needed to create a meaningful life because he believed that the universe was entirely without meaning. In a meaningless universe, the only meaning that people could find in their lives would be based on their own Sisyphean efforts to construct a sense of meaning. But this is the one place where I disagree with Camus. I think that, at root, the universe is inherently meaningful and that there are transcendent forces guiding what is happening around us. I think that each of us is here for a reason and that people have underlying purposes. I think that people's lives are inherently meaningful, as the foundations of meaning in our life have been commonplace throughout history, although in the existential vacuum of the twenty-first century many of these are currently threatened.

While I believe that the universe is inherently meaningful, you may rightfully question whether this is actually true. Is the universe really meaningful? Well, I can't prove that it is. But I also know that science has yet to prove that it is not. And I think that sometimes we should reflect on the limits of science. Don't get me wrong—I think the scientific method is the best tool that humans have ever discovered, and it works great for explaining how the world operates. It is because of science that we have been able to develop so many successful solutions for dealing with the challenges we face, and the sheer number of scientific advances that humans have come up with are themselves rather awe-inspiring. But as powerful as science is, I don't think it's particularly useful for addressing the bigger questions of life, such as: Why are we here? Why is there something rather than nothing? Why do we have consciousness? I don't think science has produced good answers to these questions, and I am doubtful that it ever can. I think there are questions that lie beyond the purview of science, and that scientists would benefit by cultivating more humility in how we understand the universe and our place within it. Thus far, science has had few answers for many of the most important questions of our lives.

But regardless of whether it's ultimately scientifically accurate to claim that the universe is meaningful, the beliefs that we have are associated with different outcomes. Much research in existential psychology finds that believing that everything is connected and meaningful is associated with some existential benefits. People who believe in something that transcends them tend to have more meaningful lives. And having a more meaningful life helps to keep us healthy, functioning, and connected with our worlds. We stand to gain much by believing we are engaged in something meaningful.

I should add that I say that I believe the universe is meaningful as someone who stopped believing in God since the age of fifteen, when I abandoned my family's Baptist faith. I abandoned it because I found the literal teachings of the Bible to be strikingly inconsistent, horribly discriminatory, and frustratingly implausible, especially as they were so frequently at odds with what science has since revealed. I have never seriously considered returning to the church, but at the same time, I have often felt there was something supernatural about the universe. I have sometimes had the subjective feeling that I am connected with something transcendent. Whenever I have these feelings, I try to embrace them rather than eschew them.

I think we would benefit by taking a page from Kierkegaard's notebook, and we should strive to leap to a meaningful life and see meaning in the world around us. We would fare better by trying to build the connections that we have with everything, shoring up our foundations of meaning, and striving to tell a meaningful life story. I think that if we can look out to the world as though it is awe-inspiring, we'll be more likely to sometimes experience awe and the feelings of meaning that come along with that. Then we'll be best poised to confront all of the challenges that we have been encountering in the existential vacuum that envelops this new age of anxiety.

# Acknowledgments

In many ways, writing a book shares a lot in common with efforts to lead a meaningful life. Both become so much easier when we can rely on our interpersonal connections. In particular, I'm grateful for all of those who took the time to read earlier drafts of chapters and provided some extremely valuable feedback along the way. Thanks goes to Eden Anbar, Karl Aquino, Miranda Bahng, Rachele Benjamin, Oliver Bontkes, Dunigan Folk, Fritz Goetz, Kate Guan, Yilin Guo, Oliver Hasegawa, Dana Hunter, Will Jettinghoff, Nick Kay, David Klonsky, Hyunjin Koo, Kristin Laurin, Darrin Lehman, Ronnie Li, Charul Maheshka, Michael Mask, Eric Mercadente, Hazuki Miyoshi, Ara Norenzayan, Christine Ou, Paniz Radjaee, Matt Ruby, Anita Schmalor, Marc Shi, Jess Tracy, Jiayin Wang, and Chenxi Wu for helping me identify ways to make these chapters more coherent. In addition, I'm also indebted to the grad students who took a class on meaning and existential psychology with Jess Tracy and me and who read some of these chapters and offered insightful thoughts on the questions that they raised. Likewise, thanks to a class of undergrad students who took a course on existential psychology with me and who read several draft chapters and discussed many of the issues in class. These experiences were invaluable for helping me to identify the best ways to frame the issues in this book.

I'm also extremely appreciative of the students and collaborators who have worked with me on the many research projects that explored these questions of how people can make meaning in their lives. Thanks to Karl Aquino, Miranda Bahng, Rachele Benjamin, Roxane Cohen Silver, Dunigan Folk, Kate Guan, Todd Handy, Michael Inzlicht, Will Jettinghoff, Darrin Lehman, Jason Martens, Eric Mercadente, Ara Norenzayan, Michael Poulin, Travis Proulx, Paniz Radjaee, Daniel Randles, Bastiaan Rutjens, Nathan Santos, Alexa Tullett, Michiel van Elk, Kathleen Vohs, and Aiyana Willard. Without their assistance, those projects could never have been done, and I wouldn't have been able to write this book.

The research that I conducted, which was discussed in this book, was all funded by the Social Sciences and Humanities Research Council of Canada. I'm grateful for the support that they have provided me throughout my career.

I greatly appreciate all of the help from my agent Max Brockman, who not only helped me formulate the early wisps of ideas into a book proposal but was also there for me throughout the long writing process. I am also grateful to the editors who I worked with at Basic Books, Emma Berry and Michael Kaler. Thanks for helping to make this a more accessible and compelling read.

I'm also thankful for discussions regarding the pursuit of a meaningful life with Martin Carroll, Allen Lehman, Bruce McMurtry, Michael Papsdorf, and Shawn Reynolds. Your friendship, and our regular gatherings, help bolster the foundation of meaning in my own life.

Finally, I'm most fortunate to have such a loving and supportive family who have helped to keep me grounded and provide

## Acknowledgments

my life with so much meaning. Thanks to my parents, Jerry and Dorothy, and my sister, Brenda, for providing me with such a well-connected and enriching upbringing. And I'm grateful to my kids, Seiji, Koko, and Elizabeth, and my wife, Christine, for making my own journey a rich and purposeful experience.

# Notes

### Chapter 1: The New Age of Anxiety

1. World Uncertainty Index. (1990–2023). *World Uncertainty Index (WUI): Global* [Graph]. https://worlduncertaintyindex.com

2. Twenge, J. M., Campbell, W. K., & Freeman, E. C. (2012). Generational differences in young adults' life goals, concern for others, and civic orientation. *Journal of Personality and Social Psychology, 102*(5), 1045–1062.

3. Putnam, R. (2020). *Bowling Alone.* Revised and updated. New York: Simon & Schuster; Kitanovska, S., Zenger News. (August 5, 2022). Average American only spends 3 dinners a week with loved ones, poll shows. *Newsweek.* https://www.newsweek.com/average-american-only-spends-3 -dinners-week-loved-ones-poll-shows-1731243; and Dew, J. P. (2009). Has the marital time cost of parenting changed over time? *Social Forces, 88,* 519–541.

4. Kannan, V. D., & Veazie, P. J. (2023). US trends in social isolation, social engagement, and companionship—nationally and by age, sex, race/ ethnicity, family income and work hours, 2003–2020. *SSM—Population Health, 21,* 101331; and Office of U.S. Surgeon General. (2023). *Our epidemic of loneliness and isolation: The U.S. Surgeon General's advisory on the healing effects of social connection and community.* https://www.hhs.gov /sites/default/files/surgeon-general-social-connection-advisory.pdf.

5. Putnam, *Bowling Alone.*

6. See Gallup. (2016). *How millennials want to work and live.* https://www.gallup.com/workplace/238073/millennials-work-live.aspx; and Bidwell, M. J. (2013). What happened to long-term employment? The role of worker power and environmental turbulence in explaining declines in worker tenure. *Organization Science, 24,* 1061–1082.

7. Jones, J. M. (2021, March 20). *U.S. church membership falls below majority for first time.* Gallup News. https://news.gallup.com/poll/341963 /church-membership-falls-below-majority-first-time.aspx; Pew Research Center. (2022, September 13). *Modeling the future of religion in America.*

https://www.pewresearch.org/religion/2022/09/13/modeling-the-future-of
-religion-in-america/; and Seybold, K. S., & Hill, P. C. (2001). The role of
religion and spirituality in mental and physical health. *Current Directions in
Psychological Science, 10,* 21–24.

8. Santos, H. C., Varnum, M. E. W., & Grossmann, I. (2017). Global
increases in individualism. *Psychological Science, 28,* 1228–1239; Oishi, S., &
Diener, E. (2014). Residents of poor nations have a greater sense of meaning
in life than residents of wealthy nations. *Psychological Science, 25,* 422–430;
and Kleiman, E. M., & Beaver, J. K. (2013). A meaningful life is worth living:
Meaning in life as a suicide resiliency factor. *Psychiatry Research, 210,*
934–939.

9. Frankl, V. E. (1946). *Man's Search for Meaning.* New York:
Washington Square Press.

10. Daniller, A. (2023, April 24). *Americans take a dim view of the
nation's future, look more positively at the past.* Pew Research Center. https:
//www.pewresearch.org/short-reads/2023/04/24/americans-take-a-dim
-view-of-the-nations-future-look-more-positively-at-the-past/.

11. Richter, F. (2019, June 18). *How U.S. family incomes have grown since
the 1950s.* Statista. https://www.statista.com/chart/18418/real-mean-and
-median-family-income-in-the-us/#:~:text=Both%20mean%20and%20
median%20family,participation%20rate%2C%20especially%20among
%20women; US Department of Commerce. (2015). *2015 characteristics of
housing.* https://www.census.gov/construction/chars/pdf/c25ann2015.pdf;
Qualman, D. (2018, May 8). *Home grown: 67 years of US and Canadian
house size data.* Darrin Qualman. https://www.darrinqualman.com
/house-size/; Ortiz-Ospina, E., Giattino, C., & Roser, M. (2020). *Time
use.* Our World in Data. https://ourworldindata.org/time-use; Statista
Research Department. (2014, June 14). *The average retirement age in the
United States from 1900 to 2010.* Statista. https://www.statista.com/statistics
/319983/average-retirement-age-in-the-us/; Merrill Lynch. (2014, March).
*Work in retirement: Myths and motivations.* Age Wave. https://agewave
.com/wp-content/uploads/2016/07/2014-ML-AW-Work-in-Retirement
_Myths-and-Motivations.pdf; and Macrotrends. (2024). *U.S. life expectancy
1950–2024.* https://www.macrotrends.net/countries/USA/united-states/life
-expectancy

12. United States Congress Joint Economic Committee. (2019,
September 5). *Long-term trends in deaths of despair.* https://www.jec.senate
.gov/public/index.cfm/republicans/2019/9/long-term-trends-in-deaths-of
-despair; Twenge, J. M., Joiner, T. E., Duffy, M. E., Cooper, A. B., & Binau,

S. G. (2019). Age, period, and cohort trends in mood disorder indicators and suicide-related outcomes in a nationally representative dataset, 2005–2017. *Journal of Abnormal Psychology, 3,* 185–199; COVID-19 Mental Disorders Collaborators. (2021). Global prevalence and burden of depressive and anxiety disorders in 204 countries and territories in 2020 due to the COVID-19 pandemic. *Lancet, 398,* P1700–P1712; and see p. 153 of Twenge, J. M., Gentile, B., DeWall, C. N., Ma, D., Lacefield, K., & Schurtz, D. R. (2010). Birth cohort increases in psychopathology among young Americans, 1938–2007: A cross-temporal meta-analysis of the MMPI. *Clinical Psychology Review, 30,* 145–154.

13. Gopnik, A. (2012, April 2). Facing history: Why we love Camus. *New Yorker.* https://www.newyorker.com/magazine/2012/04/09/facing-history.

14. Bakewell, S. (2016). *At the Existentialist Café,* 10. New York: Other Press.

15. Beauvoir, S. de (1970/1996). *The Coming of Age.* New York: W. W. Norton.

16. Proulx, T., & Heine, S. J. (2008). The case of the transmogrifying experimenter: Reaffirmation of moral schemas following implicit change detection. *Psychological Science, 19,* 1294–1300; Proulx, T., & Heine, S. J. (2009). Connections from Kafka: Exposure to schema threats improves implicit learning of an artificial grammar. *Psychological Science, 20,* 1125–1131; Randles, D., Benjamin, R. F., Martens, J. P., & Heine, S. J. (2018). Searching for answers in an uncertain world: Meaning threats lead to increased working memory capacity. *PLoS ONE, 13*(10), e0204640; Benjamin, R. F., & Heine, S. J. (2023). From Freud to androids: Constructing a scale of uncanny feelings. *Journal of Personality Assessment, 105,* 121–133; and Guan, K. W., & Heine, S. J. (2023). When good people break bad: Moral impression violations in everyday life. *Social Psychological and Personality Science, 14,* 26–39.

## Chapter 2: Becoming an Existential Ape

1. Camus, A. (1955). *The Myth of Sisyphus and Other Essays,* 3. New York: Vintage Books.

2. Bering, J. (2018). *Suicidal,* 41. Chicago: University of Chicago Press.

3. Camus, *Myth of Sisyphus,* 4.

4. Heine, S. J., Folk, D. P., Guan, K. W., Benjamin, R., Bahng, J. M., & Proulx, T. (2024). An ecology of meaning: An integrative framework for understanding human motivations. *Advances in Motivation Science, 11.*

5. Baumeister, R. F., & Landau, M. J. (2018). Finding the meaning of meaning: Emerging insights on four grand questions. *Review of General Psychology, 22*, 1–10.

6. Nietzsche, F. (1886/1973). *Beyond Good and Evil*, 19. New York: Penguin.

7. Inoue, S., & Matsuzawa, T. (2007). Working memory of numerals in chimpanzees. *Current Biology, 17*, R1004–R1005; and Martin, C. F., Bhui, R., Bossaerts, P., Matsuzawa, T., & Camerer, C. F. (2014). Experienced chimpanzees are more strategic than humans in competitive games. *Scientific Reports, 4*, 5182.

8. De Waal, F. (1982). *Chimpanzee Politics*. Baltimore, MD: Johns Hopkins University Press; and Suddendorf, T. (2013). *The Gap*. New York: Basic Books.

9. Coppins, M. (2018, October 17). The man who broke politics. *Atlantic Monthly*. https://www.theatlantic.com/magazine/archive/2018/11/newt-gingrich-says-youre-welcome/570832/

10. Warneken, F., Chen, F., & Tomasello, M. (2006). Cooperative activities in young children and chimpanzees. *Child Development, 3*, 640–663; and Tomasello, M. (2010, October). Page-Barbour lecture at the University of Virginia. For more arguments about why this is so, see Tomasello, M., Carpenter, M., Call, J., Behne, T., & Moll, H. (2005). Understanding and sharing intentions: The origins of cultural cognition. *Behavioral and Brain Sciences, 28*, 675–735.

11. Goodall, J. (1967). Mother-offspring relationships in free-ranging chimpanzees. In D. Morris, ed., *Primate Ethology*, 287–346. New York: Routledge; and Silk, J. B., Brosnan, S. F., Vonk, J., Henrich, J., Povinelli, D. J., Richardson, A. S., Lambeth, S. P., Mascaro, J., & Schapiro, S. J. (2005). Chimpanzees are indifferent to the welfare of unrelated group members. *Nature, 437*, 1357–1359.

12. Rekers, Y., Haun, D. B. M., & Tomasello, M. (2011). Children, but not chimpanzees, prefer to collaborate. *Current Biology, 21*, 1756–1758.

13. Kobayashi, H., & Kohshima, S. (2001). Unique morphology of the human eye and its adaptive meaning: Comparative studies on external morphology of the primate eye. *Journal of Human Evolution, 40*, 419–435.

14. Tamir, D. I., & Mitchell, J. P. (2012). Disclosing information about the self is intrinsically rewarding. *PNAS, 109*, 8038–8043; Dunbar, R. I. M., Duncan, N. D. C., & Marriott, A. M. (1997). Human conversational behavior. *Human Nature, 8*(3), 231–246; and Naaman, M., Boase, J., & Lai, C. H. (2010). *Is it really about me?: Message content in social awareness streams*, 189–192. Proceedings of the 2010 ACM Conference on Computer

Supported Cooperative Work (Association for Computing Machinery), Savannah, GA.

15. Heine, S. J. (2020). *Cultural Psychology*, 4th ed. New York: W. W. Norton.

16. Putnam, R. D., Leonardi, R., & Nanetti, R. Y. (1993). *Making Democracy Work*. Princeton, NJ: Princeton University Press.

17. Cullum, J. G., & Harton, H. C. (2007). Cultural evolution: Importance and the development of shared attitudes in college residence halls. *Personality and Social Psychology Bulletin*, 33, 1327–1339.

18. Shweder, R. A., Mahapatra, N., & Miller, J. G. (1990). Culture and moral development. In J. W. Stigler, R. A. Shweder, & G. Herdt, eds., *Cultural Psychology: Essays on Comparative Human Development*, 130–204. Cambridge, UK: Cambridge University Press.

19. Whiten, A., Goodall, J., McGrew, W. C., Nishida, T., Reynolds, V., Sugiyama, Y., Tutin, C. E. G., Wrangham, R. W., & Boesch, C. (1999). Cultures in chimpanzees. *Nature*, 399, 682–685.

20. Kenrick, D. T., Griskevicius, V., Neuberg, S. L., & Schaller, M. (2010). Renovating the pyramid of needs: Contemporary extensions built upon ancient foundations. *Perspectives in Psychological Science*, 5, 292–314.

21. Henrich, J. (2016). *The Secret of Our Success*. Princeton, NJ: Princeton University Press.

22. Baumeister, R. F. (2022). *The Self Explained*. New York: Guilford Press.

23. Gelfand, M. J., Jackson, J. C., Pan, X., Nau, D., Pieper, D., Denison, E., Dagher, M., Van Lange, P. A. M., Chiu, C.-Y., & Wang, M. (2021). The relationship between cultural tightness–looseness and COVID-19 cases and deaths: A global analysis. *Lancet Planetary Health*, 5(3), e135–e144; Salvador, C. E., Berg, M. K., Yu, Q., San Martin, A., & Kitayama, S. (2020). Relational mobility predicts faster spread of COVID-19: A 39 country study. *Psychological Science*, 31, 1236–1244; Fincher, C. L., Thornhill, R., Murray, D. R., & Schaller, M. (2008). Pathogen prevalence predicts human cross-cultural variability in individualism/collectivism. *Proceedings of the Royal Society B: Biological Sciences*, 275, 1279–1285; and Na, J., Kim, N., Suk, H. W., Choi, E., Choi, J. A., Kim, J. H., Kim, S., & Choi, I. (2021). Individualism-collectivism during the COVID-19 pandemic: A field study testing the pathogen stress hypothesis of individualism-collectivism in Korea. *Personality and Individual Differences*, 183, 111127.

24. Markus, H. R., & Kitayama, S. (1991). Culture and the self: Implications for cognition, emotion, and motivation. *Psychological Review*, 98, 224–253.

25. Heine, S. J. (2001). Self as cultural product: An examination of East Asian and North American selves. *Journal of Personality, 69,* 881–906; Nisbett, R. E. (2003). *The Geography of Thought.* New York: Free Press; and Henrich, J., Heine, S. J., & Norenzayan, A. (2010). The weirdest people in the world? *Behavioral and Brain Sciences, 33,* 61–135.

26. Heine, *Cultural Psychology.*

27. Heine et al., An ecology of meaning.

## Chapter 3: Understanding Ourselves and Our Worlds Through Stories

1. Camus, A. (1955). *The Myth of Sisyphus and Other Essays.* New York: Alfred A. Knopf.

2. Meagher, R. E. (2021). *Albert Camus and the Human Crisis.* New York: Pegasus; Lottman, H. R. (1997). *Albert Camus: A Biography.* Corte Madera, CA: Gingko Press; and Zaretsky, R. (2010). *Albert Camus: Elements of a Life,* 145. Ithaca, NY: Cornell University Press.

3. Whitman, W. (1855/2020). *Leaves of Grass,* 44. Independently published; and Camus, *Myth of Sisyphus,* 17.

4. Camus, *Myth of Sisyphus,* 4, 17.

5. Campbell, J. D., Trapnell, P., Heine, S. J., Katz, I. M., Lavallee, L. F., & Lehman, D. R. (1996). Self-concept clarity: Measurement, personality correlates, and cultural boundaries. *Journal of Personality and Social Psychology, 70,* 141–156.

6. Butzer, B., & Kuiper, N. A. (2006). Relationships between the frequency of social comparisons and self-concept clarity, intolerance of uncertainty, anxiety, and depression. *Personality and Individual Differences, 41,* 167–176; and Wong, A. E., Dirghangi, S. R., & Hart, S. R. (2019). Self-concept clarity mediates the effects of adverse childhood experiences on adult suicide behavior, depression, loneliness, perceived stress, and life distress. *Self and Identity, 18,* 247–266.

7. Bruner, J. (1990). *Acts of Meaning.* Cambridge, MA: Harvard University Press.

8. Miller, P. J. (1994). Narrative practices: Their role in socialization and self-construction. In U. Neisser & R. Fivush, eds., *The Remembering Self,* 158–179. New York: Oxford University Press.

9. Sartre, J.-P. (1938). *Nausea,* 39. New York: New Directions.

10. Loftus, E. F., & Pickrell, J. E. (1995). The formation of false memories. *Psychiatric Annals, 25*(12), 720–725; Ceci, S. J., Huffman, M. L. C., Smith, E., & Loftus, E. F. (1995). Repeatedly thinking about a non-event:

Source misattributions among preschoolers. *Consciousness and Cognition,* *3,* 388–407; and Porter, S., Yuille, J. C., & Lehman, D. R. (1999). The nature of real, implanted, and fabricated memories for emotional childhood events: Implications for the recovered memory debate. *Law and Human Behavior, 23,* 517–537.

11. From p. 101 of McAdams, D. P. (2001). The psychology of life stories. *Review of General Psychology, 5,* 100–122.

12. Habermas, T., & Bluck, S. (2000). Getting a life: The emergence of the life story in adolescence. *Psychological Bulletin, 126,* 748–769; and Dunlop, W. L., & Walker, L. J. (2013). The life story: Its development and relation to narration and personal identity. *International Journal of Behavioral Development, 37,* 235–247.

13. McAdams, D. P. (1996). Personality, modernity, and the storied self: A contemporary framework for studying persons. *Psychological Inquiry, 7,* 295–321.

14. Frampton, P. H. (2014). *Tricked! The Story of an Internet Scam*; and Swann, M. (2013, March 8). The professor, the bikini model and the suitcase full of trouble. *New York Times.* https://www.nytimes.com/2013/03/10/magazine/the-professor-the-bikini-model-and-the-suitcase-full-of-trouble.html

15. Dunning, D. (1995). Trait importance and modifiability as factors influencing self-assessment and self-enhancement motives. *Personality and Social Psychology Bulletin, 21,* 1297–1306; Heine, S. J., & Hamamura, T. (2007). In search of East Asian self-enhancement. *Personality and Social Psychology Review, 11,* 4–27; Cross, P. (1977). Not can but will college teaching be improved? *New Directions for Higher Education, 17,* 1–15; College Board. (1976–1977). *Student Descriptive Questionnaire.* Princeton, NJ: Educational Testing Service; and Taylor, S. E., & Brown, J. D. (1988). Illusion and well-being: A social psychological perspective on mental health. *Psychological Bulletin, 103,* 193–210.

16. Heine, S. J., & Lehman, D. R. (1997). The cultural construction of self-enhancement: An examination of group-serving biases. *Journal of Personality and Social Psychology, 72,* 1268–1283; Rose, R. (1985). National pride in cross-national perspective. *International Social Science Journal, 103,* 85–96; Belk, R. W. (2013). Possessions and the extended self. *Journal of Consumer Research, 15,* 139–168; Gawronski, B., Bodenhausen, G. V., & Becker, A. P. (2007). I like it, because I like myself: Associative self-anchoring and post-decisional change of implicit evaluations. *Journal of Experimental Social Psychology, 43,* 221–232; and Maddux, W. W., Yang, H., Falk, C. F., Adam, H., Adair, W., Endo, Y., Carmon, Z., & Heine, S. J. (2010). For

whom is parting with possessions most painful? Cultural differences in the endowment effect. *Psychological Science, 21,* 1910–1917.

17. Janoff-Bulman, R. (1992). *Shattered Assumptions.* New York: Free Press.

18. Simon, L., Greenberg, J., & Brehm, J. (1995). Trivialization: The forgotten mode of dissonance reduction. *Journal of Personality and Social Psychology, 68,* 247–260.

19. Mezulis, A. H., Abramson, L. Y., Hyde, J. S., & Hankin, B. L. (2004). Is there a universal positive bias in attributions?: A meta-analytic review of individual, developmental, and cultural differences in the self-serving attributional bias. *Psychological Bulletin, 130,* 711–747.

20. Berglas, S., & Jones, E. E. (1978). Drug choice as a self-handicapping strategy in response to a non-contingent success. *Journal of Personality and Social Psychology, 36,* 405–417; and Tice, D. M. (1991). Esteem protection or enhancement? Self-handicapping motives and attributions differ by trait self-esteem. *Journal of Personality and Social Psychology, 60,* 711–725.

21. Brown, J. D. (1986). Evaluations of self and others: Self-enhancement biases in social judgments. *Social Cognition, 4,* 353–376; and Murray, S. L., Holmes, J. G., MacDonald, G., & Ellsworth, P. C. (1998). Through the looking glass darkly? When self-doubts turn into relationship insecurities. *Journal of Personality and Social Psychology, 75,* 1459–1480.

22. Heine, S. J., Lehman, D. R., Markus, H. R., & Kitayama, S. (1999). Is there a universal need for positive self-regard? *Psychological Review, 106,* 766–794; Heine, S. J. (2005). Constructing good selves in Japan and North America. In R. M. Sorrentino, D. Cohen, J. M. Olson, & M. P. Zanna, eds., *Culture and Social Behavior: The Tenth Ontario Symposium,* 95–116. Hillsdale, NJ: Lawrence Erlbaum; and Wilson, C. (1994). Paris targets Asia's rich markets. *Asian Business, 30,* 52; see also https://www.statista.com /statistics/267733/global-revenue-share-of-gucci-by-region/

23. Baumeister, R. F. (1993). Understanding the inner nature of low self-esteem: Uncertain, fragile, protective, and conflicted. In R. Baumeister, ed., *Self-Esteem: The Puzzle of Low Self-Regard,* 201–218. New York: Plenum Press; Hankin, B. L. (2009). Insecure attachment dysfunctional attitudes, and low self-esteem predicting prospective symptoms of depression and anxiety during adolescence. *Journal of Clinical Child & Adolescent Psychology, 38,* 219–231; Heine, S. J., Foster, J. A., & Spina, R. (2009). Do birds of a feather universally flock together? Cultural variation in the similarity-attraction effect. *Asian Journal of Social Psychology, 12,* 247–258; Maddux et al., For whom is parting with possessions most painful? and

Alexopoulos, T., Simlesa, M., & Francis, M. (2015). Good self, bad self: Initial success and failure moderate the endowment effect. *Journal of Economic Psychology, 50*, 32–40.

24. Swann, W. B. (2011). Self-verification theory. In P. A. M. Van Lange, A. W. Kruglanski, & E. T. Higgins, eds., *Handbook of Theories of Social Psychology*, vol. 2, 23–42. London: Sage; and Swann, W. B., De La Ronde, C., & Hixon, J. G. (1994). Authenticity and positivity strivings in marriage and courtship. *Journal of Personality and Social Psychology, 66*, 857–869.

25. Mercadente, E., Heine, S. J., & Aquino, K. (2023). Leadership in the eye of the beholder: Follower self-esteem is associated with divergent perceptions of leadership ability for dominant and prestigious leaders. *Journal of Personality, 91*, 1253–1270.

26. Bakewell, S. (2016). *At the Existentialist Café*, 210. New York: W. W. Norton; and de Beauvoir, S. (1949/2011). *The Second Sex*, 684, 757. New York: Vintage.

27. Knowles, C. (2019). Beauvoir on women's complicity in their own unfreedom. *Hypatia, 34*, 242–265; and James, S. (2003). Complicity and slavery in *The Second Sex*. In C. Card, ed., *The Cambridge Companion to Simone de Beauvoir*, 149–167. Cambridge, UK: Cambridge University Press.

28. P. 16 in Zinn, H. (2002). *Disobedience and Democracy: Nine Fallacies on Law and Order*. Cambridge, MA: South End Press.

29. New York Times staff. (2020, November 3). National exit polls: How different groups voted. *New York Times.* https://www.nytimes.com/interactive/2020/11/03/us/elections/exit-polls-president.html; Huang, J., Jacoby, S., Strickland, M., & Lai, K. K. R. (2016, November 8). Election 2016: Exit polls. *New York Times.* https://www.nytimes.com/interactive/2016/11/08/us/politics/election-exit-polls.html; and Gest, J. (2016). *The New Minority: White Working Class Politics in an Age of Immigration and Inequality*. New York: Oxford University Press.

30. Jost, J. T. (2020). *A Theory of System Justification*. Cambridge, MA: Harvard University Press.

31. Wilkinson, R. G., & Pickett, K. E. (2010). *The Spirit Level: Why More Equal Societies Almost Always Do Better*. London: Penguin; and Mijs, J. J. B. (2021). The paradox of inequality: Income inequality and belief in meritocracy go hand in hand. *Socio-Economic Review, 19*, 7–35.

32. Dickens, C. (1843/1971). *A Christmas Carol and the Chimes*, 99. Vol. 1 in *The Christmas Books*. London: Penguin Books; Hagerty, M. R., & Veenhoven, R. (2003). Wealth and happiness revisited—growing national income does go with greater happiness. *Social Indicators Research, 64*,

1–27; and Kay, A. C., & Jost, J. T. (2003). Complementary justice: Effects of "poor but happy" and "poor but honest" stereotype exemplars on system justification and implicit activation of the justice motive. *Journal of Personality and Social Psychology, 85,* 823–837.

33. Lerner, M. J., & Miller, D. T. (1978). Just world research and the attribution process: Looking back and ahead. *Psychological Bulletin, 85,* 1030–1051; and Hafer, C. L., & Begue, L. (2005). Experimental research on just-world theory: Problems, developments, and future challenges. *Psychological Bulletin, 131,* 128–167.

34. Raine, N. V. (1998). *After Silence.* New York: Crown; and Stokols, D., & Schopler, J. (1973). Reactions to victims under conditions of situational detachment: The effects of responsibility, severity, and expected future interaction. *Journal of Personality and Social Psychology, 25,* 199–209.

35. Janoff-Bulman, R. (1979). Characterological versus behavioral self-blame: Inquiries into depression and rape. *Journal of Personality and Social Psychology, 37,* 1798–1809; Kennedy, A. C., & Prock, K. A. (2018). "I still feel like I am not normal": A review of the role of stigma and stigmatization among female survivors of child sexual abuse, sexual assault, and intimate partner violence. *Trauma, Violence, & Abuse, 19,* 512–527; and Bulman, R. J., & Wortman, C. B. (1977). Attributions of blame and coping in the "real world": Severe accident victims react to their lot. *Journal of Personality and Social Psychology, 35,* 351–363.

### Chapter 4: How Our Brains Ensure Our Lives Make Sense

1. Reynolds, S. (2011). *Retromania: Pop Culture's Addiction to Its Own Past,* xiii. London: Faber and Faber.

2. Hoban, A., & Gannon, V. (2021, June 8). *Why we were mad for nostalgia in the last year.* RTE. https://www.rte.ie/brainstorm/2021/0608/1226852 -nostalgia-millennials-pandemic-tv-film-music-marketing-brands/

3. Dostoevsky, F. (1880/2005). *The Brothers Karamazov,* 716. New York: Dover.

4. Wildschut, T., Sedikides, C., Arndt, J., & Routledge, C. (2006). Nostalgia: Content, triggers, functions. *Journal of Personality and Social Psychology, 91,* 975–993.

5. Sedikides, C., & Wildschut, T. (2018). Finding meaning in nostalgia. *Review of General Psychology, 22,* 48–61; and Routledge, C. (2015). *Nostalgia: A Key Psychological Resource.* London: Routledge.

6. Van Tilburg, W. A. P., Igou, E. R., & Sedikides, C. (2013). In search of meaningfulness: Nostalgia as an antidote to boredom. *Emotion, 13,* 450–461.

7. Routledge, C., Arndt, J., Wildschut, T., Sedikides, C., Hart, C. M., Juhl, J., Vingerhoets, A. J. J. M., & Schlotz, W. (2011). The past makes the present meaningful: Nostalgia as an existential resource. *Journal of Personality and Social Psychology, 101,* 638–652.

8. Hakulinen, C., Pulkki-Raback, L., Virtanen, M., Jokela, M., Kivimaki, M., & Elovainio, M. (2018). Social isolation and loneliness as risk factors for myocardial infarction, stroke and mortality: UK Biobank cohort study of 479,054 men and women. *Heart, 104,* 1536–1542; Pressman, S. D., Cohen, S., Miller, G. E., Barkin, A., Rabin, B. S., & Treanor, J. J. (2005). Loneliness, social network size, and immune response to influenza vaccination in college freshmen. *Health Psychology, 24,* 297–306; Holt-Lunstad, J., Smith, T. B., & Layton, J. B. (2010). Social relationships and mortality risk: A meta-analytic review. *PLoS Medicine, 7*(7), e1000316; and Caspi, A., Harrington, H., Moffitt, T. E., Milne, B. J., & Poulton, R. (2006). Socially isolated children 20 years later: Risk of cardiovascular disease. *Archives of Pediatric & Adolescent Medicine, 160,* 805–811.

9. Baumeister, R. F., & Leary, M. R. (1995). The need to belong: Desire for interpersonal attachments as a fundamental human motivation. *Psychological Bulletin, 117,* 497–529.

10. Dunbar, R. (2021). *Friends,* 154. London: Little, Brown; and Dunbar, R. I. M., & Spoors, M. (1995). Social networks, support cliques, and kinship. *Human Nature, 6,* 273–290.

11. Buss, D. M., Goetz, C., Duntley, J. D., Asao, K., & Conroy-Beam, D. (2017). The mate switching hypothesis. *Personality and Individual Differences, 104,* 143–149.

12. Rochat, P. (2009). *Others in Mind: Social Origins of Self-Consciousness,* 21. Cambridge, UK: Cambridge University Press; and Williams, K. D. (1997). Social ostracism. In R. Kowalski, ed., *Aversive Interpersonal Behaviors,* 133–170. New York: Plenum Press.

13. MacDonald, G., & Leary, M. R. (2005). Why does social exclusion hurt? The relationship between social and physical pain. *Psychological Bulletin, 131,* 202–223.

14. Lieberman, M. (2013). *Social: Why Our Brains Are Wired to Connect.* New York: Crown.

15. Eisenberger, N. I., Lieberman, M. D., Williams, K. D. (2003). Does rejection hurt?: An fMRI study of social exclusion. *Science, 302,* 290–292.

16. DeWall, C. N., MacDonald, G., Webster, G. D., Masten, C. L., Baumeister, R. F., Powell, C., Combs, D., Schurtz, D. R., Stillman, T. F., Tice, D. M., & Eisenberger, N. I. (2010). Acetaminophen reduces social pain: Behavioral and neural evidence. *Psychological Science, 21,* 931–937.

17. Quirin, M., Loktyushin, A., Arndt, J., Küstermann, E., Lo, Y.-Y., Kuhl, J., & Eggert, L. (2012). Existential neuroscience: A functional magnetic resonance imaging investigation of neural responses to reminders of one's mortality. *Social Cognitive and Affective Neuroscience, 7*(2), 193–198; van Veen, V., Krug, M. K., Schooler, J. W., & Carter, C. S. (2009). Neural activity predicts attitude change in cognitive dissonance. *Nature Neuroscience, 12*(11), 1469–1474; and Botvinick, M. M., Cohen, J. D., & Carter, C. S. (2004). Conflict monitoring and anterior cingulate cortex: An update. *Trends in Cognitive Science, 8*(12), 539–546.

18. Seeley, W. W. (2019). The salience network: A neural system for perceiving and responding to homeostatic demands. *Journal of Neuroscience, 39,* 9878–9882; Menon, V., & Uddin, L. Q. (2010). Saliency, switching, attention and control: A network model of insula function. *Brain Structure and Function, 214,* 655–667; and Ham, T., Leff, A., de Boissezon, X., Joffe, A., & Sharp, D. J. (2013). Cognitive control and the salience network: An investigation of error processing and effective connectivity. *Journal of Neuroscience, 33,* 7091–7098.

19. Durso, G. R. O., Luttrell, A., & Way, B. M. (2015). Over-the-counter relief from pains and pleasures alike: Acetaminophen blunts evaluation sensitivity to both negative and positive stimuli. *Psychological Science, 26,* 750–758; Ratner, K. G., Kaczmarek, A. R., & Hong, Y. (2018). Can over-the-counter pain medications influence our thoughts and emotions? *Policy Insights from the Behavioral and Brain Sciences, 5,* 82–89; Keaveney, A., Peters, E., & Way, B. (2020). Effects of acetaminophen on risk taking. *Social Cognitive and Affective Neuroscience, 15,* 725–732; DeWall, C. N., Chester, D. S., & White, D. S. (2015). Can acetaminophen reduce the pain of decision-making? *Journal of Experimental Social Psychology, 56,* 117–120; and Randles, D., Heine, S. J., & Santos, N. (2013). The common pain of surrealism and death: Acetaminophen reduces compensatory affirmation following meaning threats. *Psychological Science, 24*(6), 966–973.

20. Randles, D., Kam, J., Heine, S. J., Inzlicht, M., & Handy, T. (2016). Acetaminophen attenuates error evaluation in cortex. *Social Cognitive and Affective Neuroscience, 11*(6), 899–906.

21. Freud, S. (1919/2003). *The Uncanny,* 144. New York: Penguin.

22. Benjamin, R. F., & Heine, S. J. (2023). From Freud to androids: Constructing a scale of uncanny feelings. *Journal of Personality Assessment, 105,* 121–133.

23. Benjamin & Heine, From Freud to androids.

24. Mori, M. (1970). The uncanny valley. *Energy, 7*(4), 33–35. https://ieeexplore.ieee.org/stamp/stamp.jsp?arnumber=6213238

25. Clinton, P. (2004, November 10). *Review: 'Polar Express' a creepy ride*. CNN.com. https://www.cnn.com/2004/SHOWBIZ/Movies/11/10/review .polar.express/

## Chapter 5: Maintaining Meaning in Our Lives

1. James, W. (1890). *The Principles of Psychology*, vol. 1, 488. New York: Dover.

2. Piaget, J. (1953). *The Origins of Intelligence in the Child*. London: Routledge & Kegan Paul.

3. Kuhn, T. (1962/1996). *The Structure of Scientific Revolutions*. Chicago: University of Chicago Press.

4. Planck, M. (1949/2020). *Scientific Autobiography and Other Papers*, 15. Montreal, Quebec: Minkowski Institute Press.

5. See p. 213 of Bruner, J., & Postman, L. (1949). On the perception of incongruity: A paradigm. *Journal of Personality, 18*, 206–223.

6. Aronson, E., & Mills, J. (1959). The effect of severity of initiation on liking for a group. *Journal of Abnormal and Personality Psychology, 59*, 177–181.

7. Heine, S. J., Proulx, T., & Vohs, K. D. (2006). The Meaning Maintenance Model: On the coherence of social motivations. *Personality and Social Psychology Review, 10*(2), 88–110.

8. Heidegger, M. (1962). *Being and Time*, 105. New York: Harper & Row.

9. Simons, D., & Chabris, C. (1999). "Selective Attention Test." YouTube video, 1:21. Posted by Daniel Simons, 2010. https://www.youtube.com /watch?v=vJG698U2Mvo

10. Rensink, R. A. (2004). Visual sensing without seeing. *Psychological Science, 15*, 27–32.

11. Proulx, T., & Heine, S. J. (2008). The case of the transmogrifying experimenter: Reaffirmation of moral schemas following implicit change detection. *Psychological Science, 19*, 1294–1300.

12. Randles, D., Inzlicht, M., Proulx, T., Tullett., A., & Heine, S. J. (2015). Is dissonance reduction a special case of fluid compensation? Evidence that dissonant cognitions cause compensatory affirmation and abstraction. *Journal of Personality and Social Psychology, 108*, 697–710.

13. Proulx, T., Heine, S. J., & Vohs, K. (2010). When is the unfamiliar the uncanny? Meaning affirmative after exposure to absurdist literature, humor, and art. *Personality and Social Psychology Bulletin, 36*, 817–829; Randles, D., Heine, S. J., & Santos, N. (2013). The common pain of surrealism and death: Acetaminophen reduces compensatory affirmation following meaning threats. *Psychological Science, 24*(6), 966–973; Randles, D., Proulx,

T., & Heine, S. J. (2011). Turn-frogs and careful sweaters: Subliminal presentations of incongruous word pairings invoke meaninglessness. *Journal of Experimental Social Psychology, 47*, 246–249; and Guan, K. W., & Heine, S. J. (2023). When good people break bad: Moral impression violations in everyday life. *Social Psychological and Personality Science, 14*, 26–39.

## Chapter 6: Learning to Live with Our Choices

1. Kierkegaard, S. (1844/1980). *The Concept of Anxiety*, 115. Princeton, NJ: Princeton University Press.

2. Carlisle, C. (2019). *Philosopher of the Heart: The Restless Life of Søren Kierkegaard*, 61, 246. London: Penguin.

3. Kierkegaard, *The Concept of Anxiety*, 61, 158.

4. Remes, O., Brayne, C., & Lafortune, L. (2014). The prevalence of anxiety disorders across the life course: A systematic review of reviews. *Lancet, 384*, S66.

5. Fox, J. A. (1978). *Forecasting Crime Data: An Econometric Analysis.* Lanham, MD: Lexington Books; and Arnett, J. J. (1999). Adolescent storm and stress, reconsidered. *American Psychologist, 54*, 317–326.

6. Schlegel, A., & Barry, H., III. (1991). *Adolescence: An Anthropological Inquiry.* New York: Free Press.

7. Trommsdorff, G. (1995). Parent-adolescent relations in changing societies: A cross-cultural study. In P. Noack, M. Hofer, & J. Youniss, eds., *Psychological Responses to Social Change: Human Development in Changing Environments*, 189–218. Berlin: Walter de Gruyter; and Dasen, P. R. (2000). Rapid social change and the turmoil of adolescence: A cross-cultural perspective. *International Journal of Group Tensions, 29*, 17–49.

8. Susman, E. J. (1997). Modeling developmental complexity in adolescence: Hormones and behavior in context. *Journal of Research on Adolescence, 7*, 283–306.

9. Cherlin, A. J. (2009). *The Marriage-Go-Round: The Stage of Marriage and the Family in America Today*, 71. New York: Knopf; United States Census Bureau. *Table MS-2. Estimated median age at first marriage, by sex: 1890 to present.* https://www.census.gov/data/tables/time-series/demo/families/marital.html; National Center for Education Statistics (NCES). (1993). *120 years of American education: A statistical portrait.* https://nces.ed.gov/pubs93/93442.pdf; Institute of Education Sciences. (2020). *The Condition of Education 2020.* https://nces.ed.gov/pubs2020/2020144.pdf; National Center for Education Statistics (NCES). (2013). *The condition of education 2013.* Washington, DC: US Department of Education. www.nces

.gov; and Levine, A., & Cureton, J. S. (1998). *When Hope and Fear Collide: A Portrait of Today's College Student*. San Francisco, CA: Jossey-Bass.

10. Arnett, J. J. (2014). *Emerging Adulthood: The Winding Road from the Late Teens Through the Twenties*. New York: Oxford University Press; and Mehta, C. J., Arnett, J. J., Palmer, C. G., & Nelson, L. J. (2020). Established adulthood: A new conception of ages 30 to 45. *American Psychologist, 75*, 431–444.

11. Bleidorn, W., Klimstra, T. A., Denissen, J. J. A., Rentfrow, P. J., Potter, J., & Gosling, S. D. (2013). Personality maturation around the world: A cross-cultural examination of social-investment theory. *Psychological Science, 24*, 2530–2540.

12. Bakewell, S. (2016). *At the Existentialist Café*. New York: Other Press; and Flynn, T. R. (2014). *Sartre: A Philosophical Biography*. Cambridge, UK: Cambridge University Press.

13. Sartre, J.-P. (1947/2007). *Existentialism Is a Humanism*, 29. New York: Yale University Books; and Sartre, J.-P. (1943/1970). *Being and Nothingness*. London: Routledge.

14. Kierkegaard, S. (1843/1997). *Søren Kierkegaard's Skrifter*, vol. 18, 306. Copenhagen: Søren Kierkegaard Research Center.

15. Bolton, J. (2007). *Surrender Is Not an Option: Defending America at the United Nations*. New York: Threshold.

16. Goldberg, R., & Kahn, S. (2005, April 28). Bolton's conservative ideology has roots in Yale experience. *Yale Daily News*. https://yaledailynews.com/blog/2005/04/28/boltons-conservative-ideology-has-roots-in-yale-experience/

17. Staw, B. M. (1974). Attitudinal and behavioral consequences of changing a major organizational reward: A natural field experiment. *Journal of Personality and Social Psychology, 29*, 742–751.

18. Bolton, *Surrender Is Not an Option*.

19. Sartre, *Existentialism Is a Humanism*, 27.

20. Brehm, J. (1956). Postdecision changes in the desirability of alternatives. *Journal of Abnormal and Social Psychology, 52*, 384–389.

21. Festinger, L., Riecken, H. W., & Schachter, S. (1956). *When Prophecy Fails*. Minneapolis: University of Minnesota Press.

22. Murray, S. L., Holmes, J. G., & Griffin, D. W. (1996). The benefits of positive illusions: Idealization and the construction of satisfaction in close relationships. *Journal of Personality and Social Psychology, 70*, 79–98.

23. Strube, M. J. (1988). The decision to leave an abusive relationship: Empirical evidence and theoretical issues. *Psychological Bulletin, 104*, 236–250; and Herbert, T. B., Silver, R. C., & Ellard, J. H. (1991). Coping with

an abusive relationship: I. How and why do women stay? *Journal of Marriage and the Family, 53*(2), 311–325.

24. Schwartz, B. (2004). *The Paradox of Choice: Why More Is Less.* New York: HarperCollins.

25. Iyengar, S. (2010). *The Art of Choosing.* New York: Twelve; Savani, K., Markus, H. R., & Conner, A. L. (2008). Let your preference be your guide? Preferences and choices are more tightly linked for North Americans than for Indians. *Journal of Personality and Social Psychology, 95,* 861–876; Savani, K., Morris, M. W., & Naidu, N. V. R. (2012). Deference in Indians' decision making: Introjected goals or injunctive norms? *Journal of Personality and Social Psychology, 102,* 685–699; Blood, R. O. (1967). *Love Match and Arranged Marriage.* New York: Free Press; and Heine, S. J. (2020). *Cultural Psychology,* 4th ed. New York: W. W. Norton.

26. Heine, S. J., & Lehman, D. R. (1997). Culture, dissonance, and self-affirmation. *Personality and Social Psychology Bulletin, 23,* 389–400.

27. Bauman, Z. (2000). *Liquid Modernity.* Cambridge, UK: Polity Press.

28. Martela, F. (2020). *A Wonderful Life.* New York: HarperCollins; and Lipka, M., & Gecewicz, C. (2017, September 6). *More Americans say they're spiritual but not religious.* Pew Research Center. https://www.pewresearch .org/fact-tank/2017/09/06/more-americans-now-say-theyre-spiritual-but -not-religious/

29. Hofstede, G. (2001). *Culture's Consequences: Comparing Values, Behaviors, Institutions, and Organizations Across Nations.* 2nd ed. Thousand Oaks, CA: Sage; and Santos, H. C., Varnum, M. E. W., & Grossmann, I. (2017). Global increases in individualism. *Psychological Science, 28,* 1228–1239.

## Chapter 7: Reckoning with the Hereafter

1. Dostoyevsky, F. (1869/2010). *The Idiot,* 62. New York: Signet; and Frank, J. (2010). *Dostoevsky: A Writer in His Time,* 181–182. Princeton, NJ: Princeton University Press.

2. Jordan, H. (2000). *No Such Thing as a Bad Day,* 216. Atlanta, GA: Longstreet; Shearer, L. (2001, September). When the friendly skies are not so friendly. *Georgia Magazine,* 64; and Noyes, R., Jr. (1980). Attitude change following near-death experiences. *Psychiatry: Interpersonal and Biological Processes, 43*(3), 234–242.

3. Peterson, C., & Seligman, M. E. P. (2003). Character strengths before and after September 11. *Psychological Science, 14,* 381–384.

4. Frankl, V. E. (1946/1986). *The Doctor and the Soul*, 64. New York: Vintage.

5. Carstensen, L. L. (2006). The influence of a sense of time on human development. *Science, 312,* 1913–1915.

6. Carstensen, L. L., Pasupathi, M., Mayr, U., & Nesselroade, J. R. (2000). Emotional experience in everyday life across the adult life span. *Journal of Personality and Social Psychology, 79,* 644–655; Blanchflower, D. G. (2021). Is happiness U-shaped everywhere? Age and subjective well-being in 145 countries. *Journal of Population Economics, 34,* 575–624; and Rauch, J. (2018). *The Happiness Curve.* New York: St. Martin's Press.

7. Tolstoy, L. (1882/1988). *A Confession and Other Religious Writings,* 35. London: Penguin Classics.

8. MacCurdy, J. T. (1943). *The Structure of Morale,* 10. London: Cambridge University Press; Shupp, R., Loveridge, S., Skidmore, M., Lim, J., & Rogers, C. (2017). Risk, loss, and ambiguity aversion after a natural disaster. *Economics of Disasters and Climate Change, 1*(2), 121–142; and Noyes, R., Jr. (1980). Attitude change following near-death experiences. *Psychiatry: Interpersonal and Biological Processes, 43*(3), 234–242.

9. Florian, V., & Mikulincer, M. (1998). Terror management in childhood: Does death conceptualization moderate the effects of mortality salience on acceptance of similar and different others? *Personality and Social Psychology Bulletin, 24,* 1104–1112; Nagy, M. (1948). The child's theories concerning death. *Journal of Genetic Psychology, 73,* 3–27; Suddendorf, T. (2013). *The Gap.* New York: Basic Books; and Matsuzawa, T. (2012). What is uniquely human? A view from comparative cognitive development in humans and chimpanzees. In F. B. M. de Waal & P. F. Ferrari, eds., *The Primate Mind,* 288–305. Cambridge, MA: Harvard University Press.

10. Heidegger, M. (1953/1996). *Being and Time,* 251. New York: State University of New York Press; and Kierkegaard, S. (1851/1991). *For Self-Examination; Judge for Yourself!,* 82. Princeton, NJ: Princeton University Press.

11. Becker, E. (1973). *The Denial of Death,* 87. New York: Free Press.

12. Rosenblatt, A., Greenberg, J., Solomon, S., Pyszczynski, T., & Lyon, D. (1989). Evidence for terror management theory: I. The effects of mortality salience on reactions to those who violate or uphold cultural values. *Journal of Personality and Social Psychology, 57,* 681–690; Greenberg, J., Pyszczynski, T., Solomon, S., Rosenblatt, A., Veeder, M., Kirkland, S., & Lyon, D. (1990). Evidence for terror management theory: II. The effects of mortality salience on reactions to those who threaten or bolster the cultural worldview. *Journal of Personality and Social Psychology, 58,* 308–318; Mandel, N., &

Heine, S. J. (1999). Terror management and marketing: He who dies with the most toys wins. *Advances in Consumer Research, 26,* 527–532; and Wisman, A., & Goldenberg, J. L. (2005). From the grave to the cradle: Evidence that mortality salience engenders a desire for offspring. *Journal of Personality and Social Psychology, 89,* 46–61.

13. Greenberg, J., Porteus, J., Simon, L., Pyszczynski, T., & Solomon, S. (1995). Evidence of a terror management function of cultural icons: The effects of mortality salience on the inappropriate use of cherished cultural symbols. *Personality and Social Psychology Bulletin, 21,* 1221–1228.

14. Hartig, H., & Doherty, C. (2021, September 2). *Two decades later, the enduring legacy of 9/11.* Pew Research Center. https://www.pewresearch .org/politics/2021/09/02/two-decades-later-the-enduring-legacy-of-9-11/; Uecker, J. E. (2008). Religious and spiritual responses to 9/11: Evidence from the Add Health Study. *Sociological Spectrum, 28,* 477–509; Norris, A. (2004). "Us" and "Them": The politics of American self-assertion after 9/11. *Metaphilosophy, 35,* 249–272; Klein, R. A., Cook, C. L., Ebersole, C. R., Vitiello, C. A., Nosek, B. A., Hilgard, J., Ahn, P. H., Brady, A. J., Chartier, C. R., Christopherson, C. D., Clay, S., Collisson, B., Crawford, J. T., Cromar, R., Gardiner, G., Gosnell, C. L., Grahe, J., Hall, C., Howard, I., & . . . Ratliff, K. A. (2022). Many labs 4: Failure to replicate mortality salience effect with and without original author involvement. *Collabra: Psychology, 8*(1), 35271; and Chen, L., Benjamin, R., Guo, Y., Lai, A., & Heine, S. J. (2024). *Assessing the Evidential Value of a Large Psychological Literature: A Systematic Review of Terror Management Theory.* Manuscript submitted for publication.

15. George, L. S., & Park, C. L. (2014). Existential mattering: Bringing attention to a neglected but central aspect of meaning? In A. Batthyany & P. Russo-Netzer, eds., *Meaning in Positive and Existential Psychology,* 39–51. New York: Springer; Costin, V., & Vignoles, V. L. (2020). Meaning is about mattering: Evaluating coherence, purpose, and existential mattering as precursors of meaning in life judgments. *Journal of Personality and Social Psychology, 118,* 864–884; and Solomon, S. (2003). Quote in G. Byrne, dir., *Flight from Death: The Quest for Immortality* [Documentary].

16. Brown, D. E. (1991). *Human Universals.* Philadelphia: Temple University Press; and Goldenberg, J. L., Pyszczynski, T., Greenberg, J., Solomon, S., Kluck, B., & Cornwell, R. (2001). I am not an animal: Morality salience, disgust, and the denial of human creatureliness. *Journal of Experimental Psychology: General, 130,* 427–435.

17. Goldenberg, J. L., Pyszczynski, T., McCoy, S. K., Greenberg, J., & Solomon, S. (1999). Death, sex, love, and neuroticism: Why is sex such a problem? *Journal of Personality and Social Psychology, 77,* 1173–1187.

18. Boyer, P. (2001). *Religion Explained.* New York: Perseus.

19. Norenzayan, A., & Hansen, I. (2006). Beliefs in supernatural agents in the face of death. *Personality and Social Psychological Bulletin, 32*, 174–187; and Vail, K. E., III, Arndt, J., & Abdollahi, A. (2012). Exploring the existential function of religion and supernatural agent beliefs among Christians, Muslims, atheists, and agnostics. *Personality and Social Psychology Bulletin, 38*, 1288–1300.

20. Inzlicht, M., McGregor, I., Hirsh, J. B., & Nash, K. (2009). Neural markers of religious conviction. *Psychological Science, 20*, 385–392.

21. Jim, H. S. L., Pustejovsky, J. E., Park, C. L., Danhauer, S. C., Sherman, A. C., Fitchett, G., Merluzzi, T. V., Munoz, A. R., Login, G., Mallory, A. S., & Salsman, J. M. (2015). Religion, spirituality, and physical health in cancer patients: A meta-analysis. *Cancer, 121*, 3760–3768; Abu, H. O., Ulbricht, C., Ding, E., Allison, J. J., Salmoirago-Blotcher, E., Goldberg, R. J., & Kiefe, C. I. (2018). Association of religiosity and spirituality with quality of life in patients with cardiovascular disease: A systematic review. *Quality of Life Research, 27*, 2777–2797; Seybold, K. S., & Hill, P. C. (2001). The role of religion and spirituality in mental and physical health. *Current Directions in Psychological Science, 10*, 21–24; and Giles, T., Hungerman, D. M., & Oostrom, T. (2023). *Opiates of the masses? Deaths of despair and the decline of American religion.* NBER working paper.

22. Folk, D., Rutjens, B. T., Van Elk, M., & Heine, S. J. (in press). Dare to know! The existential costs of a faith in science. *Journal of Positive Psychology.*

23. Prinzing, M., Van Cappellen, P., & Fredrickson, B. L. (2023). More than a momentary blip in the universe? Investigating the link between religiousness and perceived meaning in life. *Personality and Social Psychology Bulletin, 49*, 180–196.

24. Lipset, S. M. (1996). *American Exceptionalism: A Double-Edged Sword.* New York: W. W. Norton; Jones, J. M. (2021, March 20). *U.S. church membership falls below majority for first time.* Gallup News. https://news .gallup.com/poll/341963/church-membership-falls-below-majority-first -time.aspx; and Pew Research Center. (2022, September 13). *Modeling the future of religion in America.* https://www.pewresearch.org/religion/2022 /09/13/modeling-the-future-of-religion-in-america/

25. Stroope, S., Draper, S., & Whitehead, A. L. (2013). Images of a loving God and sense of meaning in life. *Social Indicators Research, 111*(1), 25–44; Prinzing, M., Van Cappellen, P., & Fredrickson, B. L. (2021). More than a momentary blip in the universe? Investigating the link between religiousness and perceived meaning in life. *Personality and Social Psychology Bulletin*, 01461672211060136; and Koenig, H. G., King, D. E., & Carson, V. B. (2012). *Handbook of Religion and Health.* 2nd ed. New York: Oxford University Press.

26. Van Tongeren, D. R., DeWall, C. N., Chen, Z., Sibley, C. G., & Bulbulia, J. (2021). Religious residue: Cross-cultural evidence that religious psychology and behavior persist following deidentification. *Journal of Personality and Social Psychology, 120*(2), 484–503.

27. NORC. (2011, May 11). *Spirituality and religion in the United States, 1998–2020.* https://www.norc.org/PDFs/Center%20for%20the%20 Study%20of%20Politics%20and%20Society/Spirituality%20and%20 Religion%20in%20the%20United%20States,%201998-2020.pdf; Lipka, M., & Gecewicz, C. (2017, September 6). *More Americans now say they're spiritual but not religious.* Pew Research Center. https://www.pewresearch .org/fact-tank/2017/09/06/more-americans-now-say-theyre-spiritual-but -not-religious/; and Gilbert, E. (2006). *Eat Pray Love,* 230. New York: Penguin.

28. Jettinghoff, W., Folk, D., Radjaee, P., Willard, A., Norenzayan, A., & Heine, S. J. (2024). *The varieties of nonreligious experience: Meaning in life among believers, nonbelievers, and the spiritual but not religious.* Manuscript submitted for publication.

## Chapter 8: When Life Breaks Our Stories

1. Maercker, A., & Guski-Leinwand, S. (2018). Psychologists' involvement in repressive "Stasi" secret police activities in former East Germany. *International Perspectives in Psychology, 7*(2), 107–119.

2. The Stasi Museum in Berlin documents many of the atrocities and cruel tactics that were employed; see also Dennis, M. (2014). *The Stasi: Myth and Reality.* New York: Routledge.

3. Van Tilburg, W. A., & Igou, E. R. (2012). On boredom: Lack of challenge and meaning as distinct boredom experiences. *Motivation and Emotion, 36,* 181–194.

4. Fromm, E. (1963). *The Dogma of Christ and Other Essays,* 150. New York: Holt, Rinehart, & Winston.

5. Moskos, P. (2011). *In Defense of Flogging,* 55. New York: Basic Books; and Pfattheicher, S., Lazarevic, L. B., Nielsen, Y. Z., Westgate, E. C., Krstic, K., & Schindler, S. (2023). I enjoy hurting my classmates: On the relation of boredom and sadism in schools. *Journal of School Psychology, 96,* 41–56.

6. Wilson, T. D., Reinhard, D. A., Westgate, E. C., Gilbert, D. T., Ellerback, N., Hahn, C., Brown, C. L., & Shaked, A. (2014). Just think: The challenges of the disengaged mind. *Science, 345,* 75–77; and see p. 100 of Baumeister, R. F. (1990). Suicide as escape from self. *Psychological Review, 97,* 90–113.

# Notes for Chapter 8

7. Grose, J. (2021, April 7). The main reason for your pandemic boredom. *New York Times.* https://www.nytimes.com/2021/04/07/parenting /boredom-coronavirus-pandemic.html

8. Elpidorou, A. (2014). The bright side of boredom. *Frontiers in Psychology, 5,* 1245; and Van Tilburg, W. A., Igou, E. R., Maher, P. J., Moynihan, A. B., & Martin, D. G. (2019). Bored like hell: Religiosity reduces boredom and tempers quest for meaning. *Emotion, 19,* 255–269.

9. Janoff-Bulman, R. (1992). *Shattered Assumptions.* New York: Free Press; and Janoff-Bulman, R. (1989). Assumptive worlds and the stress of traumatic events: Application of the schema construct. *Social Cognition, 2,* 111–136.

10. Silver, R. L., Boon, C., & Stones, M. H. (1983). Searching for meaning in misfortune: Making sense of incest. *Journal of Social Issues, 39,* 81–102; and Silver, R. C., & Updegraff, J. A. (2013). Searching for and finding meaning following personal and collective traumas. In K. D. Markman, T. Proulx, & M. J. Lindberg, eds., *The Psychology of Meaning,* 237–256. Washington, DC: American Psychological Association.

11. Randles, D., Heine, S. J., Poulin, M., & Cohen Silver, R. (2017). Experienced adversity in life is associated with polarized and affirmed political attitudes. *Social Psychological and Personality Science, 8,* 652–659.

12. Rusnell, C., & Russell, J. (2016, April 25). *Alberta report details 'heartbreaking' life stories of 7 indigenous youths who committed suicide.* CBC News. https://www.cbc.ca/amp/1.3551181

13. CBC News. (2016, April 16). *5 more Attawapiskat youth attempt suicide in 'spiralling situation.'* https://www.cbc.ca/news/indigenous /attawapiskat-youth-attempt-suicide-1.3539564

14. Chandler, M. J., & Proulx, T. (2008). Personal persistence and persistent peoples: Continuities in the lives of individual and whole cultural communities. In F. Sani, ed., *Self Continuity: Individual and Collective Perspectives,* 213–226. Hove, UK: Psychology Press; and Kirmayer, L. (1994). Suicide among Canadian aboriginal peoples. *Transcultural Psychiatric Research Review, 31,* 3–57.

15. Chandler, M., & Ball, L. (1990). Continuity and commitment: A developmental analysis of the identity formation process in suicidal and non-suicidal youth. In H. Bosma & S. Jackson, eds., *Coping and Self-Concept in Adolescence,* 149–166. Heidelberg, Germany: Springer; and Sokol, Y., Ridley, J., Goodman, M., Landa, Y., Hernandez, S., & Dion, L. (2021). Continuous identity cognitive therapy: Feasibility and acceptability of a novel Intervention for suicidal symptoms. *Journal of Cognitive Psychotherapy: An International Quarterly, 35,* 64–80.

16.  Chandler, M. J., Lalonde, C. E., Sokol, B. W., Hallett, D., & Marcia, J. E. (2003). Personal persistence, identity development, and suicide: A study of native and non-native North American adolescents. *Monographs of the Society for Research in Child Development, 68*, 1–138.

17.  Baumeister, R. F. (1990). Suicide as escape from self. *Psychological Review, 97*, 90–113; and Durkheim, E. (1897/1963). *Suicide, 367*. New York: Free Press.

18.  Baumeister, R. F. (1991). *Escaping the Self.* New York: Basic Books.

19.  McAdams, D. P., Reynolds, J., & Lewis, M. (2001). When bad things turn good and good things turn bad: Sequences of redemption and contamination in life narrative and their relation to psychosocial adaptation in midlife adults and in students. *Personality and Social Psychology Bulletin, 27*, 474–485; and Dunlop, W. L., Guo, J., & McAdams, D. P. (2016). The autobiographical author through time: Examining the degree of stability and change in redemptive and contaminated personal narratives. *Social Psychological and Personality Science, 7*, 428–436.

20.  Klonsky, E. D., & May, A. M. (2015). The three-step theory (3ST): A new theory of suicide rooted in the "ideation-to-action" framework. *International Journal of Cognitive Therapy, 8*(2), 114–129.

21.  Eliot, T. S. (1935, February). Literature and the modern world. *The Teaching Church Review: A Journal for Students of Religion, 5*, 11–15; and Zareian, B., & Klonsky, E. D. (2020). Connectedness and suicide. In A. C. Page & W. G. K. Stritzke, eds., *Alternatives to Suicide*, 135–158. Cambridge, MA: Academic Press.

22.  Heisel, M. J., Moore, S. L., Flett, G. L., Norman, R. M. G., Links, P. S., Eynan, R., O'Rourke, N., Sarma, S., Fairlie, P., Wilson, K., Farrell, B., Grunau, M., Olson, R., & Conn, D. (2020). Meaning-centered men's groups: Initial findings of an intervention to enhance resiliency and reduce suicide risk in men facing retirement. *Clinical Gerontologist, 43*, 76–84.

23.  National Institute of Mental Health. (2024). *Suicide.* https://www.nimh.nih.gov/health/statistics/suicide#part_2557

24.  Bryan, C. J., Bryan, A. O., Rozek, D. C., & Leifker, F. R. (2019). Meaning in life drives reductions in suicide risk among acutely suicidal soldiers receiving a crisis response plan. *Journal of Social and Clinical Psychology, 38*, 774–787.

25.  Nietzsche, F. (1889/1990). *Twilight of the Idols, 33.* London: Penguin Classics.

26.  Seery, M. D., Holman, E. A., & Silver, R. C. (2010). Whatever does not kill us: Cumulative lifetime adversity, vulnerability, and resilience. *Journal of Personality and Social Psychology, 99*, 1025–1041.

27. Baumeister, R. F., Vohs, K. D., Aaker, J. L., & Garbinsky, E. N. (2013). Some key differences between a happy life and a meaningful life. *Journal of Positive Psychology, 8*, 505–551.

28. Oishi, S., & Diener, E. (2014). Residents of poor nations have a greater sense of meaning in life than residents of wealthy nations. *Psychological Science, 25*, 422–430.

29. Frankl, V. E. (1946/1984). *Man's Search for Meaning.* New York: Washington Square Press.

30. Bonanno, G. A. (2021). *The End of Trauma*, 14. New York: Basic Books.

31. Frankl, *Man's Search for Meaning*, 146; and George, L. S., & Park, C. L. (2022). Do violations of global beliefs and goals drive distress and meaning making following life stressors? *Illness, Crisis, & Loss, 30*, 378–395.

32. See p. 6 of Tedeschi, R. G., & Calhoun, L. G. (2004). Posttraumatic growth: Conceptual foundations and empirical evidence. *Psychological Inquiry, 15*, 1–18.

33. Park, C. L. (2005). Religion as a meaning-making framework in coping with life stress. *Journal of Social Issues, 61*, 707–729.

34. Lindstrom, C. M., Cann, A., Calhoun, L. G., & Tedeschi, R. G. (2013). The relationship of core belief challenge, rumination, disclosure, and sociocultural elements to posttraumatic growth. *Psychological Trauma: Theory, Research, Practice, and Policy, 5*, 50–55.

35. Pennebaker, J. W. (1997). Writing about emotional experiences as a therapeutic process. *Psychological Science, 8*, 162–166.

36. Pavlacic, J. M., Buchanan, E. M., Maxwell, N. P., Hopke, T. G., & Schulenberg, S. E. (2019). A meta-analysis of expressive writing on posttraumatic stress, posttraumatic growth, and quality of life. *Review of General Psychology, 23*, 230–250.

**Chapter 9:** Building a Meaningful Life

1. Camus, A. (1955). *The Myth of Sisyphus and Other Essays*, 123. New York: Vintage Books.

2. Steele, C. M. (1988). The psychology of self-affirmation: Sustaining the integrity of the self. In L. Berkowitz, ed., *Advances in Experimental Social Psychology*, vol. 21, 261–302. San Diego, CA: Academic Press; and Nelson, S. K., Fuller, J. A. K., Choi, I., & Lyubomirsky, S. (2014). Beyond self-protection: Self-affirmation benefits hedonic and eudaimonic well-being. *Personality and Social Psychology Bulletin, 40*, 998–1011.

3. Cohen, G. L., Garcia, J., Apfel, N., & Master, A. (2006). Reducing the racial achievement gap: A social-psychological intervention. *Science, 313*, 1307–1310; Schmeichel, B. J., & Martens, A. (2005). Self-affirmation and mortality salience: Affirming values reduces worldview defense and death-thought accessibility. *Personality and Social Psychology Bulletin, 31*, 658–667; Steele, C. M., Spencer, S. J., & Lynch, M. (1993). Self-image resilience and dissonance: The role of affirmational resources. *Journal of Personality and Social Psychology, 64*, 885–896; and Walton, G. M., & Cohen, G. L. (2011). A brief social-belonging intervention improves academic and health outcomes of minority students. *Science, 331*, 1447.

4. Van Tilburg, W. A. P., Sedikides, C., Wildschut, T., & Vingerhoets, A. J. J. M. (2019). How nostalgia infuses life with meaning: From social connectedness to self-continuity. *European Journal of Social Psychology, 49*, 521–532; and Routledge, C. (2015). *Nostalgia: A Key Psychological Resource.* London: Routledge.

5. Dovey, C. (2015, June 15). Can reading make you happier? *New Yorker.*

6. Keltner, D., & Haidt, J. (2003). Approaching awe, a moral, spiritual, and aesthetic emotion. *Cognition and Emotion, 17*, 297–314; and Piff, P. K., Dietze, P., Feinberg, M., Stancato, D. M., & Keltner, D. (2015). Awe, the small self, and prosocial behavior. *Journal of Personality and Social Psychology, 108*, 883–899.

7. Tsun-Wai-Chu, S., & Mak, W. W. S. (2020). How mindfulness enhances meaning in life: A meta-analysis of correlational studies and randomized controlled trials. *Mindfulness, 11*, 177–193.

8. Brown, K. W., & Ryan, R. M. (2003). The benefits of being present: Mindfulness and its role in psychological well-being. *Journal of Personality and Social Psychology, 84*, 822–848.

9. Jerome, L., Feduccia, A. A., Wang, J. B., Hamilton, S., Yazar-Klosinski, B., Emerson, A., Mithoefer, M. C., & Doblin, R. (2020). Long-term follow-up outcomes of MDMA-assisted psychotherapy for treatment of PTSD: A longitudinal pooled analysis of six phase 2 trials. *Psychopharmacology, 237*, 2485–2497; Hendricks, P., Thorne, C., Clark, C., Coombs, D., & Johnson, M. (2015). Classic psychedelic use is associated with reduced psychological distress and suicidality in the United States adult population. *Journal of Psychopharmacology, 29*, 280–288; and Nutt, D., King, L. A., & Phillips, L. D. (2010). Drug harms in the UK: A multicriteria decision analysis. *Lancet, 376*, 1558–1565.

10. Griffiths, R. R, Richards, W. A., McCann, U., & Jesse, R. (2006). Psilocybin can occasion mystical-type experiences having substantial and

sustained personal meaning and spiritual significance. *Psychopharmacology, 187,* 268–283; Lyubomirsky, S. (2022). Toward a new science of psychedelic social psychology: The effects of MDMA (Ecstasy) on social connection. *Perspectives on Psychological Science, 17,* 1234–1257; and Moreton, S. G., Arena, A. F. A., Foy, Y., & Menzies, R. E. (2023). Reduced death anxiety as a mediator of the relationship between acute subjective effects of psychedelics and improved subjective well-being, *Death Studies, 47,* 1115–1126.

11. Yaden, D. B., & Griffiths, R. R. (2021). The subjective effects of psychedelics are necessary for their enduring therapeutic effects. *ACS Pharmacology & Translational Science, 4,* 568–572; and Timmermann, C., Kettner, H., Letheby, C., Roseman, L., Rosas, F. E., & Carhart-Harris, R. L. (2021). Psychedelics alter metaphysical beliefs. *Scientific Reports, 11*(1), 1–13.

12. Murray, W. H. H. (1873). Ministerial vacations: Their necessity and value. In *Park-Street Pulpit: Sermons,* 283–284. Boston: James R. Osgood; and McMahan, E. A., & Estes, D. (2015). The effect of contact with natural environments on positive and negative affect: A meta-analysis. *Journal of Positive Psychology, 10,* 507–519.

13. Schertz, K. E., & Berman, M. G. (2019). Understanding nature and its cognitive benefits. *Current Directions in Psychological Science, 28,* 496–502; and Oppezzo, M., & Schwartz, D. L. (2014). Give your ideas some legs: The positive effect of walking on creative thinking. *Journal of Experimental Psychology: Learning, Memory, and Cognition, 40,* 1142–1152.

14. Baumeister, R. F. (1991). *Meanings of Life.* New York: Guilford Press; and Heine, S. J., Proulx, T., & Vohs, K. D. (2006). The Meaning Maintenance Model: On the coherence of social motivations. *Personality and Social Psychology Review, 10,* 88–110.

15. Baumeister, R. F., Vohs, K. D., Aaker, J. L., & Garbinsky, E. N. (2013). Some key differences between a happy life and a meaningful life, *Journal of Positive Psychology, 8,* 505–516.

16. Lambert, N. M., Stillman, T. F., Baumeister, R. F., Fincham, F. D., Hicks, J. A., & Graham, S. (2010). Family as a salient source of meaning in young adulthood. *Journal of Positive Psychology, 5,* 367–376.

17. Hayden-Evans, M., Milbourn, B., & Netto, J. (2018). 'Pets provide meaning and purpose': A qualitative study of pet ownership from the perspectives of people diagnosed with borderline personality disorder. *Advances in Mental Health, 16,* 152–162; Shim, B., Barroso, J., Gillis, C. L., & Davis, L. L. (2013). Finding meaning in caring for a spouse with dementia. *Applied Nursing Research, 26,* 121–126; Glass, J., Andersson, M. A., & Simon, R. W. (2016). Parenthood and happiness: Effects of work-family reconciliation policies in 22 OECD countries. *American Journal of Sociology,*

*122*, 886–929; and Kahneman, D., Krueger, A. B., Schkade, D. A., Schwarz, N., & Stone, A. A. (2004). A survey method for characterizing daily life experience: The day reconstruction method. *Science, 306*, 1776–1780.

18. Stavrova, O., & Luhmann, M. (2016) Social connectedness as a source and consequence of meaning in life, *Journal of Positive Psychology, 11*, 470–479.

19. Choi, J., Catapano, R., & Choi, I. (2017). Taking stock of happiness and meaning in everyday life: An experience sampling approach. *Social Psychological and Personality Science, 8*, 641–651.

20. Pascal, B. (1670/1995). *Pensées*, 208. London: Penguin Classics; and Terkel, S. (1997). *Working*, ix. New York: New Press.

21. Grant, A. (2016, May 6). *Three lies about meaningful work*. Huffington Post. https://www.huffpost.com/entry/three-lies-about-meaningful-work_b _7205036

22. Seybold, K. S., & Hill, P. C. (2001). The role of religion and spirituality in mental and physical health. *Current Directions in Psychological Science, 10*, 21–24.

23. Jettinghoff, W., Folk, D., Radjaee, P., Willard, A., Norenzayan, A., & Heine, S. J. (2024). *The varieties of nonreligious experience: Meaning in life among believers, nonbelievers, and the spiritual but not religious.* Manuscript submitted for publication.

24. Kierkegaard, S. (1843/2022). *Fear and Trembling*. New York: Liveright.

25. Prinzing, M., Van Cappellen, P., & Fredrickson, B. L. (2021). More than a momentary blip in the universe? Investigating the link between religiousness and perceived meaning in life. *Personality and Social Psychology Bulletin*, 01461672211060136.

26. Dostoevsky, F. (1912/2005). *The Brothers Karamazov*, 230. Mineola, NY: Dover.

27. Alimujiang, A., Wiensch, A., Boss, J., Fleischer, N. L., Mondul, A. M., McLean, K., Mukherjee, B., & Pearce, C. L. (2019). Association between life purpose and mortality among US adults older than 50 years. *JAMA Network Open, 2*(5), e194270; and Hill, P. L., Turiano, N. A., Mroczek, D. K., & Burrow, A. L. (2016). The value of a purposeful life: Sense of purpose predicts greater income and net worth. *Journal of Research in Personality, 65*, 38–42.

28. Mask, M., Folk, D. P., & Heine, S. J. (2024). *Which sources of purpose predict the good life across cultures?* Manuscript submitted for publication.

29. Oishi, S., & Westgate, E. C. (2022). A psychologically rich life: Beyond happiness and meaning. *Psychological Review, 129*, 790–811.

30. Kim, J., Holte, P., Martela, F., Shanahan, C., Li, Z., Zhang, H., Eisenbeck, N., Carreno, D. F., Schlegel, R. J., & Hicks, J. A. (2022). Experiential appreciation as a pathway to meaning in life. *Nature Human Behaviour, 6,* 677–690.

31. Campbell, J. (1949). *The Hero with a Thousand Faces,* vol. 17. Novato, CA: New World Library.

32. Rogers, B. A., Chicas, H., Kelly, J. M., Kubin, E., Christian, M. S., Kachanoff, F. J., Berger, J., Puryear, C., McAdams, D. P., & Gray, K. (2023). Seeing your life story as a hero's journey increases meaning in life. *Journal of Personality and Social Psychology, 125*(4), 752–778. https://doi.org/10.1037/pspa0000341

33. Baumeister, *Meanings of Life*; and Heine et al., The Meaning Maintenance Model.

# Index

# Index

# Index

# Index

# Index

# Index

# Index

*Paul Joseph*

**Steven J. Heine** is distinguished university scholar and professor of social and cultural psychology at the University of British Columbia. He is the author of *Cultural Psychology*, the top-selling textbook in the field, and his research has been covered in outlets like the *New York Times, Washington Post, Guardian, Newsweek,* and *New Scientist*. He lives in Vancouver, British Columbia, Canada.